ABOUT THE ~~AUTHOR~~

Neena Gupta, LL.B., is a partner with the Toronto-based firm Goodman Carr LLP. Her practice focuses on employment and human rights law, including employee training on diversity in the workplace, race relations, prevention of sexual harassment, and the duty to accommodate. Ms. Gupta has taught at the Faculty of Law of both the University of Toronto and Queen's University, and at Seneca College. She was awarded the Queen Elizabeth the II's Golden Jubilee Medal in 2002 for her numerous contributions to the legal profession on a local and national level.

To my parents, Haragauri Narayan Gupta and Manjula Gupta, who taught me
the importance of fairness;

To my husband, Brad Svorkdal, who has always been
supportive and understanding;

and

To my daughter, Kirsten Joya, in the hope she will never
experience a sexual harassment.

PREFACE

As an employment lawyer, I am often approached by clients and other lawyers to handle harassment investigations. In many cases, however, employers cannot afford to retain outside legal counsel to conduct an investigation. In my 15 years of practice, I have seen harassment investigations conducted by ill-equipped human resource and corporate security managers.

There are many excellent resources on the substantive law of sexual harassment and discrimination.[1] This book cannot replace those superb resources. Many of my clients have indicated that they would like a "how to" manual. An investigator needs an understanding of the law as well as patience, thoroughness and commonsense. These qualities are not in the exclusive purview of a lawyer.

As a lawyer involved in expensive and messy litigation involving allegations of harassment, I began to discern a pattern. A timely, thorough and fair investigation often led to cost-effective resolutions. Complainants who were satisfied with the result often chose not to avail themselves of their administrative remedies under various human rights codes. Respondents who believed that they had been given a fair audience chose not to sue for wrongful dismissal, defamation and the like. A rapid response often prevented problems from festering and encouraged efforts at mediation and reconciliation.

This book focuses on sexual harassment. In some senses, allegations of sexual harassment are the most difficult types of harassment cases to investigate. An allegation of sexual harassment may impact not just on a respondent's career, but also on his or her family and personal relationships. While the focus is on sexual harassment, many of the basic principles apply in any kind of harassment investigation.

It is my hope that this book will provide practical assistance to human resource managers, in-house counsel and anyone else tasked with investigating harassment. Throughout the text, I have provided examples of problems which routinely occur in the workplace. These examples, while inspired by cases on which I have worked, are completely fictitious.

---

[1] This book frequently refers to Arjun Aggarwal *et al.*, *Sexual Harassment in the Workplace*, 3d ed. (Toronto: Butterworths, 2000). An excellent overview of the development of case law regarding sexual harassment is also provided in Walter S. Tarnopolsky *et al.*, *Discrimination and the Law* (Scarborough: Carswell, 2001) at §8.7 to 8.8.

Names, characters, places and incidents are either products of my imagination or used fictitiously.

This book would not have been possible without the support of my beloved husband, Brad Svorkdal. I would like to thank Tamara Jordan and Dayna Arron whose enthusiasm, insight and contribution made this book possible. In particular, their enormous contribution to Chapters 1, 2 and 3 are gratefully acknowledged. My summer students, Emily Joyce and Shawn Pulver, displayed remarkable insight. Their help was invaluable in completing this book.

TABLE OF CONTENTS

PART I

CHAPTER 1[*]

WHAT IS SEXUAL HARASSMENT?

A. OVERVIEW

The term "sexual harassment" is sometimes difficult to define. When asked for specifics, people often respond, "I know when I see it." The law is not comfortable with such an ambiguous and amorphous response.

An investigator should be guided by an understanding of the legal definition of sexual harassment. While the investigator need not be a lawyer, it is easy to dismiss a complaint as being unfounded unless there is a sophisticated understanding of the types of sexual harassment recognized by the law. There are excellent resources available on what constitutes sexual harassment.[1] This chapter provides a quick overview of the definition of sexual harassment.

The Ontario *Human Rights Code* defines harassment as "engaging in a course of vexatious comment or conduct that is known or ought reasonably to be known to be unwelcome".[2] The *Canada Labour Code* defines sexual harassment broadly as being any "conduct, comment, gesture or contact of a sexual nature (a) that is likely to cause offence or humiliation to any employee; or (b) that might, on reasonable grounds, be perceived by that employee as placing a condition of a sexual nature on employment on any opportunity for training or promotion".[3] The statutory provisions codify case law[4] which defined harassment as a specific type of discrimination.

---

[*] I wish to acknowledge the enormous contribution made to this chapter by Tamara Jordan, an associate at Goodman and Carr LLP, in researching and providing materials for inclusion in this chapter. Any errors, however, are solely my responsibility.

[1] See, for example, Arjun Aggarwal *et al.*, *Sexual Harassment in the Workplace*, 3d ed. (Toronto: Butterworths, 2000).

[2] Ontario *Human Rights Code*, R.S.O. 1990, c. H.19, s. 10(1) "harassment". Appendix A contains a synopsis of the relevant legislation across the country.

[3] *Canada Labour Code*, R.S.C. 1985, c. L-2, s. 247.1.

[4] See the discussion of sex harassment as sex discrimination, *Janzen v. Platy Enterprises Ltd. (Man. C.A.)*, [1989] 1 S.C.R. 1252.

Most provinces or territories prohibit harassment explicitly.[5] Some jurisdictions prohibit discrimination on the basis of sex or other protected category. Harassment on the basis of sex or other protected ground (*e.g.* race, religion, disability, age) is recognized as a form of discriminatory conduct. Before acting on any complaint, an employer should review the nature of the complaint to ensure that it falls within the broad rubric of discrimination or harassment. There are many kinds of unpleasant conduct that might not constitute sexual or illegal harassment.[6] For example, in *Broadfield v. DeHavilland -Boeing of Canada Ltd.*,[7] a supervisor complained about disputes she had with one of the union committee men. They had a number of confrontations, replete with profane language. The Board of Inquiry ruled that while the language may have been profane, it did not constitute sexual harassment. The tribunal found:

> In the first place, most of his commentary and conduct was not directed to degrading her because of her gender; it was instead directed to confronting her own aggressive style as a supervisor. ... [The] language was often profane. ... Despite her claims to be offended, she did as much as Mr. O'Neall [the respondent] to establish this as the linguistic norm between them and this undercuts her claim that his use of profanity generally was directed to degrading her on the basis of sex and gender.

Increasingly, some experts are concerned about the phenomenon of "status-blind" harassment, *i.e.* harassment that is not directed at an individual on the basis of one of the protected grounds of sex, race, age, sexual orientation, disability, *etc.* One U.S. expert indicated that many complaints lodged with the U.S. Equal Employment Opportunity Commission involved unresolved issues of workplace bullying, rather than legally-prohibited harassment. In the education sector, bullying is being recognized as a problem that undermines students' ability to enjoy and participate in school. Regardless of the lack of legislation in this area, employers should seriously consider being proactive in prohibiting bullying.[8] While this type of "status-blind" harassment might not constitute illegal harassment at law, employers may wish to promulgate internal codes of ethics or policies prohibiting this type of conduct.

---

[5] See Appendix A for relevant excerpts of legislation.

[6] For example, a supervisor who disciplines employees in harsh and unpleasant language may be engaged in a form of abuse that is not sexual.

[7] (1993), 19 C.H.R.R. D/347 at D/366 (Ont. Bd. of Inquiry).

[8] Although outside of the scope of this book, it is useful to review some of the information available on the internet. I recommend <http://www.workdoctor.com> and <http://www.bullying.org> as a useful start.

An investigator should be aware of the developing law with respect to harassment before proceeding to commence an investigation. Because this book is focused on investigating sexual harassment, it may be helpful to review some of the basic Canadian principles involved.

B. THE SUPREME COURT OF CANADA'S DEFINITION OF "SEXUAL HARASSMENT"

In 1989, the Supreme Court of Canada considered various definitions of sexual harassment and ultimately set out the following:

> Sexual harassment in the workplace may be broadly defined as *unwelcome conduct of a sexual nature that detrimentally affects the work environment or leads to adverse job-related consequences for the victims of the harassment.* It is an abuse of both economic and sexual power. It is a demeaning practice that constitutes a profound affront to the dignity of the employees forced to endure it. By requiring an employee to contend with unwelcome sexual actions or explicit sexual demands, sexual harassment in the workplace attacks the dignity and self-respect of the victim both as an employee and as a human being.[9]

Essentially, the court broke down the definition of sexual harassment into three constituent elements:

1. unwelcome conduct;
2. of a sexual nature;
3. that detrimentally affects the work environment or leads to adverse job-related consequences for the victims of the harassment.

The definition provided by the Supreme Court of Canada in *Janzen* left some uncertainty regarding the interpretation of the three constituent elements above. Subsequent federal and provincial courts and human rights tribunals have helped to bring meaning to these elements.

1. What Constitutes Unwelcome Conduct?

The first element in the definition of sexual harassment as provided by the Supreme Court of Canada is that the conduct must be "unwelcome". It must be conduct that makes an employee feel uncomfortable or conduct in which an employee engages *unwillingly*. In short, consent (either express or implied) is a complete defence to a charge of sexual harassment.

---

[9]   *Janzen v. Platy Enterprises Ltd.*, [1989] 1 S.C.R. 1252 at 1284 (emphasis added).

Consent or the lack thereof can be difficult to establish on the evidence. In certain cases, an employee may subjectively feel compelled to participate in an activity that makes her feel uncomfortable, but not voice any objection. This issue was squarely addressed in the well-known Ontario Court of Appeal case, *Simpson v. Consumers' Association of Canada.*[10]

In this case, a senior employee at the Consumers' Association of Canada testified that she attended a strip club during a business trip, but after business hours, with the respondent, Simpson. She also testified that he engaged in sexually-charged conversations. Although there was conflicting evidence regarding who initiated some of the conversations, Simpson admitted that he had had conversations with the employee about sex. He clearly viewed the conversations and the visit to the strip club as being voluntary on the part of the employee.

The Court of Appeal found that simply because an employee participates in certain conduct, one cannot assume that the participation was voluntary. The real issue is whether the employee had the power to object without fear of reprisal. The reality of some work environments is that employees are unable to object to the conduct of a supervisor, or even other employees, without feeling that their jobs are being compromised. In fact, one recent study has demonstrated that women rarely report sexual harassment for a number of reasons, including fear of losing their job, making the problem worse, fear of retaliation, or disbelief that they are actually experiencing sexual harassment.[11] Earlier studies established that there are a variety of reasons why women do not report their experiences of sexual harassment, including feelings of embarrassment, shame, discomfort, or more practical considerations like a belief that nothing would be done about the sexual harassment even if it were reported.[12]

In the course of any investigation, the investigator cannot assume that the lack of an explicit objection constitutes consent. There are many subtle signs of discomfort. An employee may avoid certain areas of the workplace, ensure that she is never alone with a particular individual, or absent herself suddenly in certain circumstances. In cases I have investigated, employees have exhibited behaviours that are consistent with a lack of consent, without saying a word:

    (a)   requested shift changes or transfers without cogent explanation;

---

[10]   (2001), 57 O.R. (3d) 351 (C.A.).
[11]   Sandy Welsh, "Gender and Sexual Harassment" (1999) 25 Ann. Rev. Sociol. 169.
[12]   See Aggarwal, *supra*, note 1 at 191-94.

(b)   refused or made excuses not to attend departmental or company social events;

(c)   experienced higher levels of absenteeism or "stress leaves";

(d)   complained to a trusted friend or co-worker, but not a managerial employee, about the harassment; and

(e)   conducted an active job search, including lesser paying positions.

Supervisors must be particularly careful regarding conduct with subordinate employees. As the Court of Appeal for Ontario has set out in *Bannister v. General Motors of Canada Ltd.,*[13] those in a position of power within a workplace cannot ignore their supervisory roles. Supervisors must realize that subordinate employees simply do not have the power to object to conduct they find offensive or harassing. Their position in the workplace hierarchy vests them with power that they would not have in a purely social setting. Investigators must be careful about weighing the evidence. One of the seminal Canadian decisions regarding supervisory conduct vis à vis a subordinate is *Bell v. Ladas*, in which the adjudicator observed, "an invitation to dinner is not an invitation to a complaint". The adjudicator wished to balance the need for normal, healthy social interaction in the workplace against the evils of sexual harassment. His analysis is important for investigators to remember:

> One must be cautious that the law not inhibit normal social contact between management and employees or normal discussion between management and employees. It is not abnormal, nor should it be prohibited, activity for a supervisor to become socially involved with an employee. An invitation to dinner is not an invitation to a complaint. *The danger or evil that is to be avoided is coerced or compelled social contact where the employee's refusal to participate may result in a loss of employment benefits. Such coercion or compulsion may be overt or subtle, but if any feature of employment becomes reasonably dependent on reciprocating a social relationship proffered by a member of management, then the overture becomes a condition of employment and may be considered to be discriminatory.*[14]

Certain conduct should be presumptively considered unwelcome, regardless of the position of the perpetrator of the conduct. Most physical contact of a sexual nature by an employee against another will generally be viewed

---

[13]   (1998), 40 O.R. (3d) 577 (C.A.).

[14]   (1980), 1 C.H.R.R. D/155 at D/156 (Ont. Bd. of Inquiry *per* Chairman Shime). Although Chairman Shime recognizes the reality that there will be social interaction at work, companies now regularly publish an anti-nepotism policy. The companies' concern is the impact a *consensual* relationship may have on workplace morale as well as the perceived and actual fairness of performance reviews, disciplinary actions and decisions regarding promotions.

as unwelcome conduct (*e.g.* pinching, slapping the rear end of another employee, or grabbing a person's breasts or genitals).[15] This type of conduct would also constitute the chargeable offence of assault under the *Criminal Code* of Canada.

While it is likely that only one incident of serious physical contact would constitute sexual harassment, other physical touching such as tickling, or rubbing an arm or back, may require repeated occurrences before it is considered sexual harassment.[16] Non-physical conduct, such as propositions or unwelcome comments, may also need to be persistent and repeated before a tribunal or court will characterize the conduct as harassment.

In determining whether or not conduct is unwelcome, the relevant consideration is whether the perpetrator of the alleged harassment "knew or ought reasonably to have known" that the behaviour was unwelcome.[17] The investigator must measure the conduct against the standards of a reasonable person. It is an objective standard. Whether or not the victim of the harassment objects to certain conduct, if a "reasonable person" in the same circumstances would experience the conduct as unwelcome, the investigator should conclude that the perpetrator "ought reasonably to have known" the conduct was unwelcome, even if the respondent testifies that he or she did not believe that the conduct was unwelcome.

The hypothetical "reasonable person" is a difficult legal construct. A female complainant may have a very difficult perspective on what constitutes unwelcome conduct than a male respondent. The gender differences in perspective have been both legally and academically documented.[18] In some cases, the type of conduct is so egregious that it is self-evidently offensive. In other cases, the investigator may have difficulty in determining whether the conduct, viewed objectively, is inappropriate. In such cases, there may

---

[15] See, for example, *Tellier v. Bank of Montreal* (1987), 17 C.C.E.L. 1 (Ont. Dist. Ct.); *Gonsalves v. Catholic Church Extension Society of Canada* (1998), 164 D.L.R. (4th) 339 (Ont. C.A.).

[16] Aggarwal, *supra*, note 1 at 140-44.

[17] See The Law Society of Upper Canada's, "Guide to Preventing and Responding to Workplace Harassment and Discrimination: A Guide to Developing a Policy for Law Firms", March 2002, available on the Internet at <http://www.lsuc.on.ca/pdf/news_modelharassmentpolicyfinal.pdf>. See also, Aggarwal, *ibid.* at 129.

[18] An excellent discussion of the conflicting standards — "reasonable person" and "reasonable victim" is discussed in Aggarwal, *supra*, note 1 at 129 to 133. Jeanne Henry and Julian Meltzoff, "Perceptions of sexual harassment as a function of target's response and observer's sex" in *Sex Roles: A Journal of Research* (August, 1998).

be ways of resolving the complaint without making a finding of sexual harassment.[19]

2.   Is the Conduct of a Sexual Nature?

The second element in the test is whether the conduct was of a sexual nature. The unwelcome conduct must be related to a person's sex or gender to constitute sexual harassment. Although obvious in many cases, a co-worker or manager who is consistently rude and offensive to all employees may not be guilty of sexual harassment. Such behaviour may contravene an employer's internal code of conduct and in extreme cases, constitute tortious behaviour. Nonetheless, it does not constitute sexual harassment.[20]

Some conduct, while unwelcome to the recipient, simply does not form proper grounds on which to launch a harassment complaint. There may be various areas of conversation that are unwelcome to an employee, but would not be of a prohibited nature. A graphic description of the consequences of war, famine or child poverty may be distressing, but would not constitute conduct of a "sexual nature".

It may be that the conduct at issue does not constitute *sexual* harassment, but rather another form of discrimination or harassment prohibited by human rights legislation, for example, on the basis of race, class, age or disability. In some cases, the conduct may have elements of two or more types of harassment, *e.g.* both race and sex or disability and sex. Investigators should be sensitive to the fact that a victim of harassment sometimes may complain simply about "sexual harassment" without realizing that there are other factors at play, such as age, race or disability.[21] The law prohibits harassment on the basis of any of these protected categories. While this book focuses on sexual harassment, the investigator must be alert to any type of illegal harassment, even if the complainant does not frame the complaint explicitly on other grounds. Furthermore, some conduct may not constitute sexual harassment, but may violate another workplace policy or norm. In one case I

---

[19]   As indicated in Chapter 6, section 5, "Where the Parties Want to use Mediation", mediation is often an excellent tool to resolve workplace conflicts that may not fall squarely within the definition of illegal harassment.

[20]   *Bailey v. Anmore (Village)* (1992), 19 C.H.R.R. D/369 (B.C.C.H.R.). It was found that the supervisor engaged in puerile and offensive behaviour. The behaviour lacked a "sexual" component. It was clear that the supervisor treated all his employees — male and female — poorly.

[21]   For an academic perspective on how multiple factors in discrimination, sometimes termed "intersectionality", impact on human rights cases, see Nitya Duclos, "Disappearing Women: Racial Minority Women in Human Rights Cases" (1993) 6 C.J.W.L. 25.

investigated, a senior vice-president downloaded enormous amounts of violent pornography on his work computer. The IT Director was shocked to stumble upon the images during a routine investigation of bottlenecks in the computer system. While the conduct did not violate the company's sexual harassment policy, it did violate the company's internet and technology use policy. The senior vice-president was reprimanded and suspended without pay. He was required to prove he was getting professional help for his Internet addiction before returning to the workplace.

In other cases, the conduct reflects a personality conflict or an abusive boss, without a sexual component. While this type of conduct should be prohibited by internal workplace policies, human rights legislation and policies often do not address these types of issues. Most human rights legislation focuses on workplace barriers due to stereotypical assumptions or abusive conduct based on certain specific prohibited grounds, like sex.

An investigator needs to be sensitive to the scope of the policy which governs the investigation. In some cases, more than one workplace policy may be involved. In other cases, an investigation formulated in terms of "sexual harassment" may morph into something else. In these cases, the investigator may have to expand or re-do certain portions of the investigation to reflect the changing reality of the investigation.

3. Does the Conduct Detrimentally Affect the Work Environment or Lead to Adverse Job-related Consequences for the Victims of the Harassment?

In order for conduct to constitute sexual harassment, there must be an impact on either the work environment or the victim of the harassment. This 1989 requirement imposed by the Supreme Court of Canada has been rendered less important, since subsequent court decisions have recognized that working relationships often extend beyond the physical boundaries of the workplace and even beyond normal working hours.

The Ontario Court of Appeal commented:

> [i]t would be artificial and contrary to the purpose of controlling sexual harassment in the workplace to say that after-work interaction between a supervisor and other employees cannot constitute the workplace for the purpose of the application of the law regarding employment-related sexual harassment.[22]

An earlier decision of the Canadian Human Rights Tribunal also held that activities which may fairly and reasonably be said to be incidental to the

---

[22]   *Simpson, supra*, note 10 at 371.

employment or logically and naturally connected with a person's employment will also constitute the "workplace" for the purposes of examining sexually harassing conduct.[23] The determination of whether an activity that occurs after hours or outside the physical premises of the business is work-related must be considered by an investigator. An incident that occurs during working hours on the workplace is clearly work-related. An office Christmas party is work-related. A few co-workers deciding informally to go out for drinks after work may or may not be work-related. An investigator has to be sensitive to the background of any incident in order to determine whether it is work-related or not.

C. *QUID PRO QUO* HARASSMENT OR SEXUAL SOLICITATION

Legal commentators and legislation have recognized two distinct kinds of sexual harassment. The first type is often called *quid pro quo*. *Quid pro quo* is a Latin term which essentially means "this for that".

In the context of sexual harassment, it refers to the situation whereby a person in a position of power or authority either explicitly or implicitly offers a benefit or reward to a subordinate in exchange for sexual favours. For example, a classic situation of *quid pro quo* harassment is the manager who says to an entry-level employee, "Have a sexual relationship with me and I will make sure you get a permanent job."

Alternatively, *quid pro quo* harassment may take the form of a sexual proposition coupled with a threat or reprisal if the proposition is refused. For example, if a manager says to an employee, "if you don't have a sexual relationship with me, say goodbye to your promotion", this is another example of *quid pro quo* sexual harassment.

The Ontario *Human Rights Code* explicitly prohibits *quid pro quo* harassment:

7(3) Every person has a right to freedom from,

(a) a sexual solicitation or advance made by a person in a position to confer, grant or deny a benefit or advancement to the person where the person making the solicitation or advance knows or ought reasonably to know that it is unwelcome; or

(b) a reprisal or threat of reprisal for the rejection of a sexual solicitation or advance where the reprisal is made or threatened by a person in a position to confer, grant or deny a benefit or advancement to the person.

---

[23] *Cluff v. Canada (Department of Agriculture)* (1992), 20 C.H.R.R. D/61 (Cdn. Human Rights Trib.).

In one of the leading Ontario Court of Appeal cases on sexual harassment, *Simpson v. Consumers' Association of Canada*,[24] the court considered whether the following scenario constituted sexual harassment. Mr. Simpson suggested that if an assistant engaged in a "personal relationship" with him, then "opportunities could arise" for the assistant. He also mentioned that he "could make things happen" for the assistant, including getting the assistant a window office.

The assistant refused Mr. Simpson's advances. The assistant did not complain at the time, but later resigned due to her discomfort with his conduct. She also testified that Mr. Simpson became sarcastic and unpleasant with her. She attributed this to her refusal of his proposition, while he testified that he was genuinely concerned about certain work-related deficiencies.

In finding that Mr. Simpson's conduct with respect to his assistant constituted "one of the most serious and classic examples of sexual harassment", the Court of Appeal focused on the power imbalance. The assistant was a young secretary hired by Mr. Simpson. He was married and almost twice her age. He offered her job advancement if she acceded to his proposition. The Court of Appeal concluded:

> Where a supervisor in a position of authority offers advancement in employment in exchange for sexual favours, this conduct represents the clearest abuse of power. It is also a breach of duty both to the employee and to the employer, who is obliged to offer advancement fairly and equally on the basis of merit.[25]

The power imbalance is sometimes difficult to assess. In the *Simpson* case, there was a direct reporting relationship in a small organization. The age gap was significant. The connection between work advancement and the personal relationship was made explicitly. Many cases are not so clear cut and require careful consideration. Employees who are not in a direct reporting relationship may feel at a great disadvantage when propositioned by a more senior member of a company. Even co-workers may feel pressured where great emphasis is placed on getting along with members of a "team".

D.   HOSTILE ENVIRONMENT

In many cases, the conduct complained of does not relate to a specific sexual proposition. Rather, it is gender-specific conduct that impacts negatively upon an individual. The concept of a "hostile work environment" essentially

---

[24]   *Simpson v. Consumers' Association of Canada* (2001), 57 O.R. (3d) 351 (C.A.).
[25]   *Ibid.*, at 373.

recognizes that employees cannot help but be affected emotionally or psychologically by what is happening in the workplace, even when a sexual proposition is not directly involved.

A hostile work environment may be created even in the absence of direct harassment of a specific employee directly. Images (*e.g.* computer screen savers or cartoons), posters (*e.g.* pin-ups, quotes), and discussions via e-mail or in person in the workplace are all examples of conduct that can make an individual feel uncomfortable on the basis of sex.

A classic example was discussed by the British Columbia Human Rights Tribunal in *Burton v. Chalifour Bros. Constructions Ltd.*[26] Ms. Burton complained about a nude pin-up poster in the lunchroom. After she complained, the poster was removed. Unfortunately, the matter did not end there. Ms. Burton was subjected to ongoing demeaning comments after the poster was removed. The tribunal found that she was sexually harassed on the basis of a hostile work environment. The tribunal awarded relief to the woman, including $4,500 for injury to feelings caused by the poisoned environment.

The *Burton* case illustrates a number of important points relating to hostile environment harassment. The men employed by Chalifour Bros. did not find the poster offensive. Accordingly, there was no hostile environment harassment until such time as an employee found it offensive. When Ms. Burton found the poster offensive and expressed her discomfort, the employer had the obligation to deal with the poster issue effectively. It was insufficient to remove the poster. The employer also had to ensure that the employee experienced no negative consequences because of her complaint. By allowing the demeaning and nasty remarks to continue, the employer itself became liable for sexual harassment.

E. SEXUAL HARASSMENT BY WOMEN AND PERSONS OF THE SAME SEX

The reported instances of sexual harassment demonstrate that men are overwhelmingly the perpetrators, and women the victims, of this form of harassment. Men have traditionally occupied positions of power over women in the workplace. Men historically have been afforded more opportunities to abuse their positions of power.[27]

---

[26] [1994] B.C.C.H.R.D. No. 41.

[27] The power dynamic behind sexual harassment is well-documented in Catherine MacKinnon, *Sexual Harassment of Working Women* (New Haven: Yale University, 1979).

This does not preclude the possibility that men themselves can be sexually harassed. Female sexual harassment of men is simply a more infrequent occurrence. Men do experience sexual harassment by other *men* more routinely in areas other than the workplace, for example in the sports industry and in the military.[28]

Same-sex sexual harassment experiences are less widely reported, but do occur in the workplace against men and women, regardless of their sexual orientation. However, when the victim of the same-sex sexual harassment is gay or lesbian, this person may be less likely to report the discrimination.[29]

F. INTERRELATIONSHIP BETWEEN SEXUAL HARASSMENT AND OTHER FORMS OF DISCRIMINATION

The way in which a person experiences sexual harassment may be compounded by other personal characteristics. In addition to sexual orientation, a person's race, disability, or age, for example, may also contribute to the way a person views unwelcome sexual conduct.

While it is beyond the scope of this book to explore the interrelationship between harassment and discrimination on the basis of sex and other grounds, it is imperative that employers learn to recognize and respond appropriately to other forms of harassment in the workplace.

The following chapters provide a template for investigating sexual harassment in the workplace. Much of this information can be applied to the investigation of other forms of harassment. The author encourages the reader to make use of the following information for that additional purpose.

---

[28]   Aggarwal, *supra*, note 1 at 76-86.

[29]   David Corbett, "The Crystal Closet: Sexual Harassment of Lesbians and Gay Men in the Workplace" in *Managing Workplace Harassment: Practical Strategies* (Toronto: CBA, 2000).

APPENDIX 1.1

CHECKLIST OF QUESTIONS FOR INVESTIGATOR TO CONSIDER BEFORE DETERMINING COMPLAINT INVOLVES SEXUAL HARASSMENT

☐ Was it unwelcome conduct?

☐ Did the complainant explicitly advise that the conduct was unwelcome?

☐ Was the nature of conduct such that a reasonable person in the complainant's position would find the conduct unwelcome?

☐ Was the conduct physical? Consider frequency and seriousness of conduct.

☐ Was the conduct verbal? Consider frequency or seriousness of conduct.

☐ Did the complainant act in a manner that implicitly expressed discomfort, *e.g.* avoidance of person, activities, work areas, request for transfer, request for change in job, frequent absenteeism, working from home?

☐ Was there a power imbalance that might have exacerbated the seriousness of the conduct? Examples of such power imbalance include: a direct or indirect superior harassing a subordinate, a senior member of company dealing with a junior employee, a respected or influential co-worker dealing with a newcomer, an employee complaining about waiting for a promotion or transfer, the complainant being temporary or casual employee with no job security or an intern.

☐   Was the conduct of a sexual nature?

☐   Does the harassment constitute *quid pro quo* harassment? Was there an explicit or implicit promise of advancement if employee acceded *or* an explicit or implicit threat of adverse job consequences if employee refused?

☐   Even if the conduct not specifically directed at the complainant, could it constitute a hostile work environment? Was the conduct verbal or physical? Was there a tangible component to the hostile work environment, *e.g.* posters, cartoons, sexually-charged e-mails, screensavers, *etc.*?

☐   Is the conduct otherwise illegal? Could it involve harassment on the basis of race, age, marital status or other protected ground? Could it involve a breach of another workplace policy, such as Internet and electronic mail usage or anti-nepotism in the workplace?

☐   Were there actual negative job-related consequences for the complainant? Were these consequences psychological, financial, physical?

CHAPTER 2[*]

THE ROLE OF A HARASSMENT POLICY

A. INTRODUCTION

An employer that is serious about preventing sexual harassment will focus on developing an effective harassment policy. This policy is critical in any investigation.

In a leading case on sexual harassment, Mr. Justice Cumming observed:

> The advantages of a written, published, known policy are several, including the educative function of informing employees of what type of conduct is considered sexual harassment (which can manifest itself in various ways), and also that they know the consequences of any transgression. A formal policy that is made part of the contractual terms of employment can mean that there can be a dismissal for any misconduct that is spelled out in that policy as having the consequence of re-sulting in a dismissal. In the absence of a formal policy that forms part of the con-ditions of employment, the issue of dismissal as in the instant situation turns solely upon the question as to whether or not there was just cause as seen by the common law.[1]

An investigator must be familiar with the employer's policy prior to pursuing an investigation. The policy will define the expectations of the complainant, respondent and the company. A failure to follow any pro-cedural guidelines set forth in the policy may lead to a complaint, griev-ance, or litigation against both the investigator and the employer.

Even in the case of a properly-executed investigation, one or more parties may be dissatisfied. The complainant may feel that the respondent "got off lightly", while the respondent may perceive that he or she was unfairly

---

[*] I wish to acknowledge the enormous contribution made to this chapter by Tamara Jordan, an associate at Goodman and Carr LLP, in researching and providing materi-als for inclusion in this chapter. Any errors, however, are solely my responsibility.

[1] *Tse v. Trow Consulting Engineers Ltd.* (1995), 14 C.C.E.L. (2d) 132 at paras. 26-27 (Ont. Ct. J. (Gen. Div.)).

punished because of "political correctness". Given the sensitivity of a sexual harassment investigation, a complete sexual harassment policy is a useful tool for the investigator.

B. WHAT CONSTITUTES A FULL SEXUAL HARASSMENT POLICY?

Although most corporations have a short statement affirming commitment to the principles of equality and a harassment-free workplace, an expanded policy which outlines the protocol that all parties should follow should a situation arise, assists all participants in the process. Given the complexity of an employer's obligations in the context of a harassment complaint, such declarations need to be supported by a full policy that not only affirms the importance of legal compliance, but also outlines the process by which complaints are resolved.

Section 247.2 of the *Canada Labour Code* sets forth a minimum list of what must be included in each sexual harassment policy. While the Code only governs federally-regulated businesses, the statutory guideline is helpful to all employers. Sexual harassment policies must include:

(a) a definition of sexual harassment that is substantially the same as the definition in the section in the Code;

(b) a statement to the effect that every employee is entitled to employment free of sexual harassment;

(c) a statement to the effect that the employer will make every reasonable effort to ensure that no employee is subjected to sexual harassment;

(d) a statement to the effect that the employer will take such disciplinary measures as the employer deems appropriate against any person under the employer's direction who subjects any employee to sexual harassment;

(d) a statement explaining how complaints of sexual harassment may be brought to the attention of the employer;

(f) a statement to the effect that the employer will not disclose the name of a complainant or the circumstances related to the complaint to any person except where disclosure is necessary for the purposes of investigating the complaint or taking disciplinary measures in relation thereto; and,

(g) a statement informing employees of the discriminatory practices provisions of the *Canadian Human Rights Act* that pertain to rights of persons to seek redress in respect of sexual harassment.

In drafting a policy, an employer should consider the message that a comprehensive policy sends to its employees and others involved in the workplace:

- it affirms the corporation's commitment to a harassment-free workplace;
- it conforms to requirements imposed by law on the employer;
- it educates employees about what constitutes harassment and the possible consequences of such behaviour;
- it advises employees of when, how and to whom a complaint of harassment should be made;
- it provides employees with alternatives to formal complaints;
- it advises employees of the process of complaint investigation;
- it reminds managers and investigators of the process that should be undertaken when a complaint is made;
- it assures the complainant that reprisals are illegal;
- it outlines the possible consequences of the complaint investigation;
- it delineates the possibility of both informal and formal resolution processes;
- it warns against false or frivolous complaints.

C. DEVELOPING AND IMPLEMENTING A SEXUAL HARASSMENT POLICY

While daunting, the process of developing a harassment policy can be simplified by leveraging the experience of other employers and large institutions. If the internal resources do not exist, consider retaining an external consultant to facilitate the process.

1. Do Not Reinvent the Wheel

Gather all policies which have already been developed in the company on matters of harassment (sexual or otherwise) and policies which may be related: *i.e.* anti-discrimination (sometimes called equal opportunity policies), anti-nepotism policies, workplace safety and security policies, company computer usage guidelines, disciplinary policies and termination guidelines. You need to know what has already been established in the workplace before designing a new harassment policy. Furthermore, the company's policies should be internally consistent and cross-reference each other where appropriate. Review publicly-available precedents in textbooks and on the

Internet.[2] To help you get started, we have included a comprehensive harassment policy as an Appendix. Nonetheless, each company should strive to create a customized policy that works for it. No two companies and no two workforces are identical. In order to be effective, a harassment policy should reflect the reality of the specific workplace.

2. Consult all Stakeholders

While consultation can be a painstaking process, it inevitably leads to a stronger product. Employees should know that the company is considering implementing or revising their sexual harassment policy. Employees should be explicitly invited to contribute. Solicit input from all levels of staff and from all areas of the organization. Summer casual workers may have a very different perspective than permanent unionized workers. Federally-regulated employers *must* consult with employees or their representatives before developing a policy.[3]

In unionized workforces, it is critical to include the union in the process. There are both legal and practical reasons for this observation. As discussed in Chapter 4, any attempt to discipline a member of a bargaining unit pursuant to a harassment investigation may lead to a grievance under the collective bargaining agreement. Secondly, the union often faces complex issues when one member of a bargaining unit complains against another. The union also has a right to represent an individual who might be subject to discipline as a result of a harassment complaint. The tension between maintaining confidentiality of the complaint and the union's right to represent its members should be dealt with in advance of any specific complaint.[4] Obtaining union commitment to the policy and the process is a critical factor in the ultimate success of the policy.

---

[2]   The Internet will bring up thousands of examples of harassment policies. An excellent Canadian resource is the Ontario Human Rights Commission's *Policy on Sexual Harassment and Inappropriate Gender-related Comments or Conduct* available at <http://www.ohrc.on.ca/english/publications/sexual-harassment-policy.shtml>. Many educational institutions and human resource organizations have developed excellent model policies.

[3]   *Canada Labour Code*, R.S.C. 1985, c. L-2, s. 247.4.

[4]   A horrific example of the difficulties an employee can face when a union decides to represent an individual convicted of assault without considering the rights of the victim is found in *City of London, Re*, [2001] O.L.R.D. 3565.

3. Use Plain Language

In writing a policy, the author should focus on the audience. Every employee in the workplace needs to understand this policy. While human resource managers and corporate counsel may be familiar with legal terminology, most of the employees will not.

Some employers have multilingual workforces. English may be the second or third language of some of the workers. It is important to consider translating the policy where there is a realistic concern that the workers' English literacy may be inadequate to grasp the English-language version. The author should also consider other barriers to access, such as poor literacy skills or visual impairment.

4. State the Position of the Company Simply and Clearly

The most critical message is that the company will not tolerate sexual harassment in any form.

5. Explain What Constitutes Sexual Harassment

While most employees will concur with the general sentiment that employees ought not to be subject to illegal harassment, policies should contain workplace-specific examples of what constitutes harassment and discrimination. Examples culled from academia will unlikely be relevant to a manufacturing setting. The best examples come from the workplace itself. Consider whether there have been complaints in the company's own history. Fictionalized, these examples will have great resonance with the workplace. Lawyers and human resource managers are excellent sources of information regarding past examples of harassment in similar workplaces. Human rights case law[5] can provide inspiration regarding situations which have led to formal complaints and have required legal resolution.

---

[5] The most comprehensive collection of human rights cases is available in the Canadian Human Rights Reporter, which also has a fee-for-service database of almost all reported tribunal cases involving human rights. It can be accessed at <http://www.cdn-hr-reporter.ca>. Less comprehensive summaries of cases are available on various government databases, including: <http://www.albertahumanrights.ab.ca> (Alberta); <http://www.bchrt.gov.bc.ca> (British Columbia); <http://www.chrt-tcdp.gc.ca> (Canada); <http://www.gov.mb.ca/hrc> (Manitoba); <http://www.gov.ns.ca/humanrights> (Nova Scotia); <http://www.ohrc.on.ca> (Ontario); <http://www.gov.pe.ca/human rights> (Prince Edward Island); <http://www.canlii.org/qc/cas/qctdp/index.html> (Quebec); <http://www.gov.sk.ca /shrc> (Saskatchewan).

Employers also need to be sensitive to cross-cultural and cross-generational issues that might be present in a workplace. Presenting specific examples in a policy can educate employees without creating a perception that certain employees are being "picked" on. For example, the British immigrant of a certain generation who addresses some colleagues as "luv" or "dear" may not realize that he is offending his younger Canadian-born female colleagues. Another colleague may come from a culture where it is not unusual to kiss cheeks instead of shaking hands and may not realize how "forward" she seems to someone from a more reticent background.

It is also useful to include examples regarding "poisoned work environments". The traditional example is the garage with posters of scantily-clad women on the wall. Another example might be more appropriate to a white-collar establishment. The forwarding of offensive e-mail jokes or cartoons is a prevalent practise in the wired workplace.

6. Consider Workplace Demographics and Deployment

One of the most frequent problems in designing a useful harassment policy is dealing with the complexity of organizational structure. The retail operation with 300 stores across Canada has very different logistical requirements than the large manufacturing plant located in one centralized setting. The small not-for-profit organization faces limitations not faced by large corporations or governmental departments. A Canadian branch of a U.S. corporation may face special problems. The U.S. policy may refer to trained human resources individuals and legal counsel, but make no provision for Canadian employees who need assistance. In other organizations, employees may work various shifts, but are limited to accessing competent assistance on harassment issues during the day.

It is critical to ensure that all employees can rely on the harassment policy, regardless of geographic location or the type of work they perform.

This is difficult. In a centralized workplace, employees may know the individuals responsible for the enforcement of the policy. It may be easier for such employees to access their rights. In a diffuse workforce, however, employees may never meet anyone with responsibility for the policy during their entire work history with the company.

An employee should also be provided a choice of individuals to approach for redress in a potential harassment situation. It is important not to limit the choices to direct-line supervisors or senior individuals in the human resources area. In one notorious case, the very person who had been charged with developing a harassment policy was found to have repeatedly harassed subordinates.[6]

Where possible, individuals assigned responsibility for enforcing the policy should represent the diversity of the organization. Larger organizations typically assign responsibility for the policy to both a male and female manager. Where possible, the managers should belong to different departments, geographic centres, work in different time zones or be assigned to different shifts.

In very large organizations or where shift work is prevalent, a confidential toll-free hotline may be the only way to ensure that employees feel comfortable in accessing their rights under the policy.

7. Anticipate Conflicts of Interest

Employees will be reluctant to make complaints regarding harassment against senior employees or employees who are responsible for the implementation of the harassment policy. Develop a protocol that anticipates these concerns. Suggestions include the retention of an external, independent investigator.

D. EDUCATE YOUR WORKFORCE

Once a sexual harassment policy has been developed, the next step is to ensure that it is effectively communicated to all employees. This can be accomplished through a variety of education and training strategies.

1. Management "Buy-In" is Critical

The starting point for all education about sexual harassment is a serious attitude to the subject. The most carefully developed sexual harassment policy will be undermined if the efforts to educate employees about the policy are half-hearted or accompanied by an indifferent demeanour on the part of supervisors and management.

Consequently, those employees who are designated to educate and train employees about sexual harassment in the workplace must be able to present a unified, confident approach to the topic.

There are a number of ways an employer can demonstrate a serious attitude toward sexual harassment within the workplace. For example, the

---

[6] *Simpson v. Consumers' Association of Canada* (2001), 57 O.R. (3d) 351 (C.A.).

Department of Justice Canada in its Departmental Policy, *Towards a Conflict and Harassment-Free Workplace,*[7] instructs managers to prevent harassment by acting as role models in the workplace and by demonstrating that they take the issue seriously. The policy is easily accessible to all employees on-line.

Supervisors can demonstrate commitment by enforcing the sexual harassment policy consistently, taking action to halt harassment, immediately responding to complaints, and reminding employees about the policy where opportunities permit.

Employers must motivate senior employees to lead by example and to demonstrate visible support for the policy. In many organizations, supervisors are specifically rewarded on a number of personnel-related matters, such as retention of employees, successful recruitment practices and achieving certain goals.

Employers should seriously consider rewarding managers who demonstrate an open commitment to the prevention of sexual harassment in the workplace. Criteria could include the number (or percentage) of employees who have completed training, the manager's own successful training in the area and the lack of harassment complaints in the specific department. Hours devoted to attending training could be included for bonus consideration.

2. Circulating the Policy

The first step in implementation is circulating the policy to all employees and people who regularly attend the workforce, such as temporary or free-lance workers.

The policy must be circulated upon its initial creation and after any amendments have been made to it. Depending on the workplace, the policy may be provided to employees through one or more of the following methods:

- incorporating the policy into an employee handbook or manual;
- circulating the policy as a memorandum or as part of an employer's newsletter or bulletin;
- posting the policy on a bulletin board in an area of the workplace designated for official notices and policies;

---

[7]   See <http://canada.justice.gc.ca/endept/pub/just/harassment.htm>.

- posting the policy on-line, on an employer's internal electronic network;
- providing the policy separately to each employee as a personal letter;
- providing the policy to employees as part of the employment contract.

Most importantly, the policy must also be read and understood by each employee. This may present challenges for workplaces in which there are employees with minimal English skills or visual impairments. It is incumbent upon supervisors and managers in these workplaces to ensure that written information is conveyed by an alternate method, perhaps by having other employees serve as translators or providing the policy in audio-cassette format.

Many employers simply include the harassment policy in an operational manual or handbook. Technologically-advanced companies are turning to corporate intranets to distribute important workplace information.

While all useful techniques, these efforts at distributing the harassment policy often miss the mark. Unfortunately, most employees simply skim the handbook or intranet. Their attention often is focused on the business terms of the relationship, such as pay days, vacation leave and statutory holidays. Casual and part-time employees are often hired without the formality associated with permanent employees. Because of the brevity of the employment relationship, such employees are often never advised of their rights as part of the orientation process. Casual and part-time employees are often inexperienced, young or recent immigrants. They are often least aware of their rights and most vulnerable to harassment.[8]

A simple, but critical step, is to ensure that the harassment policy becomes a specific part of the hiring process for every employee, just like signing the appropriate government forms for the payroll or insurance process. Each employee should be provided a copy of the harassment policy and be required to acknowledge receipt at the start of employment. This acknowledgment should become part of the employee's personnel file. This is critical for two reasons. It establishes that the employee was advised of the company's anti-harassment policy and precludes the defence that the

---

[8]   A groundbreaking case that was argued all the way to the Supreme Court of the United States involved a female teenage life guard at a municipal swimming pool who was routinely harassed by her supervisor, a young male in his twenties. The complainant was never advised of any of the municipality's policies with respect to her rights. The Supreme Court held the City of Boca Raton responsible. See *Faragher v. City of Boca Raton*, 524 U.S. 775 (1998).

employee did not know or was never advised of the company's expectations in this regard. Secondly, it emphasizes the importance of the anti-harassment policy at the very onset of the employment relationship.

One way to ensure effective ongoing review of the sexual harassment policy is to include it as part of an employee's annual performance review. Employees could simply be asked to confirm in writing that they have been provided and have reviewed and understood the current version of the sexual harassment policy.

For some employers, the effective circulation of a sexual harassment policy may be the sole method of educating employees about issues of sexual harassment in the workplace. While this is far from ideal, the minimum protocol as set out above will at least ensure that employees have a general understanding of the issues and the steps they should take if they encounter sexual harassment in the workplace.

3.   Providing Training to Employees

There are at least three groups of employees who should receive training in issues related to workplace sexual harassment: (a) non-supervisory employees; (b) supervisors; and (c) individuals designated with specific roles or responsibilities under the sexual harassment policy (*e.g.* investigators, union stewards, human resource managers).

a. Non-Supervisory Employees

Many employers are reluctant to provide harassment training to all their employees because of budgetary and time constraints. However, introductory training need not be greatly expensive nor extensive to be effective. It simply makes sense for the employer to provide training.

First, from a legal perspective, the more steps that employers take to prevent sexual harassment from occurring in the workplace and to ensure an effective response in the event that it occurs, the more likely it is that those employers will avoid legal liability. Second, employers benefit from healthy employees. A workplace that is free from sexual harassment will experience less absenteeism due to stress-related illnesses. Third, employees will be more likely to view sexual harassment as a serious workplace issue, if it is reinforced through additional training.

Ideally, an employer should ensure employees understand:

- the definition of sexual harassment: what it is and what it is not;
- how to avoid behaving in a manner that would constitute sexual harassment;
- the process: what to do if you have been sexually harassed and what to do if a complaint has been brought against you;
- the range of possible consequences to an employee whose conduct constitutes sexual harassment, including dismissal;
- the roles of individuals who have been designated with specific responsibilities in the complaint process;
- where to go for more information or support;
- how to make a complaint.

There should be an opportunity for employees to ask questions. Some employees may have questions that they are uncomfortable raising in public and others may not be prepared to ask questions until a later date. Employees should be provided a confidential way to contact the trainer or a designated resource person.

b. Supervisors

Employers must often rely on their supervisors to prevent conditions from occurring in the workplace that would expose the employers to liability. Supervisory employees require additional education to deal effectively with sexual harassment in order to protect the employer from such liability. Unfortunately, some supervisors will abuse their authority. Sexual harassment has been recognized as a form of abuse of power. Some of the worst cases of sexual abuse involve a supervisor and a subordinate employee. An employer is often most at risk when a supervisory employee commits sexual harassment because tribunals and courts are much more likely to impose liability on an employer for the acts of a supervisory employee.

Additional training should be provided to supervisors to ensure that supervisors understand:

- the law regarding employer's liability in sexual harassment complaints;
- their own personal legal obligation (and exposure) as supervisors;
- each component of the employer's sexual harassment policy so that it can be communicated effectively to employees;
- how to ensure employees are aware of and following the sexual harassment policy;

- how to receive and refer complaints;
- what confidentiality means and how to ensure it is maintained during any sexual harassment complaint;
- the significance of keeping detailed records.

c. Designated Individuals

Under an employer's sexual harassment policy, certain employees may be designated as having a particular role in responding to a sexual harassment complaint. These employees include human resource managers, union stewards, legal counsel or specific departmental managers. These individuals must have the information, training and tools to be enable them to perform the jobs assigned to them in an effective manner. Consequently, specialized training for these individuals is crucial. These individuals will need to be trained on their specific responsibilities under the policy, including:

- how to respond to a complaint;
- the rights of the complainant, respondent (and the union, if any);
- when to conduct an investigation;
- whether an informal resolution is appropriate;
- whether a formal investigation is appropriate;
- what constitutes a conflict of interest;
- the role of an investigator;
- whether the designated individual should conduct the investigation or not;
- when to retain an external investigator.

d. Training Format

There are a number of ways in which training can be provided to employees, including seminars with accompanying literature, interactive training with audio-visual components or role-plays, written tests, or more intensive one-day workshops. The type of training a given employer chooses to implement will vary due to factors, including the number of employees in a company or an organization, the physical and geographical location of its site(s), whether the employer has suitable facilities in which to hold training sessions, the composition of employee groups within the workplace, and, of course, budgetary constraints.

One example of a cost effective way to train a large group of employees is the sexual harassment education initiative implemented by Scotiabank in 1992. This large organization provided training to all of its employees through a video training module. All employees had an opportunity to watch a video on sexual harassment and received accompanying literature.

Another large organization developed an Internet-based training module. Managers were paid a $100 bonus if they accessed the course and completed 7 quizzes. The quizzes ensured that the managers knew their basic legal obligations, the company's policies, the definition of harassment, and required them to respond to hypothetical fact patterns. The quizzes were varied and randomized, so managers would find it difficult to cheat.

In-person training, although time consuming and expensive, has many advantages. If a suitable internal resource can be utilized to provide training, this would avoid the costs of hiring an external trainer. However, hiring an external consultant with the appropriate training, knowledge and experience in dealing with sexual harassment issues is generally preferred. Hiring an independent, third party to conduct the training will create a more neutral learning space for employees, enable employees to engage more readily with the material, and allow employees to more freely ask questions they might not otherwise.

Another workplace simply invites a consultant to attend regularly-scheduled meetings for a question and answer session on employee issues. The consultant picks an area of concern and then the floor is opened for questions. Every year, the issue of harassment is reviewed. The consultant reports that almost inevitably, delicate questions arise regarding harassment, consensual relationships gone sour and how to respond to harassment complaints.

As with any "expert" retained to provide training, there is a wide range of costs and approaches available. Before an employer decides to invest in any particular training program, it may be wise to explore non-profit or governmental resources. These entities may provide training on sexual harassment at a low or sliding scale cost, or provide basic material such as handouts and pre-packaged video resources.

It is always important to provide an opportunity for employees to submit written feedback about the training they receive in order to confirm the usefulness of the training and encourage suggestions for improvement. The comments may also help to elicit additional relevant feedback about the occurrence of sexual harassment in the employer's workplace.

Finally, employers should ensure that opportunities exist for ongoing review of the employer's sexual harassment policy and that all employees are correspondingly trained when any changes are made to the policy.

E. CONCLUSION

A comprehensive workplace harassment policy is a useful preventive tool for the employer. From the investigator's perspective, it serves as the map of the investigation. The presence (or lack thereof) of a workplace harassment policy and the manner of its distribution to employees may well be an important avenue to investigate in a specific case. It may demonstrate what employees knew about what conduct was considered inappropriate in the workplace. Knowledge of the policy may also be a factor in assessing what, if any, kind of remedies, should be recommended in a final report.

APPENDIX 2.1

CHECKLIST FOR THE DEVELOPMENT OF A HARASSMENT POLICY

☐ Review corporation's previous policies and/or precedents involving similar types of companies.

☐ Remember the policy acts as an introduction to the business' commitment to anti-harassment.

☐ Ensure internal consistency with other policies.

☐ Consult stakeholders (*e.g.* human resources, union stewards, plant managers).

☐ Design a complaints procedure that works with the specific organizational structure of employer.

☐ Make sure policy applies to all employees (casual, part-time, permanent, managerial), consultants, contractors on employer's site.

☐ Define harassment in a way consistent with applicable legislation.

☐ Provide examples of what constitutes harassment in a workplace-specific manner.

☐ Assign responsibility for receiving complaints to trained individuals.

☐ Emphasize the importance of timely complaints.

☐ Explain the right to trigger an informal resolution.

☐ Explain how to lodge a formal complaint.

☐ Explain who will receive and review the complaint, whether formal or informal.

☐ Explain the obligation of confidentiality and the limits of confidentiality.

☐ Explain who will investigate.

☐ Explain the process of investigation, including witness interviews, document reviews and the follow up process.

- Explain the rights of the complainant, including the right to access the appropriate commission or tribunal.
- Explain the rights of the respondent, including the right to seek assistance from the union or legal counsel.
- Explain the anticipated time lines to complete the investigation.
- Explain whether the report of the investigator will be treated as "confidential" or whether the parties will have a right to respond to the report.
- Guarantee the complainant's right not to suffer reprisals.
- Establish the whole gamut of disciplinary options if complaint is found to be valid, *e.g.* training, reprimand, suspension, demotion, denial of bonus or other prerequisite, dismissal.
- Explore possible remedies for victim, including counselling or monetary compensation if harassment resulted in monetary loss.
- Remind complainant of the consequences if complaint found to be malicious and distinguish between malicious complaint and an unproven complaint.
- Explain that internal process may be stayed or suspended in the case of a complaint to the human rights commission or police.
- Discuss appeal mechanisms, if any.
- Solicit input and feedback on the policy for future revisions.
- Review policy for "plain language" — ask for comments from rank and file employees.
- Translate policy where necessary.
- Design and implement roll-out policy, including distribution, education and training.

APPENDIX 2.2

CHECKLIST FOR ROLLOUT OF SEXUAL HARASSMENT POLICY (EDUCATION AND TRAINING)

☐ Do not re-invent the wheel: explore available resources and investigate other employers' training programs before finalizing training programs for your workplace.

☐ Select trainers who have credibility within the organization and have a thorough knowledge of the subject area.

☐ Choose training formats that best meet the needs of your specific workplace environment(s) — think of videos, Internet, "lunch and learn" formats.

☐ Be creative in developing training to minimize cost and to provide the most user-friendly formats available.

☐ Speak with management and supervisory employees to ensure they understand their role in projecting a serious attitude and visible commitment to the sexual harassment policy.

☐ Ensure effective circulation of the policy to all employees after its initial creation and after any revisions are made to it.

☐ Ensure the policy is read and understood by all employees, including employees with low literacy skills in English or learning disabilities.

☐ Provide training sessions for the general employee population to ensure employees understand each component of the policy and the reasons behind its development.

☐ Provide employees with contact information for individuals designated under the policy (*e.g.* counsellors, investigators, and grievance officers).

☐ Provide supervisory personnel with additional training to minimize the employer's exposure to liability.

☐ Ensure that employees designated with particular roles in responding to sexual harassment complaints are provided with sufficient training to enable them to have the information and tools necessary to effectively perform the tasks assigned to them.

☐ Incorporate the policy into the hiring and review process for every employee.

SAMPLE HARASSMENT POLICY (WORKPLACE WITH MULTIPLE LOCATIONS)

EMPLOYEE HARASSMENT OR DISCRIMINATION

ABC Company is committed to a workplace that is respectful of human rights. Our policy is based upon the principles and provisions of the Ontario *Human Rights Code* which prohibits discrimination and harassment in the workplace. Management takes harassment and discrimination seriously and such behaviour will not be tolerated. If a claim of harassment or discrimination is proven, disciplinary measures will be applied, up to and including termination of employment.

ABC Company will not permit discrimination, intimidation or harassment of, or by, employees, on the basis of race, ancestry, sex, place of origin, ethnic origin, marital status, colour, citizenship, creed, age, family status, handicap, sexual orientation, same-sex partnership status, record of offences (for which a pardon has been granted) or on the basis of any other personal characteristics protected by the Ontario *Human Rights Code* ("protected grounds"). Handicap or disability includes perceived disability and mental and physical disability.

Discrimination is not permitted at any level of ABC Company or in any part of the employment relationship. This includes the following areas: recruitment; promotion; training opportunities; salary; benefits; terminations; transfers; overtime; hours of work; holidays; shift work; performance evaluations; and discipline. ABC Company is committed, and employees are required, to sustain an environment that encourages personal respect and mutual trust. ABC Company prides itself on having one of the most diverse workforces in the country and wants its employees to share in that pride.

Differences between individuals, such as in race, sex, creed and age are to be respected by all employees. The term "employees" include temporary, casual and contract staff as well as those employees who are working to gain experience (*i.e.* work placement, volunteers).

Employees are entitled to freedom from sexual and all other forms of harassment on the basis of the protected grounds listed above. ABC Company's policy against harassment and discrimination extends beyond the physical constraints of the workplace such that employees are entitled to freedom from harassment and discrimination during business trips, company parties and other company-related functions.

Harassment means engaging in a course of inappropriate comment or conduct that is known or ought reasonably to have known would be unwelcome. It comprises objectionable conduct, comment or display based on any of the protected grounds listed above, made on either a one-time or continuous basis that demeans, belittles, or causes personal humiliation or embarrassment to an employee. Examples of harassment can include unwelcome touching, sexually-suggestive comments, demeaning nicknames, posting of sexually-revealing posters on walls, jokes which are directed at a particular religious group or sex, and comments which focus on a person's body or figure. Other forms of harassment include racial remarks, jokes or innuendoes, comments ridiculing individuals because of race or race-related grounds, comments regarding religious dress, demeaning or humiliating comments or jokes related to race, ancestry, place of origin or ethnic origin, and the display of racist, derogatory or offensive pictures, graffiti or other materials. ABC Company's policy against harassment prohibits harassment within the meaning of the Ontario *Human Rights Code*. We ask employees to use courtesy amongst each other. A good rule is this: if you wouldn't want to do something in front of your parent, spouse or religious leader, do not do it at work.

Sexual harassment can be a particular problem. Sexual harassment means any conduct, comment, gesture or contact of a sexual nature, as well as inappropriate gender-related comments or conduct that is directed to a person because of his or her gender, whether on a one-time basis or in a continuous series of incidents:

(a)   that is unwelcome;
(b)   that might reasonably be expected to cause offence or humiliation to any employee; or

(c) that the employee might reasonably perceive as placing a condition of a sexual nature on employment or on an opportunity for training or promotion.

The following is not an exhaustive list, but should assist in identifying what may constitute sexual harassment or inappropriate gender-related comments and conduct:

(i) gender-related comments about an individual's physical characteristics or mannerisms;

(ii) unwelcome physical contact;

(iii) suggestive or offensive remarks or innuendoes about members of a specific gender;

(iv) propositions of physical intimacy;

(v) gender-related verbal abuse, threats or taunting;

(vi) leering or inappropriate staring;

(vii) bragging about sexual prowess;

(viii) demands for dates or sexual favours;

(ix) offensive jokes or comments of a sexual nature about an employee or client;

(x) display of sexually offensive pictures, graffiti or other materials; or

(xi) rough and vulgar humour or language related to gender.

In addition to harassment and discrimination, ABC Company will not tolerate behaviour that results in a poisoned work environment. A "poisoned environment" is a form of discrimination. It may be created by the comments or actions of any person regardless of his or her position or status. These offensive comments or actions spoil or "poison" the work environment. The poisoned environment results in an unequal term or condition in employment and is therefore a violation of the right to be free from discrimination.

Abuse of authority is a form of harassment and occurs when an individual improperly uses the power and authority inherent in her or his position to endanger an employee's job, undermine the performance of that job, threaten the economic livelihood of the employee, or in any way interfere with, or influence the career of, the employee. It includes intimidation, threats, blackmail or coercion. All employees have a right to be treated with respect, even if they are subject to disciplinary process. Yelling, screaming, threatening or abusive behaviour is not considered acceptable or professional.[9]

Managers and supervisors should be aware that under the Ontario *Human Rights Code*, ABC Company may be liable for the actions of its employees.

Managers and supervisors, in particular, should also recognize that while it is appropriate to be cordial with staff members under their supervision, they should be careful how and when they socialize with staff members. Just because conduct is "after hours" does not mean it is not subject to the harassment policy. Managers who meet with a staff member alone after hours for non-work related purposes put themselves and the company at risk of a harassment complaint. If you have any questions regarding the appropriateness of socializing after hours, please contact: _____ _____ [insert correct name] for more information.

For a more detailed discussion of ABC Company's employment policies, the Ontario *Human Rights Code* or for confidential advice on particular issues, contact _____[insert correct name] or use the confidential hotline number _____. If you see or hear behaviour that you think might constitute harassment or discrimination, talk to your immediate supervisor. If you are not comfortable talking to your immediate supervisor, contact _____[insert correct name] or use the confidential hotline number _____. Although we encourage you to give your name on the confidential hotline, ABC Company will still respond to anonymous information. An anonymous tip, however, cannot always be investigated or dealt with properly.

Complaint Procedure:

Individuals who feel their rights have been violated have the right:

(a) to talk to their direct supervisor or if they prefer _____at head office or to access the confidential hotline at _____ about the problem. These people are familiar with ABC

---

[9] This is an example of a workplace broadening the scope of the harassment policy beyond the current state of the Canadian law. The corporation is committed to a respectful workplace. During consultation, many employees voiced concern regarding abuse unrelated to gender or other protected ground. This led to the inclusion of this paragraph.

Company's policies and procedures as well as the Ontario *Human Rights Code,* and will be able to provide advice on how to deal with the problem and file an internal complaint as well as explaining the option of approaching the Ontario Human Rights Commission with a complaint. These people will be neutral and objective, and will ensure that all issues are kept strictly confidential. Although anonymous information on the confidential hotline will be followed up, it is difficult to do a proper investigation if name and contact information is not provided.

(b) to file a formal complaint against the person who he or she feels has committed the harassment or discrimination. Although the complaint is confidential, it will be discussed to the extent necessary to conduct a proper investigation. This may include discussion with the person you accuse of harassment or witnesses.

(c) to be free from threat of reprisal or discipline as a result of making a complaint or accessing their rights under this policy. This protection from reprisal also covers others involved such as witnesses, advisors, representatives of complainants and witnesses, and any investigators or decision-makers.

(d) to ensure that a *bona fide* complaint about harassment or discrimination does not affect their employment status and that no record be placed on their personnel file;

(e) to be represented by an advisor, colleague or legal counsel;

(f) subject to the needs of confidentiality, to be informed of the response to the complaint, including any corrective measures implemented as a result of valid complaint; and

(g) to receive fair treatment and respect throughout the process.

If a formal complaint is made, the following steps will be taken by ABC Company: (1) informal dispute resolution; (2) investigation; and (3) resolution.

Informal dispute resolution is a useful way to try to resolve a complaint without the necessity for an investigation. This type of resolution may involve a neutral person using a "shuttle" technique to work with the parties individually and going between the different parties to convey positions and resolution proposals.

If the informal dispute resolution process fails to resolve the matter, a formal investigation is necessary. Investigators are responsible for examining the circumstances of the complaint, including interviewing the parties and any witnesses, and aim to be as independent and objective as possible. Wherever possible, the investigator will not be in a position of direct authority over any of the people involved in the complaint, but will report to the person with the authority to make decisions and have them enforced. The investigator will be familiar with human rights generally and the Ontario *Human Rights Code* in particular. The investigator will ensure that the investigation process remains confidential. In most cases, investigations will commence immediately after an investigator is chosen, and will be completed within 90 days. At the conclusion of the investigation, the investigator will make a finding about whether discrimination and/or harassment occurred, and this finding will be set out in a report. The investigator, together with the appropriate people in the human resources department, will decide what action must be taken and the possible resolutions that exist. Depending on the finding of the investigator, any number of the following progressive discipline measures may be applied and not in any particular order:

(a)   verbal warning given and documented in employee's personnel file;

(b)   written corrective interview, including a performance improvement plan;

(c)   suspension with pay;

(d)   suspension without pay;

(e)   final notice of performance improvement, including an Action Plan;

(f)   written termination notice to be given to the employee.

If the complaint cannot be settled through ABC Company's internal procedure, the employee will then be advised that he or she may file the complaint with the Ontario Human Rights Commission. Employees should also be aware that although ABC Company has an internal procedure in place for dealing with complaints, an individual always has the option of approaching the Ontario Human Rights Commission with the complaint. Under the Ontario *Human Rights Code*, a complaint must be filed with the Ontario Human Rights Commission within six months from the date the last act of alleged discrimination occurred, whether or not ABC Company's internal procedure has been used.

While it is appropriate to respect the choice of the employee with respect to whether a complaint is filed using the internal procedure, employees should be aware that even if a complainant elects to take no further action or to withdraw a complaint, if the Human Resources department, a supervisor, or manager has reason to believe that others have been or may be subjected to inappropriate behavior by the person complained about, ABC Company has the responsibility to deal with the matter to the extent possible without the involvement of the complainant. ABC Company has a duty to investigate and address human rights concerns, particularly where there is any chance that the behaviour may continue against the particular complainant or others.

ABC Company encourages its employees:

(a)   to make their disapproval or unease about a person's actions known within a reasonable time to the alleged offender if they feel comfortable doing so;

(b)   to keep notes of any offensive behaviour at the time it occurs to keep track of specific incidents, particularly what happened (a description of the events or situation), when it happened (dates and times of the events or incidents), where it happened and who saw it happen (names of witnesses, if any);

(c)   to keep any documents or materials, such as letters, notes, or offensive pictures that may have something to do with the complaint;

(d)   to seek immediate assistance from a supervisor, the confidential hotline or _____ when a problem occurs — problems which fester are often hard to fix or resolve; and

(e)   to cooperate with those responsible for reviewing the complaint.

A person who has been accused of harassment or discrimination also has the right to either talk to their direct supervisor or if they prefer _____ at head office or to access the confidential hotline at _____ about the situation.

Please note that while every complaint will be treated seriously, it is not always possible to determine the validity of the complaint. Nonetheless, ABC Company will make every effort to resolve any harassment, discrimination or abusive behaviour complaint it receives in a professional manner.

CHAPTER 3[*]

EMPLOYER'S LIABILITY TO A COMPLAINANT IN THE CONTEXT OF SEXUAL HARASSMENT

A. INTRODUCTION

In a landmark case, *Robichaud v. The Queen*, the Supreme Court of Canada found that human rights legislation should be interpreted in light of its broad remedial purpose. Accordingly, employers governed by federal human rights legislation could be held liable for the sexual harassment of one employee by another, *even if the employer was completely unaware of the harassment.*

The traditional common law position was that an employer was only liable for an employee's misconduct if the misconduct occurred in the course of the employee's discharge of his or her work-related duties. Although the employer was not actually guilty of the act or omission, it could be held "vicariously" liable for the conduct of its employee in these circumstances. Since sexual harassment could not be justified as part of any employee's duties, employers were able to avoid liability.[1]

The 1987 *Robichaud* decision signalled an aggressive judicial attitude against sexual harassment. The employer was legally recognized as being best positioned to stop further recurrences. In the *Robichaud* case, the Supreme Court of Canada indicated that although an employer could be held vicariously liable for the conduct of its employees:

---

[*] I wish to acknowledge the enormous contribution made to this chapter by Dayna Arron in researching and providing materials for inclusion in this chapter. Any errors, however, are solely my responsibility.

[1] Much of this history is traced in *Robichaud v. The Queen (Treasury Board)*, [1987] 2 S.C.R. 84. The traditional common law case has been further eroded by the decision of the Supreme Court of Canada in *Bazley v. Curry*, [1999] 2 S.C.R. 534, which dealt with the sexual misconduct of employees in an institutional setting.

...an employer who responds quickly and effectively to a complaint by instituting a scheme to remedy and prevent recurrence will not be liable to the same extent, *if at all*, as an employer who fails to adopt such steps. These matters, however, go to remedial consequences, not liability.[2]

The language in *Robichaud* was a clear signal that employers should and could reduce liability by taking active steps to prevent harassment in the workplace. It signalled that human rights legislation ought to be read expansively.

B.   HUMAN RIGHTS LEGISLATION

The starting point of determining an employer's obligation to an employee who has been subjected to sexual harassment is the relevant human rights legislation. Every jurisdiction in Canada has enacted legislation to establish that workplace harassment is illegal. Appendix A contains excerpts from the relevant pieces of legislation.

The language with respect to employer liability for sexual harassment differs from jurisdiction to jurisdiction. Nonetheless, employers may be exposed both directly (by having committed the act of sexual harassment) and vicariously (by being responsible for the act of its employees). Damages for sexual harassment have ranged from a low of $1,500 to a high of $8,000 for the mental and emotional component of the harm suffered. Actual measurable losses are also compensable.[3]

1.   Direct Liability in Human Rights Legislation

An employer can be directly liable for discrimination or harassment if he or she is a perpetrator. This type of liability would apply to a sole proprietor or partner in a partnership. In such cases, the liability is direct and not vicarious. Where an employer does not directly harass, but authorizes, condones, adopts or ratifies the employee's harassing conduct, the employer is directly liable because the employer has refused to rectify the situation and allowed it to continue. The failure to act in circumstances when an employer should have acted attracts direct liability.[4]

---

[2]   *Ibid.*, at 96.
[3]   An excellent overview of typical damage awards can be found in Walter S. Tarnopolsky *et al.*, *Discrimination and the Law*, 3d ed. (Toronto: Carswell, 2001) at para. 8-123 to para. 8-129.
[4]   *Olarte v. Commodore Business Machines* (1983), 4 C.H.R.R. D/1705 (Ont. Bd. Inquiry). A particularly good example can be found in *Budge v. Thorvaldson Care Homes Ltd.* (2002), 42 C.H.R.R. D/232 (Man. Bd. Adj.) where an owner ignored a

Where the employer is a corporate entity and the individual guilty of harassment can be fairly considered to be the "directing mind" of the corporation, the corporation can be found directly liable for harassment. The act of the individual can be ascribed to the corporate entity itself. This is often referred to as the organic theory of corporate liability. The analysis of what constitutes the "directing mind of a corporation" is not a straightforward exercise. Although it is clear that a chief executive officer is part of the directing mind of the corporation, what about the foreman or personnel manager? Even relatively low-level employees have been found to be part of the directing mind of the corporation.

Direct liability has been ascribed to the corporation for the misconduct of a foreman where it is clear that the foreman had significant supervisory responsibility.[5] In cases where supervisory or managerial employees are accused of harassment, an employer should anticipate being held responsible for the misconduct. The focus should be on reducing exposure by acting quickly and responsibly.

2. Vicarious Liability

Depending on the wording of the legislation, an employer may be vicariously liable under statute for the acts of an employee, even where the employee is not part of the "directing mind" of the corporation. The *Ontario Human Rights Code* restricts vicarious liability to certain specific situations. The *Canadian Human Rights Act* contains more expansive language. It is important for an investigator to consider the specific language of the relevant legislation.

To a large extent, the limited language of vicarious liability in the statutory instruments has been overtaken by two legal developments. Firstly, the tribunals have been ready to ascribe direct responsibility in many cases. Secondly, the common law of vicarious liability has grown to impose liability in certain cases of wilful misconduct.[6]

An Ontario Board of Inquiry summarized the employer's obligations in responding to sexual harassment in the workplace:

---

written communication about possible sexual harassment on the basis that the author might have an "axe to grind" and that the author was trying "to take a role beyond her jurisdiction". In an unreported decision, *Simms v. Ford Motor Company of Canada* (1979), Ont. Bd. of Inquiry (Krever), the Board of Inquiry found that an employer would be liable for discrimination if it knew racially abusive langauge was being used by co-workers and did nothing to prevent it.

[5] *Olarte v. Commodore Business Machines, ibid.*

[6] See discussion in *Bazley v. Curry*, [1999] 2 S.C.R. 534.

Briefly, the six elements are that an employer must demonstrate that: (a) it is aware that sexual harassment is prohibited conduct; (b) a complaint mechanism is in place; (c) it acted with alacrity in handling the complaint; (d) it dealt with the matter seriously; (e) it has met its obligation to provide a healthy work environment; ... (f) it met its obligation to inform the complainant of its response.[7]

3.   Remedies in the Human Rights Context

The human rights commissions are charged with broad remedial powers. Although they are entitled to (and do) award compensatory damages for losses incurred because of sexual harassment, they are also empowered to provide damages for mental distress. Furthermore, the human rights commissions have powers to order remedial measures in the workplace, both to make the complainant whole and to prevent further recurrences of similar discriminatory conduct. In the past, human rights tribunals have:

(a)   awarded full reinstatement of the complainant with no loss of seniority;

(b)   required the employer to post a copy of the Human Rights Code in the workplace;

(c)   required the employer to provide a positive letter of recommendation to the complainant to assist in future job searches;

(d)   required the employer to establish a pro-active program to end systemic discrimination in the hiring process;

(e)   required the employer to have all job advertisements vetted by the human rights commission;

(f)   required the employer to report all departures/terminations of employees from the workplace to assist in monitoring the possibility of recurrences of discrimination;

(g)   required the employer to establish a workplace education program about discrimination;

(h)   required individual respondents to attend an education course approved by the commission with respect to issues of discrimination and harassment; and

(i)   required renovation of the premises in question.[8]

---

[7]   *Jones v. Amway of Canada Ltd.* (2001), 39 C.H.R.R. D/480 at para. 74 (Ont. Bd. Inquiry).

[8]   See the excellent summary in Walter S. Tarnopolsky *et al.*, *Discrimination and the Law*, 3d ed. (Toronto: Carswell, 2001) at para. 15.4 at 15-147 *et seq.*

In short, the human rights tribunals have broad remedial jurisdiction in Canada. They can look beyond the issue of compensating the specific victim and seek to deal with the underlying causes of the problem. Many of these remedies involve significant interference in the daily operation of the workplace and go beyond what a court would award in similar cases.

C. COMMON LAW OBLIGATIONS

Lawyers acting on behalf of the victims of sexual harassment have been re-visiting traditional theories of tort and contract liability in order to obtain re-dress for their clients.

1. Constructive Dismissal

Certain courts and tribunals have recognized that serious harassment may entitle an employee to resign employment and still sue for damages on the basis of wrongful dismissal or termination. The law in this area has been largely developed in the context of human rights decisions, where tribunals have recognized that employees have been forced to quit due to the intoler-able working conditions caused by the harassment.[9]

Some courts have recognized that the existence of harassment can be legally construed as a breach of the employment contract by the employer. This area of law is still in its infancy. Much of the case law focuses on the appropriateness of the civil courts dealing with issues of harassment in light of specific human rights legislation prohibiting harassment.[10] Nonetheless, courts have allowed plaintiffs to proceed on the basis that facts which con-stitute sexual harassment under human rights legislation may also constitute constructive dismissal.[11]

---

[9]   An excellent review of cases where tribunals have found that the level of harassment justified the employee's decision to quit can be found in R. Echlin and J. Fantini, *Quitting for Good Reason: The Law of Constructive Dismissal in Canada* (Aurora: Canada Law Book, 2001) at 465-78.

[10]   *Alpaerts v. Obront* (1993), 46 C.C.E.L. 218 (Ont. Ct. J. (Gen. Div.)) and *Ghosh v. Domglas Inc.* (1986), 15 C.C.E.L. 105 (Ont. Ct. J. (Gen. Div.)).

[11]   See *Lehman v. Davis et al.* (1993), 1 C.C.E.L. (2d) 15 (Ont. Ct. J. (Gen. Div.)) and *L'Attiboudeaire v. Royal Bank of Canada* (1996), 17 C.C.E.L. (2d) 86 (Ont. C.A.) which dealt with a similar argument in the context of racial discrimination and har-assment.

Damage for constructive dismissal is measured on the basis of what would the employee have received as monies in lieu of notice, if he or she had been explicitly terminated by the employer. Since young employees with short service records often are entitled to relatively modest awards in lieu of notice, a civil claim for constructive dismissal is often not the best remedy.[12]

Although constructive dismissal is an option, it is unclear whether an employee can claim constructive dismissal on the basis of abusive treatment by co-workers or customers if management was unaware of the circumstances. As Stacey Ball observes:

> It is less clear whether an employee can claim constructive dismissal for abusive treatment by co-employees of which the employer has no knowledge. We are of the view that in such circumstances, an employee must bring any complaint to the attention of the employer. However, the employer must act positively and in a timely fashion to address the employee's concern. The manner in which the employer responds to the complaint will dictate, if any, the extent of employer liability.[13]

2. Intentional Infliction of Mental Suffering

Several victims of egregious types of harassment have been successful in pursuing a tort claim against both the perpetrators and their employer. A person who, without legal justification, intentionally causes mental suffering or nervous shock, is liable for damages caused to the victim. The intention is usually inferred from the nature of the conduct. Deliberate falsehoods or flagrant or outrageous behaviour support the inference that the conduct was intentional.

The case law, however, is not consistent. Judges have routinely expressed strong reservations about litigation which appears to focus on breaches of human rights legislation in the civil context.[14]

In *Clark v. Canada*, an experienced RCMP female officer complained that both her co-workers and supervisory officers engaged in an extended course of verbal harassment. Her complaints were supported by the evidence of a civilian secretary employed in her division. She eventually suffered from clinical depression and left the employ of the RCMP. Her supervisory

---

[12] See commentary in S. Ball, *2 Canadian Employment Law* (Aurora: Canada Law Book, 1996) at 29-41.

[13] Ball, *ibid.* at para. 29:80.2.

[14] *Bhadauria v. Board of Governors of Seneca College* (1981), 124 D.L.R. (3d) 193 (S.C.C.); see also *Allen v. C.F.P.L. Broadcasting Ltd.* (1995), 9 C.C.E.L. (2d) 56 (Ont. Ct. (Gen. Div.)).

officer did not take the complaints seriously and denied ever seeing harassment. She successfully sued for the intentional infliction of mental suffering. The court not only imposed direct liability against the co-workers and supervisory officers in question, it imposed vicarious liability on the employer, the Crown in right of Canada. The court had no difficulty in imposing vicarious liability on the Crown on the basis that supervisory officers neglected to respond and deal with Ms. Clark's complaints of harassment.[15]

3. Defamation

Some complainants have sought a remedy on the basis that verbal sexual harassment constitutes a form of defamation. The concept of defamation is a broad one:

> Defamation consists of any written, printed or spoken words or of any audible or visible matters or acts which tend to lower a person in the estimation of others or cause a person to be shunned or avoided or exposed to hatred, contempt or ridicule. Thus an assertion which does not suggest discreditable conduct by the plaintiff may still be defamatory if it imputes to him or her a condition calculated to diminish the respect and confidence in which the plaintiff is held.[16]

Some sexual harassment may also constitute defamation. A suggestion that a woman obtained her professional success by "sleeping her way to the top" may be considered to be defamatory with respect to her professional or business reputation. Negative epithets such as "slut" or "whore" may constitute an imputation of immorality. Creative lawyers have used the tort of defamation to avoid the statutory limits on damages in the Ontario *Human Rights Code* or the inadequacies of the collective bargaining regime.[17]

4. Assault and Battery

Sexual harassment usually entails offensive verbal behaviour. In certain cases, however, the verbal behaviour can constitute the tort of assault, *i.e.* "the intentional creation of the apprehension of imminent harmful or of-

---

[15] *Clark v. Canada* (1994), 20 C.C.L.T. (2d) 241 (Fed. T.D.) and *Kulyk v. Toronto Board of Education* (1996), 24 C.C.E.L. (2d) 63 (Ont. Ct. J. (Gen. Div.)); see also *Boothman v. Canada*, [1993] 3 F.C. 381 (T.D.).

[16] Charles N. MacDonald, "Defamation", *Canadian Encyclopaedic Digest (Ontario)*, vol. 8A, 3rd ed. §1.

[17] See, for example, *Kulyk v. Toronto Board of Education* (1996), 24 C.C.E.L. (2d) 63 (Ont. Ct. J. (Gen. Div.)).

fensive conduct".[18] If there is actual offensive physical contact, the victim may sue on the basis of the tort of battery.[19] Complainants have been reluctant to allege the torts of battery and assault. Traditionally, employers have escaped vicarious liability for the deliberate misconduct of an employee. It was difficult to establish that assault and battery were committed in the scope of an employee's duties. The Supreme Court of Canada has recognized that where the employer's enterprise significantly or materially increased the risk of the tortious act occurring, the imposition of liability on the employer was appropriate for various policy reasons.[20]

D. LIABILITY UNDER THE COLLECTIVE BARGAINING AGREEMENT

Increasingly, collective bargaining agreements incorporate provisions with respect to anti-harassment and anti-discrimination. This permits an employee to grieve sexual harassment using the collective bargaining process. The vast majority of grievances are commenced by individuals accused of sexual harassment and who wish to challenge the employer's discipline or dismissal. Where both the alleged victim and perpetrator belong to the same union, it is difficult for a victim of harassment to feel confident that he or she will be fully supported by the union.[21]

The grievance system is designed to deal with management decisions which adversely impact on an employee. Consequently, some employees have been successful in using the system when a member of management engages in sexual harassment.[22]

The situation becomes much more complex when a union member complains about the conduct of another union member. The union may have

---

[18] Linden, *The Law of Torts*, 7th ed. (Markham: Butterworths, 2001) at 45.

[19] *Ibid.*, at 46.

[20] *Bazley v. Curry*, [1999] 2 S.C.R. 534.

[21] See, for example, *Re Canadian National Railway Co. and Canadian Brotherhood of Railway, Transport & General Workers* (1988), 1 L.A.C. (4th) 183 wherein the adjudicator observed, "The union, on the other hand, bound as it is to fully protect the rights of the discharged employee, is bitterly accused by the female complainants of having forsaken their right to be free of sexual harassment by turning its defence of the grievor into an attack on themselves." An egregious example of the conflict which can arise can be found in *Protomanni v. C.U.P.E., Local 1165,* [1996] L.V.I. 2785-4, where the union initially chose to represent a grievor who had been convicted of sexual assault of a co-worker in criminal proceedings. The employer dismissed the grievor. The union reconsidered its position only after the complainant wrote a letter.

[22] *Re Canada Post Corp. and Canadian Union of Postal Workers* (1983), 11 L.A.C. (3d) 13 and *Re Newfoundland (Newfoundland Farm Products Corp.) and N.A.P.E.* (1988), 35 L.A.C. (3d) 165.

legitimate concerns regarding how to balance the rights of the accused and the accuser.[23]

In some cases, a victim of harassment can grieve matters that would be difficult to adjudicate in the civil system. For example, in *Toronto (City) v. C.U.P.E. (Loc. 79)*,[24] the City of Toronto was held responsible for harassment of employees by members of the public. The remedy included requiring the City of Toronto to take active steps to prevent further recurrences.

The existence of a collective bargaining agreement can also pose an obstacle to unionized employees who wish to sue in the civil courts. In many cases, the employers take the position that the matter of harassment must be dealt with in the context of a grievance arbitration and should not proceed to court. The courts have shown some flexibility in permitting certain kinds of civil suits, such as defamation, to proceed despite the presence of a collective bargaining regime.[25]

Many labour lawyers believe that the collective bargaining regime represents a great opportunity to deal with issues of workplace harassment in a timely and cost-effective manner. To date, however, it appears that this regime has been used primarily by perpetrators of harassment to grieve discipline or dismissal.

---

[23] For example, in a case involving the Toronto Catholic District School Board, the union offered to provide the complainant with separate legal representation because both the complainant and the respondent were members of the same union. The complainant felt that the union was still in breach of its duty of fair representation under the Ontario *Labour Relations Act*. See, *Toronto District School Board*, [1999] O.L.R.D. 2664.

[24] Unreported decision of Adjudicator Springate.

[25] *Kulyk v. Toronto Board of Education* (1996), 24 C.C.E.L. (2d) 63 (Ont. Ct. J. (Gen. Div.)).

CHAPTER 4

EMPLOYER'S LIABILITY TO THE RESPONDENT

A. INTRODUCTION

A review of the recent case law reveals that employees accused of sexual harassment commonly assert wrongful dismissal and/or constructive dismissal in response to discipline or termination following a harassment complaint. Employees accused of harassment in a unionized setting can also grieve the employer's discipline or discharge under the grievance procedures established under the collective bargaining process. Surprisingly, employees who have been discharged or disciplined following allegations of sexual harassment have been quite successful in Canadian courts and tribunals when challenging their employer's decisions. The courts have frequently reviewed the underlying investigation as part of assessing the merits of a wrongful dismissal claim or a grievance.

B. COMMON LAW OBLIGATIONS

1. Wrongful Dismissal and Constructive Dismissal

An employer may decide to terminate an employee accused of sexual harassment. The terminated employee will often sue for wrongful dismissal. At common law, an employer is entitled to terminate most employees only upon providing "reasonable notice" or compensation in lieu of notice. One way of avoiding paying notice is by establishing just cause for the termination of employment. It is the employer's responsibility to establish that just cause for termination exists. Sexual harassment can be, in certain circumstances, just cause for termination.[1] At trial, employees routinely challenge the defence of just cause on the basis that the employer improperly

---

[1] *Simpson v. Consumers' Association of Canada* (2001), 57 O.R. (3d) 351 (C.A.).

conducted or mishandled the investigations and accordingly, the results of the investigations are suspect.

Courts are more focused on whether sexual harassment actually occurred and if so, if the type of sexual harassment warranted dismissal. Although the primary focus appears to be on the facts, a botched investigation clearly colours the judge's perception of the legitimacy of the employer's defence.[2]

After determining what actually occurred, the courts proceed to determine whether the disciplinary action was warranted given the facts and circumstances of each incident.[3]

Employers who conduct a fair and thorough investigation will provide the courts with indispensable evidence which will also help them justify grounds for dismissal.[4]

In certain cases, employees may seek to argue that certain incidents during the investigation constitute constructive dismissal. Constructive dismissal denotes an employer's unilateral imposition of a material negative change to the terms and conditions of employment. An employee is entitled to reject such unilateral negative changes and sue for damages for wrongful dismissal.

An unpaid suspension pending the investigation could constitute constructive dismissal. An unpaid disciplinary suspension might also constitute constructive dismissal. Courts have yet to set clear rules regarding the employer's right at common law to suspend employees without pay in the absence of an express or implied right to do so in the employment contract.[5] The employee could reject the suspension and sue for damages for reasonable notice.[6]

2. Defamation

A false or overstated accusation of sexual harassment tends to diminish the reputation of the respondent. An employee wrongly accused and investigated of sexual harassment may sue the employer and the employee who

---

[2]   The best example is provided in *Buchanan v. Geotel Communications Corporation*, [2002], 18 C.C.E.L. (3d) 17, additional reasons, [2002] 26 C.P.C. (5th) 87 (Ont. S.C.J.). The trial judge rejected the defence of just cause and commented unfavourably on the calibre of the investigation.

[3]   *Shiels v. Saskatchewan Government Insurance* (1988), 51 D.L.R. (4th) 28 (Sask. Q.B.).

[4]   *Bannister v. General Motors of Canada Limited* (1998), 164 D.L.R. (4th) 325 (Ont. C.A.).

[5]   *Reininger v. Unique Personnel Canada Inc.*, (2002) Carswell Ont. 2355.

[6]   *Haldene v. Shelbar Enterprises Ltd.* (1999), 179 D.L.R. (4th) 716 (Ont. C.A.).

made the false allegations for defamation of character.[7] An investigator must be circumspect in the course of the investigation in order to minimize the possibility of a successful defamation suit.

Defamation is categorized as either libel or slander. Libel involves defamatory material which has been published and damages are presumed. Slander refers to the spoken word and damages must be proven by the plaintiff. In either circumstance, a defendant will benefit from a full defence if he can or she establish the truthfulness of the statement.[8]

Employees who allege defamation must establish that (a) the statement was conveyed to third parties; (b) the statement in itself would be viewed by third parties as an attack on the plaintiff's character; and (c) the statement identified the plaintiff. There is no doubt that a false allegation of sexual misconduct would constitute defamation.[9]

The courts recognize, however, that fear of defamation lawsuits would prevent many employees from raising legitimate concerns and would prevent employers from conducting a thorough investigation. In the employment context, both the employee and the employer have an interest in ensuring that laws regarding harassment and discrimination are respected. It is inevitable that complaints will be made that might ultimately be unproven or mistaken.

Even where a court ultimately finds that certain statements were false, exaggerated or unproven, an employer and a complainant may be protected by the defence of qualified privilege. Qualified privilege has been defined as follows:

> [a]n occasion is privileged if a statement is fairly made by a person in the discharge of some public or private duty, or for the purpose of pursuing or protecting some private interest, provided it is made to a person who has some corresponding interest in receiving it. The duty may be either legal, social or moral. The test is whether persons of ordinary intelligence and moral principle, or the great majority of right-minded persons, would have considered it a duty to communicate the information to those to whom it was published. [10]

An employer who receives a complaint of sexual harassment and during the course of the investigation, reveals or repeats some of the information received, may be able to avail itself of this defence. The employer can rely

---

[7]   R. Brown, *The Law of Defamation in Canada*, vol. 1, 2d ed. (Toronto: Carswell, 1994) at 15.

[8]   A. M. Linden, *Canadian Tort Law*, 7th ed. (Toronto: Butterworths, 2001) at 706.

[9]   R. Brown, *The Law of Defamation In Canada*, vol. 1, 2nd ed. (Toronto: Carswell, 1994) at 51-56. See, for example, *Pangilinan v. Chaves* (1988), 47 C.R.R. 371 (Man. C.A.).

[10] R. Brown, *ibid.*, at 662.

on its duty under law to receive and respond to complaints of sexual harassment. This defence applies even if it is subsequently clear that there was no truth to the allegations, unless it can be established that the employer acted maliciously.[11] The defence of qualified privilege tries to strike a careful balance between society's need to have open communication and an individual's right to preserve his or her reputation.

An employee who makes an honest, but mistaken, complaint of sexual harassment to an employer can also rely on this defence as long as there was no actual malice involved.

Before determining that the defence of qualified privilege applies, the courts will contemplate (a) the nature of the alleged defamatory publication; (b) the persons publishing the alleged untrue statements; (c) the recipients of the information; and (d) the context or occasion during which the statements were made.[12]

The protection afforded by qualified privilege is not absolute. Employers must be able to demonstrate that their disclosure was in furtherance of their duty to receive, investigate and respond to complaints of sexual harassment. An investigator may have no choice but to reveal certain portions of a complaint in the course of an investigation, but should be as circumspect as possible to prevent inadvertent disclosure of sensitive information. Qualified privilege does not protect disclosure which is unnecessary.[13]

Once the elements of qualified privilege are established, an employee would have to establish that the employer or complainant acted pursuant to an inappropriate ulterior motive in order to succeed in a defamation lawsuit.

3.   Intentional Interference with Contractual Relations

Intentionally interfering with another person's contractual relations is an actionable wrong. The employment relationship between an employer and employee is one of contract.

The Supreme Court of Canada confirmed the constituting elements of the tort in *Posluns v. Toronto Stock Exchange*: (a) a valid and enforceable contract must exist; (b) the defendant must be aware of the existence of the contract; (c) the breach of the contract must have been induced by the defendant; (d) the breach must result from the wrongful interference on the

---

[11]   See *Cantelon v. Industrial Wood and Allied Workers of Canada, Local 1-71*, [1999] B.C.J. No. 1620 (S.C.) for a discussion on qualified privilege in the context of an employer-employee relationship.

[12]   A.M. Linden, *supra*, note 8 at 670.

[13]   R. Brown *supra*, note 9 at 851-86.

part of the defendant and (e) the plaintiff must have suffered damages as a result of the breach.[14] High-level employees have been able to sue for significant amounts.[15]

An individual who files a misleading complaint about sexual harassment may be subject to liability if it can be determined that (a) the individual knew of the employment contract; (b) a contract of employment existed between the employer and employee; (c) as a result of the wrongful allegation by the individual, the employer breached the employment contract and (d) the employee suffered financial losses. It is reasonably foreseeable that an employee will suffer adverse job consequences, including termination, loss of promotions or bonuses in light of a false allegation of sexual harassment.

4. Intentional Infliction of Mental Suffering

Any individual who intentionally causes mental suffering to another person commits a tortious act. Employers who knowingly communicate false statements about employees do not escape this liability. Falsely accused employees will often suffer significant mental anguish. Wise employers must proceed cautiously with the investigation and avoid contributing to an innocent party's anguish by limiting the communication of the false statements to circumstances of necessity. Employees who deliberately fabricate harmful allegations can also be held liable for initiating the investigation and the anguish that ensued.

Our society has revealed that a single allegation of sexual harassment may have serious repercussions on a person's life even when the allegation is later proven to be false. Once the truth is established, it is often too late. An investigation that is carefully conducted under the highest standard of confidentiality will therefore benefit all parties and limit the mental anguish and vulnerabilities that may arise from the process.

5. Professional Negligence

An investigator who is retained to conduct an investigation is engaging in a sensitive activity. Particularly where that individual is a professional, *e.g.* a lawyer, accredited social worker or human resource professional, that individual will be held to a high standard. Professionals are expected to

---

[14]   [1968] 1 S.C.R. 330, aff'g [1966] 1 O.R. 285 (C.A.), aff'g [1964] 2 O.R. 547 (H.C.J.).
[15]   *Imperial Oil Ltd. v. C & G Holdings Ltd.* (1989), 62 D.L.R. (4th) 261 (Nfld. C.A.).

discharge their duties up to the standard of a qualified practitioner in the field of practice.

An investigator should be aware that he or she could be held personally liable if the investigation is conducted poorly. An action for negligence could be established if the plaintiff is able to establish that (a) he suffered an injury; (b) the damage resulted from the investigator's conduct; (c) the conduct was in breach of the standards associated with a reasonably competent professional; (d) the breach was also the cause of the harm suffered; and (e) the plaintiff was not guilty of contributory negligence and has not voluntarily assumed the risk.[16] It is typical for an employee dismissed due to the results of an investigation to sue both the employer and the investigator for damages. In some jurisdictions in the United States, negligent investigation can be the basis for a lawsuit.[17] In Canada, this area of the law is underdeveloped as the courts focus on whether the employer was correct or not in determining that it had cause to dismiss the offending employee.

6. Breach of Fiduciary Duty

Although routinely alleged, it is difficult to sustain a claim that an investigator or employer breached a fiduciary duty to an employee being investigated of harassment. Nonetheless, the scope of fiduciary duty is still developing. Lawyers involved in investigations must be careful to ensure that all participants understand that the lawyer has not accepted a retainer from any of the participants in the investigation, but is retained as a neutral investigator or counsel by the employer. Unintended confusion regarding a lawyer's role can create arguments regarding conflicts of interest and/or breach of fiduciary duty.

C. THE UNIONIZED WORKPLACE

Any unionized employee who is disciplined or discharged due to an allegation of sexual harassment may seek to invoke the grievance procedures in the collective bargaining process. The union has the right to

---

[16] Linden, *supra*, note 8 at 149-51.

[17] Montana law, for example, recognizes the concept of negligent investigation. See *Crenshaw v. Bozeman Deaconness Hospital*, 693 P. 2d 487, where an award of $150,000 was given to the employee. Note that U.S. judgments are routinely significantly higher than Canadian equivalents. American precedents with respect to judgments should be regarded cautiously.

determine whether it wishes to pursue the grievance on behalf of the employee. In cases involving sexual harassment, the union faces a difficult dilemma. The union has an obligation of fair representation to all its members. Where an employee faces termination or significant penalty, that duty is particularly onerous.[18]

The union also has an interest in maintaining a harassment-free work place. In some cases, both the complainant and respondent belong to the same bargaining unit. Before declining to pursue a grievance, the union has a duty to investigate the grievor's version of events independently. It cannot just rely on the employer's investigation.[19] In many cases, the union will deal with the conflicting interests by offering one or both parties independent counsel.[20] Complainants have also sought the right to participate separately from the union as an intervenor in grievance arbitrations involving the alleged harasser, on the basis that the union is in a complete conflict of interest position.[21]

It is clear that excessive discipline, including termination, can be grieved under the collective bargaining regime in a unionized workplace. Adjudicators routinely consider a number of factors, including the worker's previous disciplinary history, the seriousness of the offence, the employer's policies with respect to sexual harassment, the impact on the complainant and whether a lesser penalty is appropriate in the circumstances.[22]

D.   CONCLUSION

Throughout the course of the investigation, it is important to recognize that a person accused of harassment can access numerous remedies. It is not surprising that many employers, even when convinced that an employee has committed serious harassment, will offer a severance package in exchange for a full and final release.[23]

---

[18]   *Re Stolp*, [1998] C.L.R.B.D. No. 11; see also *2471256 Canada Inc. (c.o.b. Greenpeace Canada)*, [2001] O.L.R.D. No. 2364.

[19]   *Ruda and Public Service Alliance of Canada*, [1997] C.P.S.S.R.B. No. 110.

[20]   *Toronto Catholic District School Board*, [1999] O.L.R.D. 2664.

[21]   *Re 3M Canada Inc. and C.A.W. Canada. Loc. 27 (Chapman)*, 64 L.A.C. (4th) 213.

[22]   See, for example, *Eastcan Bottling Ltd. v. Soft Drink Workers Joint Local Executive Board, Local 387W* (1990), 13 L.A.C. (4th) 180 (Ont. Arb. Bd.).

[23]   See *Gonsalves v. Catholic Church Extension Society of Canada* (1998), 164 D.L.R. (4th) 339 (Ont. C.A.), where the employer made an offer to pay some severance in exchange for a release, even though the termination was motivated by Mr. Gonsalves' serious misconduct.

CHAPTER 5

THE LEGAL FRAMEWORK FOR A PROPER INVESTIGATION

A. INTRODUCTION

An investigator is faced with a complex legal situation when asked to conduct an investigation. There are significant obligations to both the person alleging harassment and the person being accused of harassment.

Employers often have to deal with these conflicting obligations to both employees. Many employers seek to discharge those obligations by creating a confidential, fair and consistent response to complaints of sexual harassment. A good investigation is a critical component of this response. An investigator must have a basic understanding of the case law surrounding what constitutes a fair investigation. This chapter is intended as a basic introduction to the concept of fairness in the context of investigations.

B. THE IMPORTANCE OF FAIRNESS TO EMPLOYEES ACCUSED OF HARASSMENT

The state of the law with respect to an employer's obligation to conduct a fair investigation in the case of a complaint of sexual harassment is clearly in a state of flux.[1] Much of the law has been developed in the context of wrongful dismissal litigation, where an ex-employee disputes whether the employer had just cause for terminating employment.

A private sector employer in the non-unionized context does not have a legal duty to provide reasons for termination or provide an opportunity to an employee to explain his or her side of the story. Nonetheless, there is a

---

[1] An excellent synopsis of the state of the case law can be found at *Leach v. Canadian Blood Services* (2000), 7 C.C.E.L. (3d) 205 (Alta. Q.B.).

strong correlation between the employer's chances of success at trial and whether the employee was given a chance to respond to serious allegations.[2]

Judges are reluctant to overturn case law which upholds the right of an employer to dismiss any employee without discussing the true reasons for such dismissal. There is, nonetheless, an intuitive judicial understanding of the unfairness of not providing the terminated employee a chance to explain his or her version of events prior to the decision being made.[3]

Given the seriousness of a dismissal based on an allegation of sexual harassment, the employer is still well-advised to ensure that there is a fair and open-minded investigation. In one of the leading textbooks on sexual harassment, Arjun Aggarwal and Madhu Gupta observe:

> ... a person who is wrongfully accused or punished for sexual harassment suffers the same righteous indignation felt by an innocent, yet indicted, corporate thief. It is the employer's responsibility to protect both the sexually harassed and the falsely accused sexual harasser. Both have a right to a fair hearing. An employer who immediately takes the complainant's side and passes judgment prematurely upon the alleged harasser may find itself faced with a court action .... The principle which must govern in such cases is that whenever such allegations are made and believed, the employer is duty-bound to investigate them and to give the person against whom they were made full opportunity to answer them.[4]

Courts have repeatedly criticized employers for acting precipitously in the context of an allegation of sexual harassment, *even when the allegations are ultimately found to be true.* In the 1997 case of *Strong v. M.M.P.*, Mr. Justice Granger found that the male employee had sexually harassed several female employees. The Court accepted that cause was established, but observed:

> I was not impressed by the manner in which General Motors carried out its investigation in this matter. In my opinion, it [the employer] should before determining the validity of such allegation, and the penalty to be imposed if it accepts the validity of the allegation, meet with the alleged perpetrator of such sexual harassment and allow him or her an opportunity to present his or her version of the events. In

---

[2] R. Echlin & M. Certosimo, *Just Cause: The Law of Summary Dismissal in Canada* (Aurora: Canada Law Book, 1998) at 1-6.

[3] An excellent example is provided in the reasons for judgment in *Buchanan v. Geotel Communications Corporation*, [2002] 18 C.C.E.L. (3d) 17, additional reasons, [2002] 26 C.P.C. (5th) 87 (Ont. S.C.J.). The case involved a serious allegation that an employee had solicited a kickback from an important customer. Justice Ferguson of the Ontario Superior Court of Justice gave very little weight to the allegations of cause, partially because Geotel failed to give Buchanan a meaningful opportunity to respond to the complaint, never provided the name of the complainant to Buchanan and had not given a copy of the written complaint to him.

[4] Arjun Aggarwal & Madhu Gupta, *Sexual Harassment in the Workplace*, 3d ed. (Toronto: Butterworths, 2000) at 301-302.

this case, the evidence ... leads to the conclusion that prior to the meeting with Mr. S .... General Motors had accepted that the allegations ... were true and that Mr. S's employment ... should be terminated.[5]

General Motors escaped any liability for its failure to act fairly towards Mr. S. because the Court accepted the evidence that he had raped a female employee. Nonetheless, the comment in his judgment is a warning to all employers.

There are, unfortunately, very few cases in which the courts have praised the conduct of an investigation. One of the major exceptions is *Leach v. Canadian Blood Services*. Despite some flaws in the process, the Court praised the employer for a professional, fair and thorough investigation, which involved:

(a) promptly notifying the employee of the complaint;

(b) providing a copy of the harassment policy to the employee;

(c) providing a copy of the written complaint to the accused employee;

(d) allowing the employee time to consider his response;

(e) advising the employee he had a right to have legal counsel present during the meetings;

(f) retaining detailed notes of the meeting.[6]

C. THE BASIC COMPONENTS OF A GOOD INVESTIGATION

The case law has highlighted some of the hallmarks of a good investigation in the context of criticizing a bad investigation.

1. Appoint an Investigator

Firstly, an employer "should identify a person charged with investigating such complaints and that individual should be able to act quickly".[7] In order for the investigator to have credibility in the eyes of all parties involved, the investigator must be, and must be perceived as being, a true neutral. It is important to make a considered decision regarding who should investigate.

---

[5] (1997), 31 C.C.E.L. (2d) 47 (Ont. Ct. J. (Gen. Div.)).

[6] *Leach v. Canadian Blood Services, supra*, note 1.

[7] *Re CUPE and Office and Professional Employees' Union* (1982), 4 L.A.C. (3d) 385 at 407 (O.L.R.B.).

Chapter 8 provides a guideline regarding some of the considerations involved in selecting an investigator.

An investigator should be appointed *even when the complainant requests that nothing more be done.* This is not an unusual request, as many victims of harassment believe that a formal complaint will invoke reprisal or accomplish nothing. In the context of a unionized workforce, a grievance arbitrator observed that the failure to proceed with an investigation can also be a serious mistake:

> The fact that the grievor was not disciplined as a result of those allegations does not mean that the employer was under no obligation to give him an opportunity to answer them. The allegations were in the mind of management, they were on file and they were believed. It is inevitable that management's view of the grievor would be influenced by the allegations which it had accepted as being truthful. ...
>
> The principle which must govern in such cases is that whenever such allegations are made and believed, the employer is duty-bound to investigate them and to give the person against whom they were made full opportunity to answer them.[8]

2. Audi Alterem Partem – Hear all Sides of the Story

A company takes a huge risk of losing a wrongful dismissal action if it fails to provide the accused employee a full opportunity to explain his or her side of the story.

At the very least, an employee accused of sexual harassment must know who the accuser is and the substance of the allegations he or she faces. The employee must be given an opportunity to respond to the allegations. It is not enough to summarize the information provided by the complainant. The accused employee should be advised of every detail of the complaint. The level of detail should be sufficient to (a) identify the complainant; (b) provide details regarding time, location and circumstances of the events; and (c) identify other parties present.

Of course, an investigator may have a concern regarding fabrication of a response or retaliation against the complainant. This fear must be balanced against the concern that without such details, it would be difficult for anyone to provide a coherent response.

---

[8] *Kahlon and Treasury Board, Re* (1991), 19 P.S.S.R.B. Decision 34.

3. Be Thorough

One of the most comprehensive statements of what constitutes a good investigation is found in the 1996 decision in *McIntyre v. Rogers Cable T.V. Ltd.*[9] The court emphasized the importance of a thorough investigation, which required:

(a) written witness statements, particularly of important witnesses;

(b) in-person interviews of crucial witnesses;

(c) interviews of all important witnesses (suggested by either party or discovered in the course of investigation);

(d) a critical inquiry about the general working relationship of the complainant and respondent in order to assist in the assessment of credibility;

(e) maintaining a proper record of the investigation, including notes, statements, and copies of important documents;

(f) a thoughtful consideration of the respondent's version of events;

(f) the actual decision-maker should conduct the investigation or have sufficiently detailed summaries to enable a fair decision.

In one of the leading Ontario cases on sexual harassment, *Bannister v. General Motors of Canada Ltd.*, the Ontario Court of Appeal observed that Bannister was provided at least four opportunities to state his side of the story and to respond to evidence that had been uncovered in the course of the investigation. The initial complaint led to the discovery of other improper conduct. General Motors interviewed about 40 witnesses, including all of the witnesses suggested by Bannister himself.[10] Bannister sought to criticize the extent of the investigation at trial. The court explicitly found favour with the careful nature of the investigation.

---

[9] (1996), 18 C.C.E.L. (2d) 116 (B.C.S.C.).

[10] See the commentary regarding the propriety of the investigation conducted by General Motors in *Bannister v. General Motors of Canada Limited* (1998), 164 D.L.R. (4th) 325 at paras. 15-19 (Ont. C.A.). See also *Shiels v. Saskatchewan Government Insurance* (1988), 51 D.L.R. (4th) 28 (Sask. Q.B.) and *Quirola v. Xerox Canada Inc.* (1996), 16 C.C.E.L. (2d) 235 (Ont. Ct. J. (Gen. Div.)).

4. Consider Alternate Explanations

An investigator should conduct a careful investigation and "be assured that they are not false complaints motivated by some collateral grudge".[11] In the *McIntyre* case,[12] the court criticized the employer for not considering the possibility that the complainant was motivated by her anger at not being able to conduct an important on-camera interview.

5. Permit Union or Legal Representation

Furthermore, in a unionized setting, an accused employee has a right to a union member to represent him or her. In a non-unionized setting, particularly where there are serious allegations of sexual harassment involved which might lead to adverse job consequences, the investigator should encourage the presence of legal counsel. Many employers take the position that an internal investigation should remain internal and legal counsel is not necessary. It is, however, much harder for an employee to suggest that the process was unfair if legal counsel is permitted to be present from the beginning.[13]

6. Consider Mitigating Factors

Even when an investigator believes that sexual harassment has occurred, consideration should be given to mitigating factors.

In *Quirola v. Xerox Canada Inc.*,[14] the court accepted that the employer had established that Mr. Quirola had harassed at least one female employee. Nonetheless, the employer failed to give any real opportunity to the accused employee to explain his side of the story. The manager of human resources failed to follow Xerox's own internal policy regarding complaints of harassment.

The court found that Mr. Quirola had sexually harassed one employee. It ultimately excused the harassment on the basis that the events occurred at a time when Mr. Quirola was seriously depressed and dependant on drugs. Such behaviour was uncharacteristic of Mr. Quirola, who otherwise had a

---

[11] *Gonsalves v. Catholic Church Extension Society of Canada* (1998), 164 D.L.R. (4th) 338 at para. 19 (Ont. C.A.).

[12] *McIntyre, supra,* note 9.

[13] See, for example, *Rajakaruna v. Purdie and Simmons* (1984), 34 Sask. R. 41 (Q.B.) where the role of union representation and involvement became, ironically, the subject matter of a defamation suit.

[14] *Supra,* note 10.

superb worker record at Xerox. Mr. Quirola had also taken steps to deal with his drug dependancy problem. In the circumstances, Xerox's decision to dismiss was viewed as inappropriate.

7. Maintain Confidentiality

An allegation of sexual harassment has the potential to devastate all parties involved. A false allegation of sexual harassment may constitute libel and slander.[15] Workplace gossip may render it impossible for either party to continue to work. The lack of confidentiality may also taint the investigatory process. If witnesses hear about details of the complaint from others, they may consciously or subconsciously dovetail their evidence to match other accounts of the events. In an excellent overview written by ScotiaBank's in-house counsel, Andrew Finlay and Patricia Stephenson Taylor comment as follows:

> The employer must balance its commitment to discretion and confidentiality with the need to investigate and ensure that the accused is apprised of the case against him or her. Witnesses should be interviewed, but only those necessary to a proper and fair investigation. ... When interviewing witnesses, disclosure of information should be limited to the extent necessary to bring forth relevant information from the witness. Instructions should be given at the end of each interview about the sensitive nature of the issues which have been discussed and the potential damage to individuals should certain information be widely circulated.[16]

Complainants and witnesses cannot be given false assurances of confidentiality. In order to be fair and neutral, the respondent must be told that he or she is being accused of specific workplace misconduct. The previous relationship of the complainant with the respondent may be critical to determining if there is an innocent explanation to the conduct. In short, once a complainant makes a complaint, he or she must be protected from reprisals. Nonetheless, the fact that he or she has made a complaint against the respondent cannot be hidden from the respondent.

Many investigators and employers are afraid that any type of disclosure of the contents of a harassment complaint would constitute defamation.[17] As long as the investigator's disclosures are in furtherance of the investigation, the defence of qualified privilege applies. Nonetheless, indiscriminate discussion would exceed the privilege. An investigator should be able to

---

[15] See Chapter 4, 2. Defamation.
[16] Paper presented on March 24, 2000 entitled *Sexual Harassment in the Workplace: Prevention Reaction and Resolution"* in Managing Workplace Harassment: Practical Strategies (Toronto: Ontario Bar Association, 2000) at 12-13.
[17] See discussion at Chapter 4, 2. Defamation.

demonstrate precautions taken to maintain confidentiality of the allegations and the investigation.

D. CONCLUSION

Investigating sexual harassment requires a thorough understanding of employment and human rights law. Courts have struggled with balancing the rights of all the parties involved. An understanding of the evolving case law can assist the investigator in completing a fair and thorough investigation. We have included a basic checklist that may assist an employer and investigator throughout the investigative process.

FILE REVIEW CHECKLIST

☐ Is there a written complaint? If not, why not? Can a written complaint be obtained? Is there another basis for the investigation?

☐ If there is a written complaint, has a copy of the complaint been given to the respondent?

☐ If there is no written complaint, does the respondent have sufficient particulars to understand the nature of the complaint against him or her?

☐ Have the respondent and complainant been given a copy of the written sexual harassment policy? If not, why not? Does a policy even exist?

☐ Has the investigator considered the internal policy and how it impacts on the conduct of the investigation?

☐ Has the respondent been advised of his/her right to counsel or union representation?

☐ Has the complainant been interviewed?

☐ Has the complainant provided a written signed statement?

☐ Have witnesses suggested by the complainant been interviewed?

☐ Has the respondent been interviewed?

☐ Have witnesses suggested by the respondent been interviewed?

☐ Have important witnesses been interviewed in person?

☐ Has the respondent been given a chance to respond to any additional information that has arisen during the course of the investigation?

☐ Has the complainant been given a chance to respond to any additional information that has arisen during the course of the investigation?

☐ Has consideration been given to alternate explanations proffered by the respondent, *e.g.* misunderstanding, workplace conflict, motivations for false complaint, consensual relationship?

☐ Are original notes and witness statements available?

☐ Are copies of any relevant documents available?

☐ Is there a synopsis of the evidence and notes of interviews sufficient to allow a proper review of the evidence?

□ Has the investigation considered the impact of the complaint (and the matters it alleges) on the complainant and respondent?

□ Was the decision regarding the discipline (if any) or termination (if appropriate) taken after the conclusion of the investigation and upon consideration of all of the evidence available?

□ Were alternatives to dismissal considered?

CHAPTER 6

IS AN INVESTIGATION NECESSARY OR ADVISABLE?

A. OVERVIEW

The first decision that has to be made is whether an investigation is required. There may be several circumstances in which an investigation is not warranted or impractical. Not every complaint merits an investigation. In other cases, there may be a way to achieve the desired goal — compliance with the law and internal policies — without an investigation.

B. COMPLAINT DOES NOT REVEAL WORKPLACE MISCONDUCT OR HARASSMENT

A decision may be made *not* to conduct a formal investigation when the complaint, even if accepted at face value, does not disclose harassment or other misconduct. Each complaint should be measured against the test of what constitutes harassment or discrimination.[1]

Example 6.1
A partner at a law firm instructs his assistant to establish a "Chinese Wall" around a new file and states that under no circumstances are two specific lawyers in the firm, both of Chinese-Canadian origin, allowed near the file. Another secretary, also of Chinese Canadian origin, overhears the instruction and complains to human resources about the usage and suggests that it is a racial slur. The partner does acknowledge he used the phrase and uses it often.

The phrase, however, is widely-used in the legal and investment community to describe measures taken to ensure that information from

---

[1] See discussion in Chapter 1 above.

one group of professionals is not transferred to another group of professionals. The phrase has been used since the stock market crash in 1929 and was coined in reference to the Great Wall of China, the only man-made structure never overtaken by hostile forces. Law firms institute "Chinese Walls" in the context of potential or actual conflicts of interest.

The secretary was unaware of this phrase in the legal field. She agrees that she jumped to a conclusion that the comment was a racial slur because the lawyers referred to were of Chinese-Canadian origin.[2]

In this case, the complaint was made in good faith. The secretary believed that the complaint was a racist slur against Chinese-Canadian lawyers and herself. Because of the obvious mistake made by the complainant, this matter should not be investigated.

C. THE PROBLEM HAS BEEN RESOLVED

If the problem appears to have been resolved between the participants and it does not involve a serious breach of any workplace policy, an investigation may not be warranted.

Example 6.2
Leona Walton works in a library. One day, she walks into her superior's office in order to deliver some reports. The screensaver on the office computer displays a naked female in a suggestive pose.

The next day, Leona reminds her boss gently about the Internet/computer use policy at the library. He deletes his old screensaver and chooses one of the standard screensavers. He apologizes for causing Leona offence.

Leona Walton does not complain. She seems satisfied with the resolution and genuinely likes her job and her superior. The whole issue comes up in a casual conversation over lunch with Maureen, who is one of the H.R. managers of the library system. Maureen decides not to pursue the matter. The library policy on Internet usage does prohibit downloading pornography or using unapproved applications. The harassment policy does encourage employees to try to work things out themselves.

---

[2]   In Ontario, many law firms now use the phrase "ethical wall" in order to avoid this type of misunderstanding. Although the complaint was based on an allegation of racial discrimination, the observation is an appropriate one.

Although this involves a judgment call, Maureen has balanced a couple of factors. Firstly, Leona appears to have resolved the issue on her own. Secondly, the breach does not appear to have been a serious one at all. Many harassment policies encourage employees to discuss their concerns in an amicable matter. Escalating every issue to a formal complaint/investigation undermines workplace morale. It can cause a "backlash." Where employees seem to have worked things out well, their resolution should be supported.

D. AN INVESTIGATION WILL NOT ASSIST WITH RESOLVING THE UNDERLYING PROBLEM

Thirdly, it may be appropriate to consider an alternative to a formal investigation when another technique is better suited to resolve the issue. In certain cases, it may be useful to consider training and education instead of a formal investigation.

Example 6.3

Lydia Hussman is the first female mechanic at a well-known and large dealership. She has excellent credentials, graduating first in the provincial exams. She comes from a long line of mechanics, starting with her great-grandfather from Germany. She's not afraid of working in a male-dominated workplace.

The manager has kept a careful eye on things. Lydia does not complain and her work is excellent. He decides to leave well enough alone. There is no formal sexual harassment or anti-discrimination policy. Management has always felt that since there are no women in the workplace, it wasn't worth the time and money.

Three weeks after she starts, Lydia hands in her resignation. She has a job offer closer to home. She comments in passing that the "guys" clearly did not want her. They never spoke to her socially and excluded her during lunch breaks and the like. She felt like she was "shunned" and she felt that she never would get anywhere without some informal coaching or mentoring. The manager cannot convince Lydia to stay, but does not want to ignore the situation.

This workplace has a significant problem. It is unlikely that an investigative method will produce helpful results. The potential complainant, Lydia, has left the workplace. She has found a better job and has moved on.

Lydia is unlikely to want to return to the workplace and certainly does not wish to be cast in the role of a complainer.

Lydia's problem underscores the basic weakness of a complaint-driven process. In certain cases, the most vulnerable person in the workplace has to challenge the workplace. It is not surprising that Lydia, like many complainants, chose to "resolve" the problem by leaving the workplace. Lydia's problem also highlights the limitations of a harassment policy. Lydia was "shunned" and "excluded". Regardless of the breadth of the harassment policy, there is a very good chance that the conduct of the co-workers would not constitute illegal harassment.

An investigation is intended to determine facts and to recommend resolutions. The investigative process may not be a useful tool in this fact pattern. The manager should seriously consider steps to make the workplace more open to female hires, including instituting a formal diversity plan. The manager may want to hire a consultant to devise a program of training and mentoring to avoid any repetition of the problems that Lydia faced. The company should immediately create a harassment policy and roll it out properly (see Chapter 2). Above all, the company needs an agenda for cultural change.

E. WHERE THERE ARE NO FACTS IN DISPUTE

In rare cases, a formal investigation may be rendered unnecessary because there is no dispute regarding the facts and it is possible to arrive at a fair resolution without an investigation. A decision not to investigate should be made carefully. Even where facts are not in dispute, an understanding of the parties' history, backgrounds or motivations may be relevant in determining the resolution.

Example 6.4
Marshall and Phillippa work at a small accounting firm. Phillippa is the office manager. Marshall is a payroll clerk. Phillippa is Marshall's superior. At the firm's Christmas party, Phillippa gets very inebriated and openly propositions Marshall in front of a number of witnesses, including the two owners. Marshall tries to laugh off Phillippa's advances and then ducks into the men's room and then out of the party. One of the owners insists on driving Phillippa home.

Phillippa calls one of the owners from home the next day. She admits that she acted inappropriately and wants to know what will happen to her. The owner says he doesn't know and has to think things through.

Marshall does come to work. The owner asks to speak to him. Marshall is candid. He was deeply embarrassed by Phillippa's conduct, but likes her as a boss and likes his job. He feels that an apology and a guarantee that this type of conduct will not happen again would suffice. Marshall does not want to complain. He feels that he can put this behind him.

Phillippa is more than ready to apologize to Marshall and to her co-workers. She recognizes that her conduct was unacceptable and is aware that she placed Marshall in an awkward position. She also believes that she destroyed her own reputation in the firm. She offers to resign. The owner's "gut instinct" is not to conduct a formal investigation.

The owner's instincts are well-founded. The facts are not in dispute and both parties have indicated an interest in an informal resolution. While an apology may suffice from Marshall's perspective, the company must also consider disciplinary consequences for Phillippa.[3] Phillippa's conduct was serious and involved a public breach of its policy. While an investigation may not be necessary, the company needs to consider what the appropriate consequences for this type of behaviour are.

F.   WHERE THE PARTIES WANT TO USE MEDIATION

Many workplaces have observed that the investigative process itself can increase the tension in the workplace and have instituted informal and voluntary mediation processes.

The investigatory process is fraught with difficulties. The complainant and respondent have conflicting interests and are often forced to take opposing viewpoints. It may be difficult to make overtures to apologize, because of a concern regarding legal implications. Many employers indicate that the investigative process often exacerbates tensions and precludes the possibility of a creative resolution. Employers are often locked into resolutions mandated by the legal system.

Mediation is a voluntary dispute-resolution process. A trained mediator can be invaluable in setting ground rules, opening up dialogue, creating trust and overcoming impasses. A mediator should be knowledgeable about issues of workplace disputes and harassment, and neutral (and perceived to be neutral). The mediator's personal qualities such as intelligence, patience, honesty, perseverance, empathy and openness are also critical to the process.

---

[3]   See chapter 14 for samples of disciplinary consequences.

There are excellent books on the dynamics of mediation in the workplace.[4] Nonetheless, there are certain ground rules:

a)   the process is voluntary. The parties must agree to mediation. The mediation process does not work if either party is coerced into participation or distrusts the process;

b)   the parties choose the mediator. This is in stark contrast to an investigation, where the company usually appoints an expert of their choice, or an adjudicative system, where a decision-maker is imposed on both parties;

c)   the process is confidential. Whatever is said in the mediation process cannot be used subsequently in the investigative, litigation or disciplinary process;

d)   the mediator is a facilitator. Unlike an investigator, the mediator is not tasked with fact-finding or recommending a resolution. The mediator's job is to assist the participants in arriving at their own resolution;

e)   the resolution, if there is one, is participant-driven. While the mediator will coordinate discussions, brainstorm, play "shuttle diplomat" and ask tough questions, the mediator will not impose a settlement. The mediator assists the parties in considering options and potential resolution;

f)   the resolution can be as creative as the parties wish.

A sample mediation agreement is included in the appendices.

Example 6.5
Garreth Anderson is a highly-skilled computer technician. He is gay. He is open about his relationship with his partner and brings him to company events.

Two years after starting work, he indicates to Madeline Prosser, the chief executive officer, that the company is quite homophobic. He has decided to start his own company. She is shocked. The company includes "sexual orientation" in its anti-discrimination policy and same-sex partners are

---

[4]   Julie Mcfarlane, *Rethinking Disputes: The Mediation Alternative* (Toronto: Emond Montgomery, 1997); Genevieve Chornenki *et al.*, *Bypass Court: A Dispute Resolution Handbook*, 2d ed. (Toronto: Butterworths, 2001); Laurence Boulle *et al.*, *Mediation: Principles, Process, Practice (Canadian edition)* (Toronto: Butterworths, 1998); Michael Silver, *Mediation and Negotiation: Representing Your Clients* (Toronto: Butterworths, 2001).

included in the company benefit packages. She is dismissive about his comments, attributing it to his "over-sensitivity".

Garrett Anderson's lawyer sends a lengthy demand letter to the CEO. The letter catalogues a series of incidents that Garrett claims result in a poisoned work environment. The incidents include:

a) *use of the epithet "poufter" and "fag" in reference to him by co-workers, i.e. the "poufter" is good at fixing those kinds of problems;*

b) *refusal of his boss to consider him for a client-service position. Garrett claims that his direct boss was very nervous about what "impression" Garrett would make if he were to interact with clients. His boss never attributed the reluctance to Garrett's homosexuality, but Garrett is convinced that this may have been a problem;*

c) *shunning of Garrett in casual work-related social interactions. Garrett indicates that in the previous two years, he was never asked to join his colleagues and/or his boss for a "quick bite" or a "drink after work". While the workplace is not overly social, these types of interactions are not uncommon in the IT workplace;*

d) *a systemic pattern of not hiring (or promoting) openly gay candidates.*

Garrett's demands are perceived to be exorbitant by the company. In off-the-record discussions, the company's lawyers learn that Garrett knows that there are many employees who are scared to come out of the closet because of the perceived homophobia. He has caused the demand letter to be written because he wants to effect systemic change. The company's lawyers suggest the possibility of a mediated resolution, prior to litigation.

Prior to the mediation, the parties discussed who should mediate the dispute. The company preferred lawyers and ex-judges. Garrett preferred individuals with a known commitment to gay and lesbian rights. In the end, they compromised on an ex-lawyer with a solid record of mediating sexual harassment disputes.

After the mediation, the company and Garrett agreed as follows:

(a)   The company would include anti-discrimination and diversity in its 3-day employee orientation course;

(b)   The company human resource department would recruit pro-actively in communities where they were under-represented, including (i) gays and lesbians; (ii) visible minorities; and (iii) recent immigrants;

(c)   The company would introduce formal mentorship programs for all new hires (in order to avoid the informal shunning at lunch);

(d)   The company's corporate retreat and one-day technical seminars would invite expert speakers who also happen to be prominent in the gay and lesbian community (and other diversity communities);

(e)   The company's managers would, as part of their training, take a course in recruiting and retaining a diverse workforce;

(f)   The company's standard performance review for managers would require a review of the manager's ability to attract, retain and lead a diverse workforce;

(g)   The company would reissue and recirculate its harassment policy to all employees and periodically include a reminder in the company's e-newsletter;

(h)   The company would pay Garrett's legal fees to date;

(i)   All parties would keep the complaint and resolution confidential; and

(j)   Garrett would not pursue his complaint in any legal forum.

The resolution of this dispute shows the potential for creativity. During the course of the mediation, Garrett indicated that the company could be unwelcoming for all employees from minority communities. Although Garrett experienced the company as a white gay male, he observed similar problems facing other employees from other communities. The resolution was, therefore, broader than Garrett's own experiences. Secondly, the resolution focused on changes in the workforce: training, e-newsletters, mentorship in the future, rather than trying to resolve past wrongs. Thirdly, the resolution was not focused on monetary damages. It also did not require the company to acknowledge any wrongdoing.

Mediation is not a panacea. There are circumstances when it is not appropriate to consider mediation.[5] Nonetheless, where the parties appear to be willing to consider mediation as an option, it may be an appropriate alternative to a full investigation. Furthermore, the parties can agree to defer the investigation for a short period while the mediation is undertaken. If the mediation is successful, the matter is resolved. If the mediation is unsuccessful, the investigation can proceed as if the mediation had not occurred.

G. WHEN THERE IS AN ON-GOING INVESTIGATION BY A REGULATORY OR LAW ENFORCEMENT AGENCY

A company must exercise significant judgment if it appears that an external regulatory authority has already commenced an investigation into a specific complaint. In such cases, great care must be taken to ensure that the company's internal investigation is not perceived as running interference or hindering the official investigation.

Example 6.6

Tracy Lord is a young, attractive sales clerk. Her job with "Clothes make the Woman" is an excellent opportunity for her. She is ambitious and wants to enter a career in fashion design and retailing. On Thursday evening, she left a message with the H.R. manager that she would not be back. On the message, she claimed she had been assaulted by the president and that she was going to the police. The H.R. manager is concerned. She knew the president was going to meet with Tracy Lord on Thursday after the store closed to discuss the possibility of a significant promotion within the organization.

There is an internal sexual harassment policy that charges the H.R. manager with investigating any accusation of sexual harassment or discrimination. She wants to ask the president what happened and why. She also wants to call Tracy Lord and set up an appointment to interview her. As the H.R. manager is reviewing the policy, the receptionist calls and advises that there are two officers from the local police force asking to see her.

---

[5] See Michael Silver, *supra,* note 4 at 51.

The H.R. manager in this case should consider adjourning any internal investigation. The H.R. manager may wish to allow the police investigation to go ahead and await the results of that investigation. Although the H.R. manager is fully within her rights to conduct an investigation, she may wish to defer to the results of the criminal investigation. Legal advice should be sought regarding how the company should best proceed. The president should retain separate legal counsel. The president may wish to consider the implications of participating in the internal investigation on the criminal proceedings. Information provided to the company's investigator may be compellable in a criminal proceeding. Given the sensitivities, the company may wish to adjourn any investigation until it can discern the direction of the criminal investigation.

The dynamic is different if the external regulatory authority is one of the provincial or federal human rights commissions. In many cases, a prompt investigation will reduce the company's exposure to liability.

Where external law enforcement agencies are involved, the H.R. manager should obtain legal advice. Where a decision is made to go forward with the internal investigation, the H.R. manager should consider retaining an external investigator. In many cases, it is appropriate to retain a lawyer in order to preserve solicitor-client privilege.[6]

H.   WHEN THE INVESTIGATION WOULD BE MOOT

In rare cases, it may be appropriate not to investigate if it appears that a company could not implement any practical resolution. The alleged harasser may have left the employ of the company or died. The events may have occurred many years previously.

I.   CONCLUSION

While this book is focused on conducting investigations, there are cases which a company may choose not to investigate. The decision not to investigate should not be because there is a desire to "sweep matters under the carpet". Rather, it should be a principled decision that honours the spirit of the company's human rights obligations. In each case, the decision-maker should consider the policy and the law and whether an investigation is required to fulfill the company's obligations.

---

[6]   See Chapter 8, Section E.

CHAPTER 7

WHAT CAN YOU DO IF THERE IS NO COMPLAINT?

A. OVERVIEW

The legal system in Canada is predicated on an adversarial model. A complainant is expected to lodge a complaint, either formally or informally. The respondent is given an opportunity to respond. The employer, after hearing all sides, is tasked with deciding what the appropriate result should be. This model, however, often does not work well in the context of sexual harassment. Because employees are often reluctant to trigger the complaint process, many instances of sexual harassment go unreported.

During the course of an investigation, it is not unusual to unearth numerous, unreported cases of offensive or illegal behaviour.[1] In many cases, employees often indicate that "everyone" knew that a particular employee routinely engaged in offensive behaviour. Employees find it difficult to believe that management could be unaware of a problem when "all" rank-and-file employees are aware of it. Management's perceived refusal to deal with a "known" problem is interpreted by employees as a strong endorsement of the harasser.

Human resource managers should be vigilant for signs that there may be a problem, even where there is no complaint. In many instances, by the time the complaint is made, much of the damage (and legal exposure) is irreparable.

Management should be alert for certain indicia of potential sexual harassment:

(a)   anonymous complaints;
(b)   rumours of harassment, abuse or inappropriate behaviour;

---

[1]   See synopsis of the facts in *Bannister v. General Motors of Canada* in Chapter 5, section C.3, "Be Thorough".

(c)   high absenteeism rates;

(d)   high attrition rates that exceed company or industry averages; or

(e)   employees refusing job transfers into certain departments without cogent explanation.

These factors do not always justify a full-blown investigation. They constitute an early-warning system that the workplace may require some kind of intervention, including sexual harassment education.

B.   ANONYMOUS INFORMATION

Human resource managers routinely receive anonymous information. Anonymous complaints are notoriously tricky. It is difficult to determine whether the information is reliable or motivated by some personal grudge. Nonetheless, it is dangerous to ignore such information completely. In many cases, employees are more candid because they are protected by anonymity.

Example 7.1
A company sets up a suggestion box. Since the suggestions are made anonymously, the company is not able to trace the suggestions. Most suggestions deal with routine matters — such as plant shutdowns, overtime, employee benefits. The company operates a manufacturing line 24/7. Because of the various shifts, most responses are posted on the company bulletin board. Recently, the company received a typed complaint:

> *Since you promoted Dave, things have gotten bad on the night shift. Dave yells and screams at employees. He uses foul language and refers to the girls as c**ts and b**tches. No one wants to work with Dave. He tells us he's been with the company for 25 years and that the bosses trust him. He is such a two-faced s.o.b. He is only nice if the owners are around.*

The company is shocked. Dave has been with the company for 25 years and has always been a trusted employee. The owner goes to Dave with the complaint. He shrugs and says that the complaint is false and must have been made by someone who is out to "get him". He even suggests the names of two employees who were recently suspended for repeated absenteeism/tardiness.

Example 7.1 is a classic situation of a true anonymous complaint.[2] Dave is a trusted employee who has delivered excellent financial results. There has never been a complaint about his performance. Many clients have praised Dave's commitment. The company's owners find it difficult to believe the complaint and are tempted to dismiss it because it is "impossible" to investigate.

Many employers believe that an anonymous complaint cannot be investigated. This is not true. An anonymous complaint is much more difficult to investigate, because there is no complainant willing to be interviewed. Given the seriousness of the complaint, however, the company must respond.

The note requires a strongly-worded response that invites employees to avail themselves of the company's harassment policy. Here is a sample response.

> *We recently received a serious anonymous complaint about one of our managers through the suggestion box. As you know, the company is committed to a harassment-free workplace.*
>
> *We have discussed the complaint with the manager in question. We are reposting our harassment policy. We invite any employee who has a concern about workplace conduct to contact Jennifer, the human resource manager or any other member of senior management. Our cellphone numbers and home phone numbers are provided. We will be investigating as best as we can the information we have received. Our ability to respond, however, is hampered by the anonymity of complaint.*

The company has a number of tools at its disposal. Existing employees should be interviewed, with an assurance that the company protects against reprisals. Employees who have recently transferred from the night shift may be a useful source of information. Employees who have recently resigned from the company are another fruitful source.

Given the anonymity of the complaint and the seriousness of the potential damage to Dave's reputation, the investigator must be careful to ask open-ended questions. These questions could include:

---

[2] In some cases, handwritten notes can be traced. In other cases, the use of certain words or grammatical errors can tip the company off as to the authorship. This problem is based on a real situation, where the company was unable to trace the author of the note.

(a) How would you rate the managers you have dealt with? Who do you rate the highest? Why? Who would rate the lowest? Why?

(b) Are you familiar with the company's harassment policy? Have you ever seen any conduct you would consider to contravene the policy? What did you do about it? If you didn't do anything about it, why was that?

(c) Have you ever heard foul language being used on the plant floor? Did you ever find it personally offensive? Do you think others found it offensive? Can you give us any instances?

(d) [For transferred employees] You recently transferred from the night shift. Why did you request the transfer? Would you ever go back to the night shift? Why or why not?

(e) [For former employees] You recently left the company. Would you ever consider coming back? Why or why not?

(f) [For employees on nightshift] Do you like working on the night shift? Is there anything that you would change on the night shift?

At this preliminary stage, the investigator should be careful to avoid accusing anyone of writing the note or even identifying the subject of the investigation. The fact that a manager is being investigated for harassment can destroy a professional reputation. The note was written anonymously. Unless the investigator has strong reason to believe that he or she can identify the author of the note, it is appropriate to use open-ended questions about the workplace in general.

Investigators are often surprised at employees' candour when asked open-ended questions. A preliminary investigation of the anonymous complaint may cause the employee to self-identify. In other cases, it may provide sufficient information to confirm that there is a serious problem with Dave and his management of the night shift. Assuming that the preliminary investigation has discovered cogent evidence supporting the possibility of harassment, a formal investigation is warranted. More specific questions can be asked.

In certain cases, an investigator senses that there is a problem, but employees refuse to confide in the employer. It may be worth considering employing someone to work undercover during the night shift and report back to the investigator or owner.

Even when the results of the investigation are inconclusive, the company should review the sexual harassment policy with Dave and remind him that they expect him to behave in a professional and courteous manner. Although this discussion is not intended to be disciplinary, the owners should remind Dave of the disciplinary consequences of sexual harassment. A note should be made of the discussion. If a complaint is made in the future, the nature of the discussion with Dave will be relevant. The note, however, is not disciplinary. It is being created only to confirm the discussion. It is a piece of evidence, but should not impact on Dave's entitlements at the workplace.

Finally, the company should monitor any unusual activity on the night shift. Dave may well be right that the note was written by an employee with a grudge. Nonetheless, the company has been alerted to a potential problem.

C. RUMOURS AND GOSSIP

Investigators are often surprised by comments made by employees that "everyone" knew that a manager harassed his employees. Often management is the last to know. Other times, management refuses to respond to innuendo, gossip and rumours on the basis that they are often unreliable and exaggerated. Even when information regarding workplace harassment is received through an untraditional channel, management should respond. Many employers are much more vigilant regarding rumours of fraud (*e.g.* "fudging" expenses or time sheets) than they are about harassment. Harassment is a serious legal and corporate problem. It should be treated proactively. The old adage, "where there's smoke, there's fire", often holds true in the context of sexual harassment.

Example 7.2
Two recently-hired managers are chatting during a break in a training session. The company is a national chain that sells upscale sporting goods and attire. The Vice-President, retail operations overhears a conversation.

Manager 1 says, "I nearly quit two weeks after I started. The senior manager at Store 111 was such an idiot. He rated every female customer on how hot they were on a scale of 1 to 10. He told everyone that only he could deal with the 10s. I felt like I was in a frathouse. I'm so glad I've finished my on-site training!"

Manager 2 responds, "That's nothing. He was a real groper. It stopped when I 'accidentally' elbowed him in the rib. He wanted to say something and I told him 'accidents happen when you get too close'. He got the message, all right! It was a hoot seeing his face. I don't think anyone has had the gumption to put him in his place.

Manager 2 chuckles, "Serves him right. Every one I talked to had a story about him. Well, we survived. ..."

The Senior Manager is respected because of the high sales and low shrinkage results he has achieved. Store 111 is used as a training location for all employees about to be given their first management assignment. The Vice-President is upset, but does not know what to do.

This example is very typical. There is no formal complaint, but senior management now has grounds to believe that there is a problem with Store 111. The Vice-President, retail operations should take action. Depending on the company's management structure, the Vice-President should consult with the human resources department. Many companies are reluctant to pursue this kind of gossip. The vast majority of sexual harassment incidents go unreported.

The company cannot afford to turn a blind eye. If a formal complaint or litigation subsequently occurs, information that "everyone" had a story about the senior manager increases the company's exposure.

The first step will be to approach each of the gossiping managers *separately* and indicate what was overheard. The managers should be reminded of the sexual harassment policy and assured that there will be no reprisal. If either of the managers confirm the information, there is a formal trigger to an investigation.

The investigator should expect the employees to be reluctant to discuss the information in a more formal setting. It is important to reassure the employees that they are not subject to discipline, but that the company is concerned about the information they overheard. If the managers decline to respond to the investigator or deny the conversation, the company is faced with a dilemma. There is no cogent evidence of harassment and the sources of information have refused to confirm the private discussion. On the other hand, the company does not have grounds to discipline the managers for engaging in a private conversation.

In the absence of a confirmation, the company does not have sufficient grounds to proceed on a traditional investigation of the *specific* complaints discussed. Nonetheless, the company cannot be naive. There are numerous reasons why employees deny experiencing sexual harassment. The company may choose to investigate the senior manager at Store 111, using the techniques discussed in the previous section.

The investigator must note that these employees were overheard in a casual conversation discussing the senior manager's conduct, but denied the conversation and denied experiencing or witnessing sexual harassment. Trainees who have recently graduated from the Store 111 programme should be asked open-ended questions to elicit responses regarding the store atmosphere or any suggestions regarding inappropriate behaviour or sexual harassment. The senior manager should be apprised of the concern that has arisen and given an opportunity to respond.

It should be made clear that there is no specific formal complaint, but the company is undertaking an investigation in order to determine whether there is reason for concern.

Even where the results of the investigation are inconclusive, the company is entitled to discuss the company's sexual harassment policy with the senior manager in a non-disciplinary manner. This discussion should include:

- an assurance that this discussion is not a disciplinary matter;
- a review of the sexual harassment policy, emphasizing that it includes customers and employees;
- a reminder that a store manager must set an example for all employees;
- a reminder that individuals need their personal space;
- a reminder that since the senior manager is responsible for training, he has a high degree of responsibility for honouring and enforcing the harassment policy.

On an on-going basis, the company should consider monitoring the flagship location. Employees who resign, request transfers or are terminated should be asked general questions regarding the atmosphere at the flagship location. When employees refuse to confirm information previously divulged in a casual setting, the company is put in a difficult position. It is inappropriate to discipline or take adverse action against an employee based on unsubstantiated gossip.

Finally, the gossiping employees need to be reminded that gossip can be harmful. Exaggeration and bravado in a conversation may be fun, but can ruin people's reputations. While this gentle reminder is not intended to be disciplinary, it serves as a useful reminder that the company does not tolerate defamation. This discussion should be noted as well.

D.   WORKPLACE REVIEWS

Experienced human resource managers are aware that many complaints of harassment go unreported. Good managers try to establish a healthy workplace. High attrition rates and high absenteeism are often early warning signs of a problem. Many employers have instituted programs to improve their human resource practices and the workplace in general. These programs include employee surveys, 360 degree reviews, engaging external consultants and exit interviews of departing staff. These techniques reveal a wealth of information regarding how employees really think about the workplace. They are designed to provide *aggregate* information regarding the workplace in general and not specific information regarding any employee.

The majority of the information gathered usually deals with compensation, benefits, training, promotions and the possibility of upward mobility. In some instances, however, credible evidence of abuse or harassment can be uncovered.

Example 7.3

A company has been experiencing high attrition rates. The human resource manager knows there is a problem, but cannot put his finger on it. The company provides excellent pay, training and opportunities for advancement.

A consultant is retained to conduct exit interviews of all employees who resign, retire or who are packaged out of a large software corporation. Employees are given written assurances that information provided to the consultant will remain to be used in the aggregate only. The consulting company provides quarterly reports to the employer. Statistical information is provided regarding why employees leave, including education, family responsibility, more money, etc.

In the last six months, eight employees have resigned from the sales force, representing a 60 per cent turnover. The consultant has had some difficulties in getting former sales employees to provide candid information.

Five of the employees have flatly refused to participate in the process. They are employed by competitors. Three employees have advised that the atmosphere in the sales department was toxic and that the sales manager was a "bully". The only female interviewed indicates that the sales manager was a "boor" and repeatedly undercut her by calling her "honey" and "darling" in front of clients.

When asked why the employee did not complain, she indicated that the industry was small and women still a significant minority. She had just landed a very well-paid position and did not need to "rock the boat". The sales manager is very powerful and is considered to be on his way to the executive levels.

The consultant referred to this information in his narrative report, but confirms he will not disclose the identities of the interviewees. The human resource manager has a gut instinct that there may be some truth to the complaint. He has found it difficult to recruit into the sales department and he, too, has been at the receiving end of some of the sales manager's caustic comments first-hand.

The consultant's information covers a gamut of problems — from workplace bullying[3] to sex discrimination. The second-hand nature and the anonymity of the information pose problems. The high attrition rate corroborates some of the anonymous information.

The human resource manager should seriously consider investigating the sales department and the sales manager, in particular. An external investigator (see Chapter 8) is crucial. Given the power of the sales manager and given the human resource manager's own experiences with the sales manager, an internal investigation may be tainted and ineffective. The company may also wish to consider non-investigative responses, including executive coaching for the sales manager.

E. THE RELUCTANT COMPLAINANT

Almost every H.R. manager has been told "confidentially" about a harassment or bullying problem. The employee, however, is reluctant to proceed with a complaint and in fact, will beg the H.R. manager to keep the disclosure "just between us".

The difficulty is that once management knows about a potential workplace problem, it cannot turn a blind eye.[4] In such a case, the H.R. manager may have to insist upon proceeding in accordance with the sexual harassment policy. A good sexual harassment policy will have potential

---

[3] Recent studies have suggested that workplace bullying is a much more frequent problem than classic sexual harassment. In this example, the bullying overlaps with sexual harassment and discrimination. For more information regarding this phenomenon, you can access <http://www.bullyinginstitute.org> or <http://www.workdoctor.com>. For U.K. information, consider <http://www.workplacebullying.co.uk>. An interesting book written for victims of bullying, *The Bully at Work* (SourceBooks, Inc., 2000) covers some of the personal and workplace costs of bullying from a U.S. perspective.

[4] See discussion of some of the legal ramifications at Chapter 3, B1, "direct liability". In order to avoid this problem, many educational institutions (Harvard University, University of Toronto, Dalhousie) and organizations (the Law Societies of Ontario, B.C. and Alberta) have created the office of the ombudsperson. The ombudsperson can serve as a resource in situations of harassment and discrimination, and is explicitly prevented from escalating the matter to the complaint stage, without consent.

informal resolution processes or the possibility of a mediated solution. It will also reassure the complainant that it is appropriate to move forward with the complaint.

Example 7.4

Justine Merrill discloses to the senior VP, human resources that one of her supervisors is a "sexist pig". He makes off-colour jokes, circulates pornography by e-mail, surfs the Internet for pornographic jokes and refers to female support staff by their bra cup size. She will not complain and warns that she will deny the information. She just wants to know why the senior VP, human resources has never done anything. Justine points out that two other women did complain about sexism in the workforce and were restructured during the next downsizing. She does not want to get involved. She just wants the senior VP to do something. She also points out that "whistleblowers" in the company get slaughtered. The two payroll clerks that discovered a senior executive's expense account fiddle were coincidentally terminated due to "outsourcing". She is the sole financial support of her family and warns that if pushed, she will deny the entire conversation. Justine says that she knows that if the company wanted, it could try to push her out due to absenteeism. Justine has recently missed a lot of time due to her elderly mother's and her young daughter's illnesses.

The senior VP, human resources has a legal obligation to deal with this problem. The senior VP is an officer of the corporation. Her knowledge constitutes the company's knowledge. She and the company have an obligation to get as much information as she can from Justine and record it. Much of what Justine has disclosed (jokes, e-mails and Internet) describe a "poisoned work environment". The conduct may also violate the company's technology use policy. In certain cases, it may be appropriate to start an investigation on the basis of the rumours of violations of both the technology use policy and the "off-colour jokes".

While Justine's personal situation is difficult, the company has a legal obligation to ensure that it maintains a harassment-free workplace. There may be ways to protect Justine during and after the investigation.

Many employers are reluctant to pursue a harassment investigation in the face of a reluctant complainant. The same employers pursue potential fraud aggressively, even when witnesses are equally reluctant. The issue of harassment is not a matter of civility (or incivility) between employees. It is the legal obligation of the corporation to strive to remove harassment in the workplace.

Large workplaces that are serious about sexual harassment should consider the "ombudsperson" model. This model establishes a "safe haven". The ombudsperson can be an external consultant or an internal individual designated as a confidential resource person for victims of harassment. The designated person should not be a member of the executive and should be explicitly instructed that information he or she receives is to be kept confidential, unless instructions are received to reveal the information. Consequently, it is clear that any victim speaking to the ombudsperson is doing so under an express guarantee of confidentiality. This model has been successfully adopted by governments, large employers, universities and law societies.[5]

F.   CONCLUSION

This chapter deals with some of the preliminary considerations which occur when there is no formal complaint. Organizations need to recognize that most victims of harassment do not exercise their rights to complain. In that type of situation, it is important to be alert for other signs of problems. The legal system is predicated on the adversarial system — formal complaint and formal response. In reality, many instances of sexual harassment come to the attention of management indirectly.

Treating indirect information seriously accomplishes many goals:

a)   it reduces legal liability by demonstrating a pro-active approach to sexual harassment;

b)   it sends a signal that the firm is committed to a harassment-free workplace; and

---

[5]   The legal profession is not immune to these quandaries. As a self-regulated profession, lawyers have an obligation to report unethical behaviour by another lawyer. Victims of sexual harassment felt that they faced an intolerable conundrum. They had a legal obligation to report sexual harassment. Most of the victims were young and economically vulnerable. Many required articling jobs to obtain their credentials as a lawyer. When they turned to their legal mentors for help, their mentors faced a conundrum. They, too, had an obligation to report unethical behaviour. Most of the victims did not wish to go public. Many of them required letters of recommendation from their harassers. In the end, almost all complaints of sexual harassment were not reported. The Law Society of Upper Canada and other law societies created a "safe haven". They used an ombudsperson model. Victims could consult the ombudsperson, without being pushed into making a complaint. Some victims chose to proceed with a formal complaint; others opted for informal resolution. Nonetheless, the existence of the office alerted the profession to the prevalence of the problem. The reader can find more information at <http://www.lsuc.on.ca/equity/program_discrimination.jsp>.

c)   it may prevent problems from festering and becoming full-blown legal complaints or litigation.

Even when the results of the investigation are inconclusive, responding to such concerns affords everyone an opportunity to be reacquainted with the company's harassment policy.

CHAPTER 8

SELECTING THE INVESTIGATOR

A. OVERVIEW

In most cases, a complaint of harassment will come to the attention of a human resources manager, senior manager or in-house counsel. Depending on the organization, these people must make two key decisions: (a) whether an investigation is necessary (see Chapter 6); and (b) if an investigation is necessary, who should investigate.

In many cases, the decision-maker may wish to conduct the investigation. In other cases, the decision-maker might want to delegate the responsibility to someone else, either internally or externally.

There are several key decisions that must be made at this preliminary stage:

(i)   Should the investigator be internal or external to the organization?

(ii)   Should the organization retain a lawyer to conduct the investigation in order to maintain solicitor-client privilege over the investigation or not?

(iii) Does the complaint require more than one investigator?

In determining the answer to these questions, the organization needs to consider both practical and legal issues. Appendix 8.1 contains a useful checklist of questions that should be considered before an investigator is picked.

B. NEUTRALITY

The bedrock principal is that an investigator must be neutral as between the complainant and the respondent. Accordingly, an employer should determine whether the investigator has any links to either party to the complaint. Where an internal investigator, *e.g.* the Director of Human Resources, is being considered for the role of the investigator, both actual neutrality and the *perception* of neutrality is critical.

Before selecting the investigator, an employer should consider a number of factors:

(a)   Does the investigator have any prior working history with any of the parties to the complaint or material witnesses?

(b)   Is either party a subordinate, superior or in a close working relationship with the proposed investigator?

(c)   Will the proposed investigator have the internal organizational clout to make recommendations that may detrimentally impact upon a party's career? For example, a human resources manager may not feel comfortable delivering an adverse report regarding the conduct of the chief financial officer of a company.

(d)   Does the investigator have a relationship with any of the parties to the complaint or material witnesses outside of work? Personal friendships, membership in community, club or sports organizations, or even connections through extended family may all raise the suspicion, however unwarranted, that the investigator was influenced by factors extraneous to the investigation.

(e)   Does the investigator have any specific knowledge of the facts leading to the complaint? For example, a human resources manager who witnessed a possible incident involving the parties to the complaint might have material information with respect to the issues in the complaint. This person may have difficulty being completely neutral and may, in fact, become a witness. This person should not investigate.

(f)   Does the investigator have any mental reservations regarding his or her ability to be neutral?

The investigator is not required to be ignorant of the identity of the participants. The law requires neutrality and fairness. If an investigator cannot be neutral or will not be perceived as neutral, another individual should be appointed.

An internal investigator has some formidable advantages. He or she has a prior history with the employer and an understanding of the corporate culture. He or she may be able to facilitate a workable resolution because of his or her unique organizational insight. An internal investigator is often very cost-effective and can determine whether there are underlying systemic issues that need to be addressed due to recurring problems. At the end of the day, both the complainant and the respondent must have confidence that the investigator has the clout to deliver an honest report, unswayed by any corporate preferences.

Despite all these advantages, an external investigator should be seriously considered when the allegations involve senior executives of the company. A complainant may have legitimate doubts about the integrity of the investigation when an internal investigator can be fired, demoted, disciplined or denied other job privileges for displeasing senior executives of the company.

An external investigator is not automatically considered to be neutral. Before deciding on an external investigator, consider some of the following factors:

(a) Does the external investigator have a previous relationship with the organization? If so, could that relationship impair the perception of neutrality?

(b) Does the external investigator have a previous relationship or knowledge of any of the potential participants in the investigation?

C. TRAINING

Investigating harassment is not easy. Many companies routinely look to their in-house counsel, human resource departments or audit departments to review complaints. The underlying assumption is that these individuals are competent because of their professional training or work experience. In some cases, companies look to professional investigation firms to deal with these matters. Good investigators come from all walks of life.

Because of the complexity of the law, the investigator should have knowledge of the laws governing harassment and discrimination. Many law schools, colleges and private training institutes provide courses on the law of harassment. Private training institutes in the United States and Canada offer workshops on the process of conducting an investigation. These courses are invaluable to anyone conducting an investigation.[1]

---

[1] For example, McGrath Systems Inc. provides sophisticated video and on-line training aimed primarily at the education market in issues relating to sexual and racial harassment and investigation in the United States. In Canada, the Edge Quality Communications Consultants provides a two-day workshop on harassment investigations. Excellent training is provided by various human rights commissions and some of the larger unions to their employees. Law schools and colleges with human resource programs often provide credit courses on issues surrounding harassment and discrimination, with a more academic focus.

Depending on the type of harassment, certain kinds of technical expertise may be invaluable. In certain cases, the harassment involves cyberstalking or sexist e-mails from allegedly anonymous sources. Since the investigation will involve computer forensics, it may be appropriate to retain that type of expertise, instead of the traditional investigator.

When retaining an external investigator, it is wise to obtain a curriculum vitae that lists seminars and training courses relevant to discrimination, harassment and workplace investigations. Furthermore, ask for references relevant to an actual investigation. During the reference check, the following questions should be asked:

(a) Was the investigator knowledgeable about harassment?
(b) Was the investigation completed in a timely manner?
(c) Did the investigator treat all parties with respect and courtesy?
(d) Was the investigator thorough?
(e) Was the report (if provided) lucid, thorough and persuasive?

D. EXPERIENCE

Investigation is an art, not a science. Experience is, therefore, invaluable. The investigator should have experience in dealing with complaints of harassment and investigating them. Many experienced investigators are consultants who previously worked in-house with human rights commissions or in large legal or human resource departments. Former law enforcement officers often have received specialized training in investigating sexual harassment and sexual assault.

E. SPECIAL CONSIDERATIONS IF USING A LAWYER

Many companies automatically retain their lawyers to conduct an investigation into a complaint. Lawyers are knowledgeable about the developments in the law and are often very experienced in resolving litigation involving issues of harassment.

Companies may also wish to avail themselves of solicitor-client privilege. Solicitor-client privilege can be defined as the protection that is afforded any communication between a lawyer and the client relating to the provision of legal advice. It is deeply rooted in the Anglo-Canadian tradition that an effective legal system requires all parties to have competent legal representation. Candid and open communication is considered to be a key to the provision of good legal representation. Protection is also granted to the lawyer's work product.

A lawyer's investigation may attract solicitor-client privilege if it is conducted as part of the process of providing competent legal advice to the client. In short, the lawyer must be acting in furtherance of his or her legal retainer. The law recognizes that lawyers do not always provide *legal* advice. Solicitor-client and work-product privilege only applies to context of providing *legal advice*. By invoking solicitor-client privilege, the client may be able to shield communications with the lawyer and the work product of the lawyer's investigation from disclosure.[2]

Many companies wish to use in-house legal resources. Since many in-house counsel provide both legal and business advice, the application of solicitor-client privilege becomes a thorny issue.

The case law is well-developed in the U.S. In *Upjohn v. United States*, in-house general counsel coordinated the receipt of questionnaires arising from an internal investigation of possible bribery of foreign officials. The IRS sought disclosure of the questionnaires. *Upjohn* involved solicitor-client and solicitor work product privilege. The Supreme Court upheld privilege and described a five-part test:

(a) communication must be for the purpose of securing legal advice;

(b) employee communicating to the investigator must be doing so at the request/direction of employer;

(c) request must be made by employer in order to obtain legal advice;

(d) the subject matter of the communication must be within scope of employee's duties;

(e) the communication must not be disseminated beyond those persons who, because of the corporate structure, need to know its contents.[3]

In 1999, Barbara Ann Sellinger, now Chief Employment and Litigation Counsel to American Standards Companies, Inc., prepared an excellent summary of how a lawyer should protect the investigative file from forced disclosure to an adverse party. Some of her recommendations include:

---

[2] There is an excellent discussion regarding these issues in *Gower v. Tolko Manitoba Inc.* (2001), 7 C.C.E.L. (3d) 1 (Man. C.A.) and *Wilson v. Favelle* (1994), 26 C.P.C. (3d) 373 (B.C.S.C.).

[3] 449 U.S. 383 (1981).

(1) The lawyer should stamp or mark documents as "Solicitor-Client Privilege". This should be on notes, legal memoranda, witness statements, tapes of interviews.

(2) Employer should request in writing that the lawyer conduct a formal investigation and the request should specifically include reference to the fact that the investigation is necessary for the purpose of securing legal advice. Employer should also indicate that the lawyer should maintain all steps to retain solicitor-client privilege. Employer should request legal advice on the potential legal ramifications of the complaint, any potential exposure to litigation, any potential cause of action that either the complainant or respondent may have. An example of a potential retainer letter is included in Appendix 8.3.

(3) If the lawyer obtains help from non-legal personnel, *e.g.* law clerks, psychologists, investigators, etc., the lawyer should coordinate the investigation and retain such personnel. Such retainer should specify that the lawyer is requesting the assistance in the context of a privileged retainer and for the purpose of providing the employer with proper legal advice and set forth the steps necessary to maintain privilege. All reports and communications of the non-legal personnel should be made directly to the lawyer and not to the employer. There should be no question that the lawyer is coordinating the investigation.

(4) The lawyer should maintain a separate file for all work product relating to the investigation, which must be marked Confidential/Solicitor-Client Privilege.

(5) Employer should communicate directly with the employees advising that the lawyer has been retained for the purpose of providing legal advice and may be contacting them for the purpose of ascertaining certain facts.

(6) Protect witness statements as legal work product. Notes which contain a lawyer's analysis or opinion is protected more carefully than simple verbatim notes or recordings of a witness's recollection. A lawyer should record mental impressions and observations, analysis of credibility, strengths and weaknesses of case, musings on how information fits into other evidence.

(7) Reports should meet the requirements of solicitor-client privilege. The report should not be a dry recitation of "he says/she says". The report should include legal advice to the client, opinions regarding litigation exposure and recommendations regarding resolution or settlement.

(8)   Privilege can be accidentally or inadvertently waived. The company and the lawyer must avoid sending the report (or accompanying materials) to external third parties, such as an insurer or government agency.

(9)   The lawyer must avoid conflict of interest. The lawyer must ensure that everyone he or she interviews knows that the lawyer represents the company. The lawyer cannot give any legal advice to any of the participants in the investigation. His or her retainer is with the company.[4]

Solicitor-client privilege is not absolute. Firstly, the company may need or want to call the lawyer/investigator as a witness as part of its defence to a lawsuit brought by either the complainant, respondent or a regulatory agency or commission. Privilege is waived if the lawyer is called as a witness. Furthermore, if the lawyer is called as a witness, he may be disentitled from acting as counsel on any litigation arising from the matter.[5]

F.   TEAM INVESTIGATIONS

Some employers prefer a team approach — one male, one female. The justification is that there will always be an investigator of the same sex as the party being investigated or interviewed. Furthermore, one investigator can ask questions and listen; the second can take notes. There are clearly gender differences in the perception of harassment.[6]

In other cases, the breadth and complexity of the investigation requires numerous investigators just to complete the task in a timely manner.[7] Team investigations have many drawbacks, not the least of which is additional cost. This book assumes that only one individual will investigate. This book

---

[4]   Barbara Ann Sellinger, Esq., "The Attorney-Client Privilege and Work Product Doctrine", presented to the 1999 American Corporate Counsel Association's Annual Meeting as part of its session on *Recent Developments in Labor & Employment Law*. The article is written for an American in-house legal audience. It provides excellent insight which is applicable in the Canadian context.

[5]   It is outside the scope of this book to discuss the intricacies of solicitor-client privilege. An excellent introduction to the topic can be found in Ronald Manes and Michael Silver, *Solicitor-Client Privilege in Canadian Law* (Toronto: Butterworths, 1992).

[6]   Jeanne Henry, "Perceptions of sexual harassment as a function of target's response type and observer's sex" in *Sex Roles: A Journal of Research* (August, 1998).

[7]   A classic example of a team approach is found in *Masters v. Ontario* (1994), 115 D.L.R. (4th) 319 (Ont. Div. Ct), where several members of a law firm investigated serious allegations of sexual harassment against Carlton Masters, who was Ontario's Agent-General in offices in New York and Boston.

also assumes that if there is a team approach, team members will be present at all critical interviews and will draft the report jointly.

In some cases, it may be appropriate to delegate a portion of the investigation. This approach should be taken carefully. The senior investigator should determine what portions of the investigation should be handled personally because they are critical, and what can be delegated. Unless there are too many complainants to interview personally, the same person should always interview the respondent and the complainant.

G. TIMELINESS

A good investigator must be able to respond quickly to the complaint and devote a significant block of time immediately to the investigation. Unfortunately, some external investigators are so busy, investigations are truncated and delayed. Internal investigators may be over-committed, having to juggle operational priorities and the pressures of the investigation.

A good investigation should be expeditious. The complainant should be interviewed within days of making a formal complaint. The investigator should be able to devote sufficient time to complete interviews, review evidence and deliver a report within a short time period, preferably one to three weeks. While some investigations are longer because of the complexity of the issues, the investigator's timetable should not be a stumbling block to a complete and rapid response to the complaint.

Timeliness is important to both the complainant and the respondent. The complainant wants to see that the complaint is being taken seriously. The respondent may wish to explain or vindicate his or her reputation. Interim measures, such as suspensions with pay, may lead to rumours and gossip in the workplace. The investigation itself is a source of enormous stress on all parties involved.

H. CONCLUSION

The choice of an investigator is important. A good investigator will complete a timely, accurate and fair investigation. The parties and witnesses will be much more forthcoming if the choice of investigator makes sense.

APPENDIX 8.1

FACT PATTERNS ILLUSTRATING CONSIDERATIONS REGARDING WHO SHOULD INVESTIGATE

EXAMPLE 1 — THE MANAGER WITH HISTORY

Janice Appleworth is the manager, human resources, of ABC Limited. It is a sales and distribution company in Canada. Arthur Kenley is the manager, sales and marketing. Arthur is a rising star at ABC Limited. He has not hesitated to go over Janice's head on H.R. issues, including demanding and getting special "stay bonuses" for some of his key people. His employees are very loyal to him. He has made it clear that he views Janice as an overpaid "payroll manager" and has asked her to "keep her nose out of the sales department". The friction has not gone unnoticed in the company, but both parties have made a real effort to be civil to each other. Despite Arthur's opinion, Janice is very well-qualified for her position.

Two days ago, Connie van Veen, a recently-hired sales agent, handed in her resignation. When Janice conducted the exit interview, Connie indicated that she didn't need to work for a guy that thought the sales department was his personal harem. When pressed, Connie states that the guy "didn't know how to take no for an answer". Connie was not interested in making a formal complaint. She was focused on finding a new job. She wanted to make sure that she got a decent reference check out of ABC Limited. Janice wants to push this matter further. She had a lot of training in her previous position in a unionized workplace and has conducted several investigations for ABC Limited.
Should Janice investigate?

Janice should not investigate. This hypothetical demonstrates several of the problems with an internal investigation. The respondent has had run-ins with the manager, human resources. He will find it difficult to believe that Janice will conduct a neutral investigation. Secondly, although Janice and Arthur are equals in the corporation, employees will know that Arthur has significant clout in the organization. Their confidence in the process (and the results) will be undermined. Finally, Connie is clearly a reluctant participant. She has not complained. She has left her position. She will not be motivated to participate in the process. In the circumstances, Janice should escalate the matter to the appropriate senior executive. It may be appropriate to consult a lawyer regarding the best response to Connie's disclosure. If a decision is made to investigate formally, the investigation should not be conducted by Janice. An external investigator is the best choice.

EXAMPLE 2 — THE GENERAL MANAGER

James Seyforth is the general manager of Millworks, Inc., a medium-sized manufacturing company based out of Winnipeg, Manitoba. Two of the women in the painting department are pregnant. They requested a transfer to the packaging department because the paint fumes were making them nauseous. The foreman responded, "don't bother me. I didn't get you knocked up." Since the ladies requested the transfer, the foreman has made jokes and comments about their pregnancy. They want it to stop and they want their transfer.

James Seyforth is appalled. Millworks, Inc. has made a real effort to recruit and keep women. James has gone to several seminars on recruiting women, harassment and discrimination, and best practices. He doesn't see the need to engage an external consultant and is completely willing to accede to the request for a transfer. James does not want an external investigator.

James is probably right. As general manager, James has clear authority over both the foreman and the pregnant employees. The scope of the complaint seems straightforward. James can always consult legal advice or other experts if the matter gets complicated. Given that the complaining employees do not want to sue, James should discuss the complaint more formally with the foreman. Depending on the results of the conversation, James may wish to consider some disciplinary consequence for the foreman.

A seminar on the business imperatives of diversifying the workforce may be important. Nonetheless, in this case, the complicated power dynamic in Example 8.1 does not exist in the second example. With assistance from external counsel or a good human resources consultant, James can probably deal with the problem.

APPENDIX 8.2

CONSIDERATIONS LIST FOR SELECTING AN APPROPRIATE INVESTIGATOR[8]

☐ Is the investigator trained and experienced in interviewing and investigating?

☐ How complicated are the facts?

☐ What is the company's legal exposure if the complaint is true?

☐ Does the proposed investigator have training in the nature of harassment?

☐ Does he or she have knowledge of the organization's policies, procedures, rules, collective bargaining agreements (if applicable)?

☐ Can he or she be objective between the parties and potential witnesses?

☐ Will he or she be perceived as objective between the parties? Think about reporting structures, previous relationship with the parties or the organization?

☐ Does the investigator have credibility within the organization and with the parties involved?

☐ Does the complaint involve senior executives of the company?

☐ Can he or she keep an open mind about the complaint and the response?

☐ Will he or she be discreet and keep the complaint (and the investigation) as confidential as possible?

☐ Does the investigator have an understanding of the legal issues at play?

☐ Will the employer want legal advice as part of the investigative report?

☐ Does the investigator have or need cross-cultural sensitivity?

---

[8] This checklist is adapted from presentation material kindly made available by Priti Shah, LL.B., Praxis Conflict Consulting of Winnipeg, Manitoba.

☐ Should the investigator be an external neutral investigator?

☐ Does the nature of the complaint and legal exposure involved warrant the cost of an external investigator?

☐ Is more than one investigator required due to the extent of the complaint or its complexity?

☐ Can the investigator move in a timely manner? How much time can the investigator devote this week? Next week? The week after?

APPENDIX 8.3

RETAINER OF EXTERNAL LAW FIRM REQUESTING LEGAL SERVICES

September 9th, 200x
Donald DiLauro
Albright, DiLauro
868 Meadow Road
North York ON M2X 1X1

Dear Mr. DiLauro:

We have received a complaint of sexual harassment from one of our employees, Janine Carruthers. Her complaint specifically refers to the conduct of her immediate supervisor, Jack Andrews, during the time period of June, 200x to August, 200x. Copies of the complaint, response and the harassment policy are enclosed. We ask that you review same prior to commencing the investigation.

We are concerned about our potential legal liability to both Ms. Carruthers and Mr. Andrews. In order to provide us a reliable analysis of our legal exposure, we would request that you conduct a thorough investigation and provide us your opinion regarding the validity of the complaint. We would also request that you provide us your recommendation regarding any potential resolution of the complaint.

You are authorized to conduct whatever investigation you think appropriate, including interviews of Ms. Carruthers, Mr. Andrews, and any other necessary witnesses. We have already apprised Ms. Carruthers, Mr. Andrews and Mr. Blackwell that you have been retained. We would be pleased to facilitate any other interviews you think are necessary. Please ensure that all interviewees are aware that you have been retained by ABC Company for the purposes of providing legal advice to us and are not acting in any other capacity.

Please take all necessary steps to ensure that your investigation and all related work-product remain solicitor-client privileged.

Please advise me if you need to inspect documents and records in the possession of ABC Company as I will coordinate the process of obtaining such records for you.

Please ensure that your invoice to ABC Company is marked simply "TO ALL LEGAL SERVICES RENDERED". Please maintain a confidential and detailed log of all interviews, telephone calls, documents received and/or reviewed. We may seek to review your log in order to verify the reasonableness of your invoice. We confirm that you will charge $x per day and that you anticipate that your investigation will take a minimum of __ days and a maximum of __ days. Travel and out-of-pocket disbursements will be reimbursed upon presentation of receipts. You confirm that you will try to complete your report by September x, 200x.

Please provide your legal advice and the factual basis for such advice in a written report directed to my attention no later than _____, 200x.

Sincerely,
ABC Company
per:
David Ricketts

Appendix 8.4

Excerpt of Formal Contract Between Lawyer/ Investigator and Employer in *Gower v. Tolko Manitoba Inc.*, Where Solicitor-Client Privilege was Upheld

(1) The Investigator will conduct an investigation as counsel on behalf of the Employer for the purpose of providing a fact finding report and giving legal advice based on the findings in the report.

(2) The Investigator's notes, fact finding report and legal advice will be protected by solicitor/client privilege. The Investigator will advise all witnesses, including the Complainant and the Respondent, that she is conducting this investigation as legal counsel for the Employer.

(3) All information supplied to the Investigator by the individuals whom the Investigator interviews, including the Complainant and the Respondent, will be supplied in confidence and will be treated by the Investigator as strictly confidential. The information will be revealed only on a "need to know" basis in order to ensure that the investigation is fair.

(4) The Investigator will meet with and interview the Complainant, the Respondent and any other employees or other witnesses whom the Investigator believes have information relevant to the investigation.

(5) The Investigator will prepare a report for the Area Manager stating her findings of fact and her conclusion as to whether the findings of fact constitute sexual harassment and a breach of the Employer's harassment policy and will provide legal advice based on those findings of fact and conclusions.

(6) The Area Manager will treat the report as strictly confidential and will review the report only with the employer's advisors.

CHAPTER 9

PRE-INVESTIGATION AND INTERIM STEPS

A. OVERVIEW

Prior to the investigation commencing, the organization should consider whether any interim measures need to be implemented. These interim measures are designed to facilitate the investigation and should not be considered as part of the disciplinary process.

B. CONFIRM THAT AN INVESTIGATION WILL BE CONDUCTED

The complainant and the respondent should be advised that a formal investigation will be conducted. Both parties should be given a copy of the sexual harassment policy. Although many employers communicate this verbally, in most cases the communication should be confirmed in writing.

1. Communicating with the Complainant

The complainant should be advised of the identity of the investigator (internal or external) and given a brief synopsis of the investigator's qualifications to do the investigation. The complainant should be assured that the law (and the policy) protect him or her from reprisals for having made the complaint. The complainant must be reminded that the complaint, response and the investigative process are highly confidential and that the complainant must not discuss these matters with anyone within the company, except the investigator or human resources. He or she should also be reminded that any other communication should be restricted to obtaining legal, medical or other professional advice.

The complainant should be asked if he or she will have problems honouring this request. In some cases, a co-worker is a major source of emotional support. This should be discussed candidly. It may be appropriate to refer the complainant to someone within the company who can serve as an adviser and source of emotional support, without jeopardizing the integrity of the investigation.

2. Communicating with the Respondent

Communicating with the respondent is much more difficult. This communication may be the first time that the respondent becomes aware that there is any question regarding his or her behaviour. The communication should be made in person. The respondent should be given a copy of the harassment policy. The respondent should be advised regarding the investigative process.

The respondent should be given a copy of the complaint (if made in writing). The respondent should be given an opportunity to provide a written response to the complaint or to provide a succinct verbal response regarding his or her position on the complaint.

The respondent must be reminded that under no circumstances can there be any suggestion that the company or the respondent have engaged in reprisals because of the complaint. Accordingly, the respondent should be advised of any protocols surrounding his or her communications involving the complainant.

The respondent should be reminded that the complaint, response and the investigative process are highly confidential and that the respondent ought not to discuss these matters with anyone within the company (except the investigator and/or human resources). The respondent should be reminded that any other communication should be restricted to obtain legal, medical or other professional advice.

C. WORK ASSIGNMENTS

The organization may have to consider whether work assignments need to be changed. The company should consider whether the complainant and the respondent are (a) in a direct reporting relationship; (b) work in close proximity to each other; or (c) required to interact with each other in order to discharge their duties. Furthermore, the seriousness of the complaint ought to be considered. The complainant may also voice an objection to working with the respondent during this sensitive period of time. While none of these factors are determinative, an employer should consider them carefully. There have been numerous cases where the initial complaint of sexual harassment has not been substantiated, but the adjudicator or court has found that reprisals or retaliation for the complaint occurred. A careful allocation of work assignments in this interim investigatory period can alleviate some of the potential for inadvertent claims of retaliation.

Where any of these factors exist, it is appropriate to consider a number of responses, including:

(a) a temporary shift in the respondent's *physical* work location. Telecommuting or transfer to another geographic location may be appropriate;

(b) a temporary change in the reporting structure;

(c) a removal of the respondent from the workplace on a temporary basis pending the results of the investigation.

These responses should not be considered disciplinary and should ordinarily be with full pay and benefits. There should be correspondence confirming the change in the work assignment and the fact that it is not disciplinary. Appendix 9.2 contains a sample letter which can be modified and used.

D. SCHEDULING WITNESSES

Upon reviewing the complaint, the investigator should draw up a list of potential witnesses revealed by the complaint. The organization should facilitate witness interviews. Where possible, a senior human resource manager should make initial contact with witnesses to advise that the investigator will be calling. At the same time, the importance of maintaining strict confidentiality should be emphasized.

Great care should be taken to maintaining the confidentiality and privacy of the process. Efforts should be taken to maintain the appearance of normalcy. It is appropriate to consider scheduling appointments either before or after normal business hours to reduce the possibility of inadvertent disclosure and gossip. While the temptation is to use the company's boardrooms, this may be inappropriate, particularly for employees who would not normally have access to these boardrooms. Neutral boardrooms (*e.g.* hotels and conference facilities), the investigator's offices, or the private residence of an employee may be preferable to the workplace.

Avoid any place where the conversation can be overheard. Restaurants, coffee shops and food courts are not appropriate. It is far too easy for confidentiality to be lost simply because a co-worker noticed an unusual conversation occurring in a public location and commences open speculation regarding the circumstances.

Leave enough time between witnesses. Witness interviews often take longer than scheduled. It is difficult to predict which witness will have a goldmine of information.

E. DOCUMENT PRESERVATION AND RETRIEVAL

In certain cases, the investigation may turn on the existence of corroborating documentation. Electronic mail records, corporate credit card invoices, security access records, travel records, time and attendance records may be of importance. In many cases, these documents have already been sent to off-site storage or exist only on backup computer tapes. Many records are routinely destroyed. Documents may take time to retrieve. The investigator should request the documents as soon as they appear to be relevant and ensure that they are preserved pending the investigation.

Electronic documents often require third-party assistance in order to retrieve and understand them. The investigator should consider how the request for assistance should be made. In many cases, information technology departments will search for information using the names of authors or by searching for a particular string of text. Investigators must be aware that asking for certain kinds of information will trigger speculation. Where third-party assistance is required, the investigator must emphasize the importance of confidentiality and warn that breach of that obligation constitutes a disciplinary offence.

F. PREVENTING INADVERTENT REPRISALS

Harassment investigations are kept strictly confidential. In large organizations, hiring and firing decisions may be made by someone who is completely unaware of the complaint. Human resources should create an alert system to ensure that no one who is participating in a harassment investigation is terminated, demoted, or given an adverse performance review without senior management approval. It is best to keep any decisions in abeyance until the investigation is completed. Examples of conduct that could be perceived as retaliatory include:

- dismissal;
- cutting back on hours;
- unilateral geographic transfer;
- unilateral shift changes;
- layoffs;
- change in office location, size or prestige;

- removal of company car privileges;
- removal of key job duties;
- reduction in compensation;
- denial of computer privileges;
- denial of customary expense or travel budget.

During the investigation, the company should strive to maintain the status quo for the complainant and any other employees involved in the investigation. Any negative change could be perceived as a direct or indirect reprisal. The company will bear the onus to prove that the conduct complained of is not retaliatory.[1]

---

[1] For an introduction to the concept of reprisals and retaliation, see the discussion in Walter S. Tarnopolsky, *Discrimination and the Law* (Toronto: Carswell, 2001) at para. 9.7.

APPENDIX 9.1

LETTER ADVISING COMPLAINANT OF SEXUAL HARASSMENT INVESTIGATION AND INTERIM STEPS

Private & confidential
to be opened by addressee only
via courier

Janine Carruthers
882 Prince's Gate Road
Streetsville ON L4V 2XL

Dear Ms. Carruthers:

Re: Sexual Harassment Complaint

We acknowledge that you have made a complaint about the behaviour of Jack Andrews. As you know, in accordance with our harassment policy, these types of serious complaints must be investigated. Given the nature of the allegations and individuals involved, we have retained Donald DiLauro to investigate your complaint (*where appropriate: and to provide us legal advice regarding the issues your complaint raises*). His contact information is as follows:

Albright, DiLauro
868 Meadow Road
North York ON M2X 1X1

tel: 416.555.8282 x 3
fax: 416.555.8283
email: Donald_DiLauro@albrightdilauro.ca

We request that you keep your complaint and the investigation process confidential. We confirm our request to you not to discuss this matter with any co-worker or potential witness. This request is made to help protect the integrity of the investigation.

We anticipate that the investigation will take ___ days. The investigator has indicated that he will be contacting you later today in order to set up an appointment with you.

During the course of this investigation, we ask that you not communicate, either directly or indirectly with Jack Andrews. If you need to communicate with him in order to discharge your duties, you can route your request through me or Evelyn, our human resource manager. Mr. Andrews has been requested to refrain from communicating with you and will not be attending at the offices during the investigation.

If you have any questions, kindly do not hesitate to contact me.

Sincerely,

David Ricketts

Appendix 9.2

Letter Advising the Respondent of Sexual Harassment Investigation and Interim Steps

Private & confidential
to be opened by addressee only
via courier

Jack Andrews
1233 Kenilworth Lane
Streetsville ON L4V 3M6

Dear Mr. Andrews:

Re: Complaint of Janine Carruthers

This is to confirm that we have received a complaint from Janine Carruthers regarding your behaviour. Her allegations, if true, would constitute a violation of the company's Anti-Discrimination and Harassment policy. A copy of the complaint and the policy is enclosed for your review. You are requested to respond in writing to the complaint by _____[insert date].

In light of the nature of the complaint and the parties involved, we have determined that it would be appropriate that you not attend at your normal workplace during the course of the investigation.

You will be permitted to telecommute from your home office pending the investigation.[2]

This is not a disciplinary response and does not prejudge the investigation in any way. We anticipate that the investigation will take _____ days to complete. The investigation will be conducted by Donald DiLauro, who has been retained by our company. His contact information is as follows:

Albright, DiLauro
868 Meadow Road
North York ON M2X 1X1
tel: 416.555.8282 x 3
fax: 416.555.8283
email: Donald_DiLauro@albrightdilauro.ca

He will be calling you to set up an appointment to speak with you in person.

Please note that you are directed not to communicate with Janine Carruthers for any reason whatsoever pending the investigation. If you need to communicate with her for business reasons, kindly route the communication through me or Evelyn, our Human Resource Manager. This directive has been issued to protect you and the company from any suggestion that illegal pressure or retaliation was directed against Janine Carruthers by reason of the complaint.

We also ask that you not discuss the investigation with anyone within the organization or any potential witnesses. I'm sure you would not want to taint the investigative process.

If you have any questions, kindly do not hesitate to contact me.

Sincerely,

David Ricketts

---

[2] This is one option. Other options include (i)You will be located out of the _____ office pending the investigation. Staff have been advised that you are on a temporary assignment, assisting the company on a special project; or (ii) You will be on paid administrative leave. You are not to attend at the offices during this leave. Your salary and benefits will continue.

APPENDIX 9.3

LETTER TO POTENTIAL WITNESS

Private & confidential
to be opened by addressee only
via courier

Timothy Blackwell
228 Marshall Drive
Oakville ON L5X 3V2

Dear Mr. Blackwell:

This is to confirm our conversation that a sexual harassment complaint has been made and you have been identified as a potential witness.

Donald DiLauro has been retained by our company in order to investigate a sexual harassment complaint. He will be contacting you in the next 48 hours regarding setting up an appointment with you. This matter has the highest priority.

Donald DiLauro's contact information follows:

Albright, DiLauro
868 Meadow Road
North York ON M2X 1X1
tel: 416.555.8282 x 3
fax: 416.555.8283
email: Donald_DiLauro@albrightdilauro.ca

The company takes its responsibilities with respect to its sexual harassment policy very seriously. We believe that a fair investigation is the best way to protect the rights of everyone involved. Your participation is critical.

Please answer Mr. DiLauro's questions honestly and to the best of your knowledge. It is important that you give your recollection and not try to tailor your evidence with anyone else. Please do not discuss this letter, the sexual harassment investigation or your evidence with anyone.

Please also note that the investigation must remain confidential in order to protect the reputations of all parties involved. You are required to keep this letter and any communications you have with respect to the investigation in the strictest confidence.

If you have any questions, call me.

Sincerely,

David Ricketts

CHAPTER 10

INTERVIEWING WITNESSES

A. OVERVIEW

Most investigations rely on witnesses. The art and science of investigation is a complex subject. Lawyers, psychologists, social workers and police officers are fortunate, because they are often given formal training in interviewing techniques and witness psychology. There are excellent resources on the art and science of interviews.[1] The interviewer must walk a careful tightrope. The manner of questioning can taint a witness's recollection. Failure to ask probing questions can diminish the reliability and accuracy of the investigative results.

B. REVIEWING THE BASICS

Most witnesses will be uncomfortable. Even before the formal interview starts, it is important to place the witness at ease. The interview room should have a few non-alcoholic drinks and snacks and the witness should be seated in a comfortable chair. The interview room should be completely private and, if necessary, off-site.

The interviewer should also try to connect on a human level. Inconsequential chitchat regarding the weather, children or weekend plans can break the ice.

On a formal preliminary note, the investigator must:

(a) explain the purpose of the interview;
(b) confirm that the investigator has been retained by the company and will report to the company;

---

[1] Most books are aimed at the law enforcement market. See, for example, Jim Euale *et al.*, *Interviewing and Investigation* (Toronto: Emond Montgomery, 1998); Charles Yeschke, *The Art of Investigative Interviewing* (2002); Rebecca Milne, *Investigative Interviewing (Psychology & Practice)* (West Sussex, England: John Wiley & Sons Ltd., 1999).

(c) explain that the investigation is being conducted under the auspices of the company's harassment policy (if there is one) and/or the company's duty to investigate complaints of harassment;

(d) emphasize the importance of the absolute confidentiality of the interview;

(e) Where appropriate, the witness should be assured that he or she is legally protected from suffering any reprisals because of his or her participation in this process. If the issue of reprisals becomes a concern, the witness should contact either the investigator or a designated person within the company. This assurance should be rephrased for the complainant and respondent. The respondent may be faced with disciplinary consequences (not reprisals) if found to have been guilty of harassment. The complainant may be faced with disciplinary consequences if the investigator determines a malicious complaint was made.

Once the investigator has reviewed these items, the ground rules of the interview should be clarified:

(a) the witness should always ask for clarification, if a question is confusing or unclear;

(b) the witness should be reminded that he or she should be candid regarding what is a clear recollection and what is not. A truthful "I don't know" or "I can't remember" is much preferable to a speculative answer.

C. TYPES OF QUESTIONS AND HOW TO USE THEM

Most witnesses find the interview process intimidating. It is the investigator's job to establish rapport with the witness. Tone of voice, body language and starting with easy questions are useful ways of putting the witness at ease.

The investigator should not start the interview on a hostile footing. All the parties — complainant, respondent and neutral witnesses — are entitled to be treated as truthful and honest. After the interviewee has had a fair opportunity to provide his or her recollection, the investigator is entitled to point out any discrepancies or concerns that might exist. The investigator should approach the interview with an open mind. Prejudging a witness or a complaint is a serious mistake. The investigator is obliged to be neutral. By prejudging a witness or a complaint, the investigator is in danger of turning a blind eye to evidence that does not support his or her theory of the case.

Investigators can also be impatient. They often want to "get to the point" and are tempted to interrupt or hurry the witness along. This is inadvisable. Most scientific studies suggest that witnesses are able to provide much more accurate testimony when they are permitted to deliver a narrative account. It is important not to derail the witness's flow by interrupting. Instead, let the witness finish his or her thought and then go back over any details that might have been missed or misunderstood.

One of the cardinal rules is to take enough time with each witness. Witnesses can sense when the interviewer is rushed for time. Leave ample time between interviews in order to ensure that each witness can get undivided attention.

1. Background Questions

Many interviewers start with background questions. The purpose of these questions is not to elicit direct information relevant to the complaint, but to establish certain baselines, including:

(1) Is the witness comfortable with the process? When a witness responds to the question with a question or gives short answers, the witness is probably uncomfortable with the process. The interviewer may wish to probe for the source of discomfort either directly or indirectly. The interviewer may also want to ask further background questions regarding the interviewee's education, work history and role in the company in order to reduce the tension that inevitably occurs at the beginning of an interview.

(2) What is the witness's capacity to recall information? A witness who is unable to recall dates about his or her own personal history and is generally vague and uncertain may be less reliable.

(3) Does the witness have any kind of underlying hostility or anxiety?

Examples of these questions include:

- "Tell me about your work history with the company?"
- "Tell me about the general atmosphere at the workplace?"

These types of questions are best used at the beginning of the interview, when it is important to establish a rapport with the witness.

2. Inviting a Narrative

Many psychologists suggest that honest witnesses can provide the best information when they are invited to go back to an incident and provide a full narrative of the events, editing nothing. This enables the witness to replay the incident in his or her mind.

> *Example 10.1*
> *Jennifer DeMarco complains that she was sexually assaulted by a co-worker, David Grand. She claims that David walked her to her room from a pub on May xx, 200x, the night before the company management retreat started. She states that the assault occurred in the resort hotel elevator and there were no other witnesses.*

After reviewing the preliminaries, the investigator chooses to use open-ended questions to invite a narrative. Here is an excerpt of their exchange:

Interviewer: *Looking at your complaint, I understand that you had a problem with David at the company retreat on May x, 200x. I'd like you to go back in your mind's eye to that date and tell me everything you recall about your interaction with David. Don't hold anything back. Don't worry about me taking notes or what is relevant or not. Just tell me what you remember.*

Complainant: *I remember that day really clearly. I arrived late — about 7:00 p.m. I was exhausted. The drive had been treacherous up the mountain roads. It was already dark. I checked into my room and checked messages. There was a short message from David indicating that the "gang" would be saving a place for me at the Bear Pit, a local watering hole a short walk away. Look I don't know if I'm answering your question....*

Interviewer: *Yes, I'm listening. This will be very helpful. Keep going.*

Complainant: *I changed into some casual clothes — jeans and a sweatshirt & put on my sneakers. I walked over. The weather was still pleasant, but it was going to be chilly at night. I arrived at the Bear Pit about 7:30 p.m. David, Sofia, Sylvana, Russell and Barry were already there. One of them, I can't recall whom, said that a few others were no-shows until tomorrow a.m.*

	Things were very pleasant. We were talking about dogs, vacations, cars — nothing too important. About 10:00, I said I was going to turn in. (Pause)
Interviewer:	*What happened then?*
Complainant:	*David said he thought it was a good idea. He offered to walk me back. The rest of the gang accused us of being "party-poopers". (Pause)*
Interviewer:	*What happened then?*
Complainant:	*I told them I wasn't 21 any more and needed my beauty rest. David grabbed his jacket and we headed out. (Pause)*
Interviewer:	*What happened after David grabbed his jacket?*
Complainant:	*We walked back. It was a short walk, maybe 5 to 10 minutes. Once we got to the hotel, David invited me up for a "nightcap". I said "No, I really do need my beauty rest." (Pause)*
Interviewer:	*What was David's response?*
Complainant:	*He said, "Suit yourself." (Pause)*
Interviewer:	*What happened then?*
Complainant:	*We went into the elevator. When the doors closed, he put his arm around me and pulled me towards him. He said he'd been, "waiting all night for this". I told him to get off me. He said, "don't play hard to get. You know you've been waiting for this." I told him, "it's over. Grow up and get over it." (Pause)*
Interviewer:	*What do you remember next?*
Complainant:	*The elevator doors opened and I pulled myself away and ran to my room. David didn't follow me. I was so mad. I wanted to call the police, but then thought better of it. David was being stupid and probably had too much to drink. I was exhausted. I felt I would be better able to deal with everything and put it in perspective after a good night's sleep.*

In the example, the investigator uses questions like "tell me what you recall" or "what happened next" to encourage the complainant to complete her narrative. Although the investigator has a number of questions arising from the narrative, he refrained from interrupting the complainant's flow.

3. Review Questions

It is important to review answers at an interview and ask questions regarding details or facts that may have been missed the first time around. In the DeMarco narrative, the investigator should get the full names and job titles of all the people that were at the *Bear Pit*. If it appears that alcohol consumption may be a factor in the incidents, the investigator may wish to probe further on this point. Finally, there is a cryptic reference in the complainant's narrative that she responded, "It's over. Grow up and get over it." This may be a critical detail and it is important to explore both the comment and the nature of the relationship to which the complainant referred. Once the witness has completed the narrative, the investigator can ask specific questions to review matters.

> *Investigator: You indicated that you told David to "Grow up ... it's over." What did you mean by that?*
>
> *Answer: I guess you don't know. It's not a big secret. David and I were dating for a few months. I broke up with him about six months ago. It wasn't anything serious. We had a lot of fun for a short time. He was looking to settle down, find a wife, have kids, etc. I wasn't ready for that. I was looking for a bit of fun. Once I realized we were on different wavelengths, I broke it off. Told him he should look for someone who was ready for commitment.*
>
> *Investigator: How did David take that?*
>
> *Answer: He was disappointed. We were having a lot of fun. He took it well. I really didn't have any problems with him. He was always a big one to keep work out of our personal relationship.*

4. Using Specific Questions

Investigators usually prefer to obtain the witness's own recollection of events. They are aware that it is easy to encourage certain responses by the manner of questioning. In some cases, a narrative approach is ineffective. The witness may not have much to offer by way of narrative. In such cases, more specific questions will have to be drafted. Even then, it is important for the investigator to avoid putting words in the witness's mouth.

Example 10.2
Devraj Choudhry complains that while he worked in the IT department, Ralph Ng, was openly-hostile to him and called him derogatory names like "the poufter" and "the fag". Ralph denies the accusation. He states that he never called Devraj anything like "fag" or "poufter".

The investigator determines that it is necessary to interview a number of Dev Choudhry's co-workers, who worked in the other cubicles in the IT department. The investigator is cautious, because he knows that the interview process may damage Dev's and Ralph's reputation. The investigator chooses to use open-ended questions.

Interviewer: *Did Ralph ever use nicknames about any of his employees? Did he have a nickname for all staff members? What were the nicknames?*
Answer: *I guess so. He called me Sacha. That's what my Russian friends call me. He called Devraj, Dev. I'm not sure that he had nicknames for the others.*
Interviewer: *Did you hear Ralph ever use any nicknames that you thought were unpleasant or unprofessional?*
Answer: *I'm not sure what you mean. Ralph is very professional.*

As the previous section demonstrates, it is sometimes difficult to get the witness to provide information regarding the specific complaint, unless very specific questions are asked. Such specific questions inevitably tend to reveal the identity of the parties involved and the nature of the complaint. The investigator can only remind witnesses of the importance of maintaining confidentiality and not discussing the interview with anyone, not even their boss, friends or spouse.

Interviewer: *Did Ralph have a nickname for Devraj?*
Answer: *Yes, Devraj was often called Dev by Ralph and everyone.*

In this example, the witness is truthfully answering the questions. The neutral word "nickname", however, may not be sufficient to elicit the kind of information that the investigator needs.

Interviewer: *Did Ralph ever use the word "fag" or "poufter"?*
Answer: *Yes, a few times.*

5. Dangerous Leading Questions

Leading questions suggest the answer that the investigator wants. While they are a very useful technique in court for lawyers cross-examining witnesses, they are dangerous at the investigative stage. The investigator should not suggest in any way the "correct" answer to the witness. By using leading questions, the investigator taints both the witness and the investigation. Witnesses often try to "please" or "help" an investigator by giving the answers they think the investigator wants.

> *Interviewer*
> *(improper question):*
>   *You heard Ralph call Devraj a "fag" and "poufter", didn't you?*
> *Answer:*   *I guess so. Maybe, I'm not sure.*
>   *A much better way to ask the question is for the investigator to ask:*
> *Interviewer:* *You said you had heard Ralph use the word "fag" or "poufter". Do you recall in what context?*
> *Answer:*   *I heard him use the word "fag" a number of times.*
> *Interviewer:* *Please tell me when you recall Ralph using the word fag?*
> *Answer:*   *A number of times. I don't recall specifics.*
> *Interviewer:* *Did you ever hear him call Dev a fag or poufter?*
> *Answer:*   *I'm not sure. He might have.*

While the last two questions clearly reveal the nature of the complaint, at some point in time the investigator has to ask a specific question to determine the witness's recollection. It is quite possible that a witness may have been able to provide excellent information in response to the earlier questions. The investigator has chosen to put a very specific question to the witness, "did you ever hear him call Dev a fag or poufter?" only after asking a series of general questions.

The investigator should note the specific questions and answers. The response, "I'm not sure. He might have," demonstrates a certain amount of uncertainty. This should be noted in any report.

6. Credibility Questions

One of the tasks of the investigator is to determine the credibility of witnesses. The investigator should ask certain questions to determine if the witness has been pressured or tampered with in any way. Some investigators choose to ask these questions up front. Others prefer to leave them to the end, once the witness has established a rapport with the investigator.

(a)   Has the witness discussed his or her evidence or recollection with anyone (aside from the formal interview)? If so, who?

(b)   Has the witness been contacted by anyone (except the investigator or HR) regarding giving evidence or what transpired?

(c)   Does the witness feel pressured to give evidence in a particular way to assist a friend, the company, *etc.*?

This type of information is critical. The investigator needs to determine whether there has been any deliberate witness tampering or if the conversation was more innocent. In a recent investigation involving an allegation of sexual assault during a ride home, several witnesses were asked if the respondent had ever given a drive home to other female co-workers. The witnesses all responded, "yes, but he never offered the ride". It later became evident that the respondent had telephoned his juniors and instructed them on how to answer the question. Some exchanges can be quite innocent:

Investigator: *As I indicated to you, I've been asked to investigate a complaint involving David Grand made by Jennifer DeMarco. Aside from myself and the HR manager, have you had any discussions regarding this matter?*

Witness: *Well, Jennifer DeMarco called me the next morning and was sobbing on the phone. She said that David Grand had mauled her the night before and she couldn't believe that something like this could happen to her. She wanted me to help her.*

Investigator: *Anything else?*

Witness: *No, there's not much I could do. I didn't want to get into the specifics. I'm the one who down-loaded the [harassment] policy from the intraweb and sent it to her. I told her that she should trust the HR manager and that the company would play straight with her.*

Investigator: *Anything else?*

Witness: *No, I don't think anyone else knows about what is going on.*

Investigator: *Have you talked to her since?*

Witness: *No, she left me a message confirming she got the harassment policy.*

Investigator: Any other contact?
Witness: No.
Investigator: Do you know why she contacted you?
Witness: She's a fairly new employee. When she first started, I was her mentor. We've been friendly since then. I guess she felt she could trust me.
Investigator: You say you are friendly, could you describe the friendship?
Witness: We're workplace friends, I guess. We go out for lunch once a month. She's a lot younger than I am, but a decent enough kid. We don't socialize outside of work.

This exchange helps the investigator to determine whether this witness's evidence has been influenced by a workplace friendship or any communication between the complainant and the witness.

It is not unusual for witnesses to feel torn. In many cases, witnesses genuinely like both the complainant and respondent and do not want either to face problems at work. In some cases, witnesses may volunteer comments like "the respondent is a nice guy and has a family ... I don't want him to get into trouble." These types of responses should be noted and go into an assessment into credibility.

Here is a sample exchange:

Investigator: As I indicated to you, I've been asked to investigate a complaint of harassment involving Devraj and Ralph. Aside from myself and the HR manager, have you had any discussions regarding this matter?
Witness: Well, that's all that's being discussed at work. Devraj phoned me to tell me to watch carefully and that fireworks would start. I asked him what he meant, but he told me to be patient.
Investigator: Anyone else?
Witness: Ralph told me that I would probably be contacted by HR and asked me to cooperate. He told me that he would appreciate me letting him know when I was going to be away from the office. He sounded a bit chastened, if you want my opinion.
Investigator: Anything else?
Witness: Listen, I'd really like to be kept out of this. Ralph is a good manager and I need this job. All the other IT staff

have been gossiping about this complaint and what it will do to Ralph's career. I just want to keep out of it.

In this case, the investigator is now aware that the witness is anxious about being forced to give evidence against his manager. Ralph's contact with the witness appears to be professional and correct. Devraj's contact with the witness may or may not be relevant. The gossip in the IT department may have to be managed in some way by the human resources department.

7. Soliciting Other Relevant Information

Investigators often comment on how their decision often turns on un-covering "similar fact" evidence. In the *Bannister v. General Motors* case, an initial complaint by a summer student uncovered numerous instances of inap-propriate conduct. This is often the norm. People behave consistently. Accordingly, the witness should always be asked if he or she might be able to suggest other witnesses the investigator should interview. In many cases, the investigator may stumble into a more significant problem than first anticipated.

Investigator: *Thank you for your help. I was wondering if you think I should interview anyone else in connection with the issues we've discussed.*

Witness: *You mean about Ralph using the words "fag" or "poufter".*

Investigator: *Yes, or anything else you think might be relevant.*

Witness: *Well, I don't know if this is relevant or not, but you might want to ask Alain Desjardins about his experience with Ralph.*

Investigator: *I haven't heard that name. Who is Alain Desjardins?*

Witness: *Alain was our former network specialist. Nice guy. He was very obvious about his sexual orientation. When he left, he told me that he didn't need to work with a redneck homophobe. I'm not sure what he meant, but it might be relevant. He trained Devraj to be his replacement.*

Investigator: *Where's Alain Desjardins now?*

Witness: *He's the manager, IT systems of a small law firm. I think I have his contact information .....*

By simply asking for further witnesses, the investigator has potentially discovered a similar fact witness who may or may not be able to provide cogent evidence. Similarly, the witness should be asked of any documents (electronic or paper) that the investigator should review.

Similar fact witnesses should be treated carefully. If they have information about other incidents that are similar to the main complaint, the respondent must have a chance to respond to the additional allegations. Even though the information is not directly relevant to the complaint itself, it may weigh heavily in an assessment of credibility. The respondent should have an opportunity to confront that evidence as well. Circumstances that may seem similar on the surface can be significantly different upon review.[2]

D.   FOLLOW-UP INTERVIEWS

It is not unusual to interview the complainant, the respondent and key witnesses more than once. In certain cases, the purpose is simply to clarify some detail in the narrative that may have been lost in the notes or investigate an issue that seemed unimportant before.

In other cases, there is a direct contradiction between witnesses or between documents and witness testimony. In such cases, the investigator should return to the complainant, participant or witness in question and confront them with the contradiction. In some cases, the seeming contradiction is simply a misunderstanding on the investigator's part. In other cases, the investigator has discovered a common problem. Honest witnesses will remember different things. If the discrepancy is critical, the investigator may have to resolve a credibility issue. In other cases, the discrepancy simply confirms the fallibility of memory.

In some cases, the witnesses are being evasive or lying. Responses to follow-up questions can help the investigator determine credibility. At the follow-up stage, it may be perfectly appropriate to disclose that other witnesses or documents have suggested other information and ask the witness to explain the discrepancy. The witness's demeanour — helpful, defensive, angry, loud, thoughtful — may provide some clue to the

---

[2]   One of the best discussions of the dangers of using so-called similar fact evidence is in the arbitral decision of *Samra v. Treasury Board* (1996) PSSRB File # 166-2-26543. In *Samra*, the grievor admitted that he had acted inappropriately and overly familiarly with one employee. When accused of serious sexual harassment by a second employee, he firmly denied the allegations. The internal investigators were significantly swayed by the previous complaint. The arbitrator, however, found that the two complaints were very dissimilar in substance and found for the grievor.

credibility of the witness as well. These types of questions challenge the witness.

In certain cases, it may be helpful to use other evidence to control the witness.[3]

Example 10.3

Paige Langdon claims that she was working late one night in August, 200x. While she was at the photocopier, she claims Peter Barnett, one of the sales executives, came up from behind and gave her a bear hug and then proceeded to feel up her skirt. Paige was wearing high heel shoes. She shoved her heel into his instep and broke the right heel. Peter apparently released her. Paige Langdon claims he smelled of "booze and cigarettes". Peter denies the allegation. He acknowledges returning to the office that evening to check his messages and check his e-mail. He admits seeing Paige and saying "hello, you're working late, aren't you."

Assume that after the initial investigation, one of the issues in a case is how much Peter Barnett drank. In an initial interview, Peter Barnett claimed he had only a couple of drinks. Other witnesses have suggested the respondent "drank heavily", but have no specifics. The complainant's recollection is that Peter Barnett smelled of "booze and cigarettes".

In the course of the investigation, the company has produced an expense report that suggests that eight premium scotches and three domestic beers were consumed that night. The investigator is inclined to believe that Peter Barnett drank all eight premium scotches, but is uncomfortable jumping to that conclusion. He decides to follow up with Peter Barnett with respect to this and other discrepancies.

An appropriate line of questioning may proceed as follows:

Interviewer: Mr. Barnett, thank you for agreeing to see me again. I only have a few questions. Do you recall me asking you about how much you had to drink that night?

Barnett: Yes, I do. I told you I had a couple of drinks at the Brew Pub.

---

[3] Most litigation lawyers understand the importance of using techniques to control the witness. Investigators, including those with a legal background, should not try to use courtroom techniques in a neutral investigation. Nonetheless, cross-examination techniques can be useful once the investigator is working on resolving contradictory accounts. For a good introduction on courtroom questioning techniques, see Chapters 4 to 7 of Steven Lubet (Canadian adaptation by Sheila Block and Cynthia Tape), *Modern Trial Advocacy Canada*, 2d ed. (National Institute for Trial Advocacy, 2000).

Interviewer: Yes, that's what my notes say you told me. You also told me that Morton Chambers was drinking beer. Do you recall that?

Barnett: Yes, that's right. Morty always drinks beer in the summer.

Interviewer: Were you drinking beer?

Barnett: No, it was Morty. Like I told you.

Interviewer: Did anyone else join you that night?

Barnett: No, like I told you before, it was only Morty and I that evening — discussing our proposal.

Interviewer: Any chance Morty tried some scotch that night?

Barnett: Morty, no he hates that stuff. He's a rye & coke type of guy.

Interviewer: In the course of my investigation, I had a chance to look over your expense report for that week. You submitted an invoice from the Brew Pub for that night — eight premium scotches and three domestic beers. I want to show you that.

```
Brew Pub
August xx, 200x
Server: Sonali Patel
1 tasting platter        18.50
1 veggie & dips           7.50
3 domestic beer          18.00
8 premium scotches       64.00
***

Paid in full
Credit card J. Barnett
xxxx xxxx xxxx xxxx
```

Can you explain to me why you were charged and paid for eight premium scotches that night? The Brew Pub bill leads me to believe that you had eight premium drinks that night.

Barnett: I guess I had more than I thought. Look, I honestly believed that I only had a couple. I guess it was more.

In this sample exchange, the investigator has already heard Barnett's story and has three sources of concern: (a) other witnesses who talk about

Barnett "drinking heavily"; (b) the complainant's complaint and subsequent interview complaining he stunk of "booze and cigarettes" and (c) the invoice from that evening. The investigator wishes to resolve the concern regarding the potential discrepancy by giving Barnett a chance to explain himself.

The investigator used the invoice to control the witness. The investigator also ensured that the background facts were agreed upon, *i.e.* who was drinking what and who was present. This signalled that the investigator had control of the facts gathered to date and would not be gulled by some kind of contrived story. Nonetheless, Barnett has been given a full opportunity to address the investigator's concern.

E.   FINISHING THE INTERVIEW

Before the interview concludes, the investigator should review the complaint and the notes in order to determine whether all the necessary issues have been covered. In a complex investigation, it is easy to miss some aspect that should be covered with the witness.

At the end of the interview, the investigator should explain how the witness's evidence will be recorded. Depending on the technique used, a second meeting may be required to obtain a signed statement. A signed statement is not legally mandated, but is a useful way to guard against errors.

The witness should be invited to ask any questions he or she may have. Common questions include, "how long will the process take? Will I have to testify in court? What happens to my job?" The investigator should respond to the questions candidly or refer them to someone authoritative in the organization.

The witness should also be reminded of the importance of confidentiality. It is important to impress upon the witness that casual conversations can start career-damaging gossip and innuendo. The witness should be instructed not to discuss the interview or any information he or she learns in the process with anyone.

It is important to invite the witness to add anything else that he or she thinks is germane. In some interviews, the most important information comes just as the witness is leaving the door and flings out some piece of information that may be critical, but the witness has been uncertain about disclosing.

An investigator should always leave follow-up contact information. The investigator should always invite the witness to call if a correction might be required or the witness wants to provide further information.

F.   INTERVIEWING THE PARTIES INVOLVED

The interviews of the complainant and the respondent are the two most critical interviews in any investigation. In the majority of cases, the final decision ultimately rests on the credibility of these parties.

A complainant may be emotionally shaky, frightened, angry or exhausted. He or she may be overwhelmed by the process that has been triggered. The complainant may also view the investigator as her "ally" and "advocate". While the investigator is supportive of the principle that a workplace should be harassment-free, he or she cannot be the complainant's champion. The respondent may be angry, confused and upset. He or she may be concerned about the career consequences of the complaint. He or she may want advice regarding how to protect his or her reputation or pursue the complainant for defamation.

Both parties may want a spouse, family member or lawyer to accompany them during the interview. Unless the complainant or respondent is a minor child, it is inappropriate to allow a family member or spouse accompany them to the interview. Most investigators prefer to interview the complainant and respondent alone. In most cases, tough and embarrassing questions may have to be asked. The presence of the family member will influence the candour of the witness.[4] A better option is to request that the friend or family member wait outside the interview room and assure the interviewee he or she can take a break, if necessary.

Although different investigators have different approaches, most professionals permit a complainant or respondent to have a lawyer present, provided that the lawyer does not interfere in the questioning. The refusal to allow a party to have a lawyer involved may be interpreted subsequently as an effort by the employer to "railroad" one of the parties.

Furthermore, the investigator should be prepared to discuss with the complainant and the respondent the anticipated time to completion. If the timetable subsequently turns out to be unrealistic, the investigator should initiate a quick telephone call to the party and explain that the investigation is still underway, but will take longer than expected. Parties can be very understanding about delays, *as long as they feel that the investigator is being candid and giving the investigation priority.*

---

[4]   For example, the complainant and the respondent may have had a previous consensual extra-marital relationship. The family member may be unaware of this relationship and the complainant may be forced to be less than candid in order to preserve "face" in front of the family.

G. LEGAL CONCERNS

Complainants and respondents will ask investigators difficult legal questions. The investigator cannot become a legal resource for either party, as it would impinge on the principle of neutrality.

If the complainant asks about making a human rights complaint, he or she should be referred to the appropriate human rights commission.[5] In a unionized workforce, many of the larger unions have resources dedicated to victims of sexual harassment in the workplace.

Many respondents will also be concerned about the legal ramifications of the complaint. They may wish to discuss defamation, wrongful dismissal or grievances. The investigator is not in a position to discuss these matters. He or she should emphasize that the investigation is part of a complex process and that at the preliminary stage, no decisions have been made. Legal questions should be handled by a referral to the union (if appropriate) or a lawyer experienced in employment matters.

Many complainants will be concerned about the impact of the complaint. They will ask, "what happens if I can't prove the complaint". The investigator should respond frankly (see Chapter 15). There are three distinct possibilities:

(1)   The complaint has been made in good faith, but the investigator determines that there was no harassment, but rather a misunderstanding or miscommunication or that the complaint does not constitute sexual harassment.

(2)   The complaint was made in good faith, but the investigator determines that it cannot be proven or disproven.

(3)   The complaint was not made in good faith, but rather maliciously or mischievously.

The complainant should be told that in the first two cases, there will be no negative consequences for the complainant.

In the third case (rare), there would be disciplinary consequences for the complainant. A deliberately false complaint of sexual harassment is defamatory. It can ruin the reputations of both the respondent and the company.

---

[5]   Appendix B contains a list of the provincial human rights commissions. British Columbia no longer has a commission, but complaints can be made to the tribunal. Many of the provincial law societies maintain a database of lawyers who are accepting cases. Furthermore, it is often helpful to maintain a roster of employment law lawyers who have experience in sexual harassment cases.

In many cases, either the complainant or the respondent will retain legal counsel. Legal counsel will insist on participating in the process. While most investigators are cautious about the presence of legal counsel, it is inappropriate to refuse to interview a party because he or she has retained legal advice. Nonetheless, the investigator should ensure that the lawyer knows that interference with the actual investigation will not be allowed and that adverse inferences will be drawn if the witness refuses to answer questions that are relevant without a coherent explanation.

H.   EMOTIONAL AND HEALTH CONCERNS

Many complainants are fragile and embarrassed. They may seek emotional counselling from the investigator. Respondents may find the investigative process stressful and may need support. Most investigators are not trained to provide this type of intervention. Certainly, the role of emotional support conflicts with the role of neutral fact-finder.

Many Employee Assistance Programs (EAPs) have trained social workers and psychologists who are able to deal with issues of workplace harassment. Many local sexual assault crisis services are equipped to deal with workplace harassment.

The complainant or respondent should also be encouraged to go to his or her family doctor and seek a qualified referral. The investigator should indicate that he or she does not have the appropriate training to deal with these types of issues. It is inappropriate for the investigator to step into the role of amateur psychologist or psychiatrist.[6]

In rare cases, the complainant's or respondent's medical records may be relevant. The complainant may have indicated that he or she delayed making a complaint, but disclosed the problem to a family doctor. A respondent may suggest that part of the reason for his or her uncharacteristic behaviour is due to medical problems. The investigator should seek medical disclosure. This is a sensitive area. The party involved may have legitimate reasons not to

---

[6]   An excellent web-based resource for referrals is a registry maintained by the Canadian Registry of Health Service Providers in Psychology at <http://www.crhspp.ca/findlist.htm>. The search engine allows the researcher to search by issue, *e.g.* "workplace issues" and city. The results provide contact information and short resumes of psychologists who counsel individuals who need help working through workplace issues, including harassment. The website also provides the names and contact information of the various provincial associations of psychologists. Many of these organizations provide free referral services. There is also a plain language guide for complainants on the internet: *Workplace Harassment: An Action Guide for Women* located at <http://www.owjn.org/issues/s-harass/guide.htm>.

wish to disclose his or her full medical history. The investigator should be open to tailoring the level of medical disclosure required to what is strictly necessary for the purposes of the investigation.

The investigator may wish to consider obtaining partial or full disclosure from the appropriate doctors or health-care workers. Consents must be obtained from the patient. A health-care provider is not entitled to release any information without such an authorization. Sample authorizations are enclosed at Appendix 10.1 and 10.2. Many provinces have strict regulations regarding the disclosure of medical information.

I.   REQUESTING INPUT ON RESOLUTION

It is also appropriate to ask both the complainant and respondent what he or she hopes will transpire as a result of the complaint and whether they have any ideas as to a resolution. The investigator can make no promises or assurances. Nonetheless, the parties' responses to this critical question can assist during the resolution phase of the investigation. The complainant's wishes do not govern legally, however. The author has been involved in numerous cases where the complainant has urged that the company not punish a respondent. The complainant will emphasize that the respondent has family obligations, needs the money, was under stress or cannot afford to be unemployed. While the complainant's concerns should be considered, the employer bears final responsibility for an appropriate response.

APPENDIX 10.1

GENERAL MEDICAL AUTHORIZATION FORM

MEDICAL AUTHORIZATION

TO:

FROM: [Name of Patient]
           D.O.B.:

This is to authorize you to furnish to _____ [name of investigator or company] with:

(Check one)

☐ all information, records, opinions and reports which they may request from you from time to time regarding the physical and psychological condition and treatment of myself and your full co-operation is respectfully requested; or

☐ all documents, notes, records or opinions relating to your treatment of me for _____. [insert description, *e.g.* work-related stress, anxiety disorder, etc.]

A facsimile of this medical authorization is to be treated as an original.

DATED:

Signature: _____

_____
Name of Patient: Witness
Please Print

APPENDIX 10.2

MENTAL HEALTH ACT DISCLOSURE FORM (ONTARIO)

Ministry of Health	Form 14 Mental Health Act	Consent to the Disclosure, Transmittal or Examination of a Clinical Record under Section 35 of the Act

I, _____
(Print full name of person)

of _____
(Address)

hereby consent to the disclosure of or transmittal to the examination by

_____, of the
(Print name)

clinical record compiled in _____
(Name of psychiatric facility)

in respect of _____ .
(Name of patient and date of birth)

Date:

_____

Witness to the signature

_____

Signature

If other than the patient, state relation to the patient: .

Dated this _____ day of _____, 200x.

CHAPTER 11

OBTAINING OTHER EVIDENCE

A. OVERVIEW

The vast majority of the investigator's time is devoted to interviews. Nonetheless, it is important to consider other evidence that may be of assistance. In most investigations, documentation is a critical type of evidence. Depending on the case, an investigator should consider what information, other than witness testimony, can help prove or disprove the complaint.

In terms of documents, there are effectively three kinds:

(a) Documents that are part of the substance of the complaint, *e.g.* a pornographic poster, an offensive e-mail or sexist cartoon;
(b) Documents that bolster the credibility of a witness's account (*e.g.* an expense report that establishes the time when the complainant and respondent finished lunch);
(c) Documents that refresh the memory of a witness.

Documents encompass any record that can be retrieved or reviewed. Electronic documents, security videos, punch cards, letters, receipts, bills, expense reports, personnel documents, resumes, letters, payroll records are just a few examples of documents that this author has reviewed during the course of an investigation. Appendix 11.1 contains a list of documents that may be useful. The list should be modified, depending on the nature of the complaint.

B. COMPELLING PRODUCTION

This book is aimed at internal investigations authorized by an employer. As an employer's agent, the internal investigator has the power to review the corporation's records, such as personnel files, electronic mail messages sent to and from the corporate computing system and corporate expense reports.

Internal investigators do not have the power to *compel* an employee or witness or other third-party to provide documents belonging to them. For example, in the sample case file in Part II, the respondent refuses to release his personal telephone records to the investigator. The investigator may not be able to obtain this information.[1] By contrast, law enforcement agencies and human rights investigators have broad powers to compel production.[2] An investigator can, however, draw an adverse inference against a witness or party who refuses, without a cogent explanation, to release apparently relevant documents.

C. SECURING THE DOCUMENTS

One of the first pre-investigation steps is to ensure that any documents that may be relevant to an investigation are secured. Many companies have automatic document destruction protocols. In other cases, the documentary information is transitory by nature. For example, in the case of e-mails, some sites retain "sendmail" logs for only short periods of time. E-mail that could be traced, if the trace were immediately commenced, may no longer be traceable after 24 hours. Time is of the essence.

Documents have been known to have been inadvertently destroyed, even though there was an on-going investigation. An investigator may not realize what, if any, documents, are relevant to the inquiry until the investigation is underway. The investigator should secure documents as soon as it becomes evident they may be relevant. In a recent case, video surveillance tapes were routinely re-used. Because the significance of the tapes became evident several weeks after the incident, they were no longer available to confirm or deny the complainant's allegation of sexual assault about the videotape. The tape was erased and re-recorded every 72 hours. If the human resource

---

[1] It is an open question whether refusal to cooperate in an internal investigation constitutes just cause for termination. Although a single act of insubordination can constitute cause for termination, an employee may be able to proffer a legitimate excuse for non-compliance. Furthermore, recent legislative changes support an employee's right to privacy. For an excellent discussion of the concept of insubordination as cause for termination, see Stacey Ball, *1 Canadian Employment Law*, looseleaf (Aurora: Canada Law Book, 1996) at para. 11:90.

[2] Appendix 11.1 provides excerpts of the B.C. and Ontario human rights legislation, which defines the scope of an investigator's powers and sets forth the protocol for obtaining a warrant. These mechanisms are available to investigators appointed by the applicable human rights commission and not to an internal investigator. All investigators appointed under the various human rights regimes have broad powers to compel production of documents. Section 487 of the Canadian *Criminal Code*, R.S.C. 1985, c. C-46 sets forth the procedures for a law enforcement officer to obtain a search warrant.

manager had secured the tape, there may have been persuasive evidence supporting or undermining the complainant's account.

D. DOCUMENTS WHICH ARE THE SUBSTANCE OF THE COMPLAINT

In some cases, the complainant is able to produce documents that are alleged to be offensive. In some cases, the nature of the offence is self-evident, *e.g.* a pornographic poster or sexist cartoon. In other cases, the document itself is neutral, but the complainant draws an inference from the document. The investigator may have to determine whether the inference is appropriate or not.

In cases in which an employee alleges that he or she experienced a reprisal for declining a sexual solicitation or making a complaint, a thorough review of performance reviews, job descriptions, compensation packages and other personnel information may be critical in determining whether there was indeed a linkage between the harassment and the job-related consequences of which the complainant complains. It may be necessary to review not just the complainant's personnel file, but also the files of co-workers as well in order to determine if the complainant was being treated consistently with previous corporate practice. This raises some difficult issues regarding privacy.[3]

Example 11.1
After her performance review, Lalita is devastated. Previously, she had received average-to-good reviews. This review contained numerous detailed criticisms of her inability to complete tasks on a timely basis, her failure to delegate work to subordinates and her refusal to learn a new

---

[3] It is out of the scope of this book to fully review the implications of privacy legislation on investigations. Nonetheless, the *Personal Information and Protection of Electronic Data Act* (PIPEDA) applies to any personal information about employees held by federally-regulated employers. The definition of personal information is broad. It includes any information other than the name, job title, and *business* contact information of an employee. PIPEDA does permit employers to rely on *implied* consent to the release of information. The privacy commissioner has warned, however, that the more sensitive the data, the more cautious a company should be. Quebec and Alberta have enacted their own privacy regimes that apply to provincially-regulated employers in those jurisdictions. Investigators and employers should tread cautiously when reviewing personnel files or other documents, where there clearly would be an expectation of privacy. The application of privacy law to private internal investigations is still developing. The federal privacy commissioner has indicated that much of this law will develop in the context of complaints from employees.

computer system. Her supervisor presented the document to her at her annual review on February 1. Lalita is firmly convinced the performance review is a reprisal because she had turned down the supervisor's proposition at the company's Christmas party the previous year. The supervisor does not deny the proposition, but states that it was irrelevant to his assessment. He points out that he asked Lalita once and when rebuffed, never renewed his attention. He admits that he exercised poor judgment with respect to his conduct at the Christmas party, but denies the retaliation. He has three major justifications for his review: (i) the review is true and he has documented these concerns before; (ii) the company has recently received ISO certification and is much more professional and strict with respect to performance reviews; and (iii) he is a new supervisor. The previous supervisor was notoriously lax with respect to employees and their performance. He is tough on all employees.

A negative performance review is not, in and of itself, sexual harassment. A manager is entitled to manage his employees. In this case, however, it may be critical to review the previous reviews and the performance documentation that the manager claims he has. It may also be necessary to compare the previous year's and current year's reviews of all employees in this manager's department in order to test the defence that he is "tough on all employees". This example is drawn from an investigation conducted by the author. A thorough review of the documents revealed the following:

(a) Lalita had refused two times to attend the in-house computer training session and had sent her assistant instead. She had bitterly objected to the new computer system in several reports.

(b) There were four e-mails in which the supervisor complained about Lalita's inability to complete certain tasks, along with a comment that she had to learn to delegate.

(c) Co-workers resented Lalita, because her failure to complete tasks meant that they often had to stay late. The overtime budget in Lalita's department was disproportionately high.

(d) Lalita's six-month review, written before the Christmas party, was consistent with the performance review, but was not so strongly-worded.

(e) The supervisor had written several critical performance reviews of his subordinates and in general, was "tough" on his employees.

In light of the totality of the evidence, the performance review was tough, but justified. The supervisor was reprimanded for his conduct at the Christmas party. The much more serious allegation regarding reprisal, however, was held to be unfounded.[4]

E. DOCUMENTS THAT ASSIST THE RECOLLECTION OF A WITNESS

There are two kinds of documents which assist witness testimony. In legal jargon, they are distinguished as "past recollection recorded" or "present recollection refreshed". In most cases, witnesses should be encouraged to refresh their recollection from contemporaneous notes or other documents. The investigator should obtain copies of any such documents in order to test the accuracy of the witness's recollection. While there are limits to the use of these types of documents in litigation, they can be an invaluable resource to an internal investigator.[5] Note that in some cases, it is important to review the originals of the documents, to ensure that the documents are contemporaneous and/or that nothing of importance has been erased or amended.

Example 11.2

Patricia Fenton complains about verbal sexual propositions, physical sexual harassment and stalking against her former supervisor, John DiFilipis. She claims that she maintained an accurate diary on her

---

[4] Note that in this case, it was determined that Lalita had made her complaint in good faith. She *believed* that her negative review was motivated by her refusal of the supervisor's proposition. Lalita was not subject to any discipline as a result of the complaint, but was required to work on her computer skills and to delegate certain tasks.

[5] In the Anglo-Canadian court system, "past recollection recorded" is a document which records a witness's recollection of events. Such documents include notes of witness interviews, transcripts, a complaint made when the complainant remembered the events and diary entries made contemporaneously with events. The witness may no longer remember the events due to the passage of time or impairment due to age or disease and may seek to rely on the document in lieu of actual recollection. In most cases, "past recollection recorded" is not admissible on its own as evidence of the events recorded in the document. There are some limited exceptions to this rule. By contrast, documents which jog a witness's memory may "refresh" the recollection. Technically speaking, the witness is providing the evidence, but needs the document to refresh the recollection. In such cases, parties are entitled to the documents used, partially to test the accuracy of the refreshed recollection. This distinction is relevant in court proceedings. During an internal investigation, an investigator should determine what weight, if any, should be placed on the documents and the information they provide.

personal hard drive at work regarding the events as they occurred. She explained that she had delayed complaining against John until she had successfully applied for a job transfer. The computer log contained details that Patricia said she could no longer recall. John, however, insisted that the computer itself be examined. Through some basic forensic examination, it was established that the document was created months after some of the events. Patricia then indicated that she had just created a new document to "clean up" her previous, messy document. A further forensic investigation of the computer and the company's extensive computer archives revealed that in fact no previous versions (or excerpts) existed.

This example illustrates the importance of not accepting documents at face value. Although it may require technical expertise to verify the authenticity of electronic or other documents, it may be a crucial step where there is a serious dispute regarding the document's validity.

F.   CORROBORATING DOCUMENTS

In most cases, the documentary evidence is secondary. It corroborates a witness's narrative, but is rarely determinative of the issues.

In Part II, a sample case file is enclosed. In this case file, receipts and cell phone records may be of assistance in corroborating aspects of each party's case, but will not be able to prove or disprove the complainant's complaint.

Nonetheless, a thorough investigator will demand any documentation that might be of assistance. The documentation might reveal the names of other witnesses or establish that a witness has been less than truthful with respect to a non-critical aspect of his or her testimony.

In today's technological world, people's movements are tracked in much greater detail and in ways that many investigators might not be able to easily access. Depending on the nature of the complaint, it may be important to retain technical assistance to preserve electronic data immediately.[6] In most cases, however, the documentary evidence is more prosaic. It may include credit card receipts, cellphone records and date books.

---

[6]   For a good introduction to the complexities of electronic evidence from a Canadian perspective, see Alan Gahtan, *Electronic Evidence* (Carswell, 1999). A more detailed book, aimed at information technology professionals, is Albert J. Marcella and Robert S. Greenfield, eds., *Cyber Forensics: A Field Manual for Collecting, Examining, and Preserving Evidence of Computer Crimes* (Auerbach Publications, 2001).

Medical records may also be relevant in corroborating allegations of mental stress as a result of the harassment. An investigator can only access such information upon receiving the written consent of the witness. Mental health records may require a more detailed consent.[7]

G.   EXPERT DOCUMENTARY ANALYSIS

In most cases, the documentary evidence is quite straightforward. The document is what it purports to be. The investigator must decide what inferences can be drawn from the document.

In Example 11.1, the authorship of the performance review is not in question. Ultimately, the investigator will determine if the performance review was retaliatory or not. Traditional techniques — such as interviews and review of previous performance reviews — may be all that is required.

In rare cases, the documentary issues are complex. Anonymous hate messages, e-mails from dummy accounts or allegedly forged signatures may become an issue. Unless the investigator has the appropriate expertise, an expert must be retained. Such experts can sometimes resolve seemingly intractable problems.

A forensic document examiner may be able to:

- obtain fingerprints and conduct fingerprint analysis to identify who handled the document in question;
- identify signatures, handwriting and printing by comparing the document in question with other samples;
- perform ink analysis to assist in establishing provenance;
- analyze the paper itself to determine age, manufacturer, country of origin;
- review a photocopied or computer-printed document to confirm or deny if the document was produced by a particular machine;
- review a typewritten document to confirm or deny whether it was produced by a particular machine;
- assess whether the document has been altered or forged.

Forensic linguists can be of assistance. This is an emerging and somewhat controversial area of study. Experts in forensic stylistics, a sub-specialty of forensic linguists, can examine writing style "for the express purpose of

---

[7]   See Chapter 10, section 4.

resolving litigated questions related to disputed authorship or meaning".[8] For example, in the well-publicized case of the anthrax letters in the United States in the fall of 2001, the FBI used forensic stylistics to develop a profile of the perpetrator.[9] Forensic stylistics can assist in determining:

- the level of education of the author;
- his or her place of origin;
- whether the author is a native speaker of English or not;
- whether the author has had certain kinds of technical or specialist training.

Example 11.3
An employee complained that she had received numerous racist and sexist messages. She had ignored them at first, thinking they were some kind of sick joke. They continued. They had been placed under her car's windshield wiper at the company's parking lot, sent to her in a plain envelope by inter-office mail and slipped under her office door. Most of them were computer-generated messages or obscene photographs. She and the company could not determine authorship and had no idea why she was receiving this mail. There were no viable suspects. Traditional investigatory techniques proved to be fruitless.

The employee indicated that she would resign because the company was unable to stop the messages. She threatened a human rights or wrongful dismissal case. Out of frustration, the company retained a forensic document examiner. This expert was able to determine that most of the messages had been generated by a specific printer at the workplace. The IT department could determine who had access to that printer and when. In combination with a review of vacation records, building entry records and witness interviews, the company was able to pinpoint the employee. When

---

[8] G. McMenamin, "Forensic Stylistics" (1993) 58 Forensic Science Int'l 1 at 45. Note that some U.S. courts in criminal cases have expressed concern regarding the reliability of forensic stylistics and have refused to allow the prosecution to adduce this type of expert testimony in court. See, for example, *United States v. Van Wyk*, 83 F.Supp.2d 515 (D. New Jersey, 2000). In most cases, forensic linguistic analysis can help eliminate suspects, but is unable to determine exactly who authored the document.

[9] See FBI briefing — November 9, 2001: Amerithrax Press Briefing, Linguistic/Behavioral Analysis of Anthrax Letters, Critical Incident Response Group, National Center for the Analysis of Violent Crime (reproduced at <http://web.bham.ac.uk/forensic/>).

confronted, the employee confessed and was astonished that he had been tracked down.

There are excellent tools available to help trace "anonymous" e-mail messages, particularly if the tracing procedures are commenced immediately upon receipt. An employer's internal information technology department may already have the expertise.[10]

H. TAKING A VIEW

In some cases, it is important to take a view of where an event occurred in order to determine the veracity of the complainant's and respondent's account. The physical setting can be crucial in certain complaints. Complainants have complained about pornographic posters within the workplace or a "sexually-charged" atmosphere (fireplace, wine, music, candles and low-lighting).[11]

Once the investigator takes a view, it may prompt further questions. The investigator should consider:

- location of the event;
- location of potential witnesses;
- sightlines – who could or could not have seen what happened?
- lighting (what could be seen and by whom).

Example 11.4
Genevieve Sharpe complains that her boss, Alvin Watson, fondled her breasts and groin from behind while she was working the cash. Genevieve told him to stop, but Alvin continued. She claims that she elbowed Alvin and ran away. Alvin denies the charge. He points out that the store has large windows and that security is right in front of the store. Alvin states he didn't do it and if he did, security would notice. During a telephone interview, security confirms that they look right into the store

---

[10] Although many IT departments already have this type of expertise, caution should be exercised. It is inappropriate to use internal resources if there is any chance that a member of the IT department could be responsible for the impugned messages. External consultants can provide surprisingly cost-effective assistance. Many of the tools used are available at little or no cost. Some of the best information is available on the internet. See, for example:<http://www.abika.com/reports/traceemails.htm>; <www. support.netfronts.com/email/tracing_emails.htm>; <www.catalog.com/mrm/security/ trace-forgery.html>; <www.networking-earthweb.com/reports/index.php/31>.

[11] See discussion in the case of *Mahmoodi v. Dutton (No. 4)* (1999), 36 C.H.R.R. D/8 (B.C. H.R.T.), aff'd 95 B.C.L.R. (3d) 186 (S.C.).

most of the time and would normally have noticed something. Genevieve agrees that the store has large windows and is surprised that security did not notice anything. When taking a view, the investigator noticed a large display of new product arrivals. After looking from the security desk, it is clear that most of the store is visible, but the cash register area is blocked by the display.

Example 11.4 demonstrates the importance of looking at the physical setting. Furthermore, it illustrates the importance of a rapid response to the complaint. Since retail displays change frequently, it is possible that the investigator would have missed the detail if he or she had delayed taking a view.

I. CONCLUSION

Many investigators focus on witness interviews. In many cases, this does a disservice to both the complainant and respondent. Many instances of sexual harassment occur in private. Without corroboration, the investigator is faced with a stark exercise of determining credibility. In many cases, the documents or a view can help establish the veracity of one of the parties on critical details. Furthermore, an investigator who demonstrates a mastery of the documents is often able to control witnesses.[12] Accordingly, an investigation should not ignore this valuable source of information.

---

[12] An example of this technique is provided in Example 10.3 in Chapter 10 on *Interviewing Witnesses.*

APPENDIX 11.1

CHECKLIST OF SOURCES OF DOCUMENTARY EVIDENCE

☐ Complainant's and respondent's personnel files
☐ Complainant's and respondent's electronic mail messages
☐ Complainant's and respondent's internet surfing records
☐ Computer hard drive
☐ Expense reports including:
 ☐ Parking receipts
 ☐ Hotel bills
 ☐ Restaurant receipts
 ☐ Car rental invoices
 ☐ Credit card receipts
 ☐ Telephone usage records
 ☐ Cellphone usage records
☐ Instant messaging usage records
☐ Datebook/diary (electronic/paper form)
☐ Payroll records for vacation, holidays, days off, sick days
☐ Medical records (consent required)
☐ Psychiatric records (consent required)
☐ Prescription records (consent required)
☐ Building security entry logs
☐ Building security videos
☐ Building security elevator usage records
☐ Building access/egress records
☐ Punch card records
☐ Parking usage records

APPENDIX 11.2

POWERS OF A HUMAN RIGHTS INVESTIGATOR

The British Columbia, *Human Rights Code*, R.S.B.C. 1996, c. 210 (Supp.), ss. 23 and 24 provide:

Investigation – 23 (1) The commissioner of investigation and mediation may designate an employee appointed under section 17(1), or any other person, as a human rights officer for the purpose of conducting investigations of complaints.

(2) The commissioner of investigation and mediation must assign a human rights officer to investigate a complaint unless that commissioner determines that the complaint can be disposed of under section 26 without an investigation.

(3) A human rights officer must submit to the commissioner of investigation and mediation a report of the findings of an investigation.

Powers of investigation — s. 24 (1) For the purpose of investigating a complaint, the commissioner of investigation and mediation or a human rights officer may:

(a) require the production of books, documents, correspondence or other records that relate or may relate to the complaint, and

(b) make any inquiry relating to the complaint of any person, in writing or orally.

(2) If a person refuses to:

(a) comply with a demand under subsection (1)(a) for the production of books, documents, correspondence or other records, or

(b) respond to an inquiry made under subsection (1)(b),

the commissioner of investigation and mediation or a human rights officer may apply to the Supreme Court for an order requiring the person to comply with the demand or respond to the inquiry.

(3) A judge of the Supreme Court, on application under subsection (2), may

(a) make an order requiring a person to

(i) produce a book, document, correspondence or other record to the commissioner of investigation and mediation or a human rights officer under subsection (1)(a), or

(ii) respond to an inquiry made under subsection (1)(b), and

(b) make any other order that the judge considers necessary to enforce the demand or inquiry under subsection (1).

(4) For the purpose of investigating a complaint, the commissioner of investigation and mediation or a human rights officer may, with the consent of the owner or occupier, enter and inspect any premises that in the opinion of that commissioner or the human rights officer may provide information relating to the complaint.

(5) A person exercising a power of entry under subsection (4) must, on request, produce identification and give reasons for requiring entry to the premises.

(6) If consent to enter any premises is withheld by the owner or occupier under subsection (4), the commissioner of investigation and mediation or a human rights officer must not enter the premises unless authorized by a warrant under subsection (7).

(7) A justice, if satisfied by information on oath or affirmation that access to any premises is necessary for the purposes of an investigation under section 23, may issue a warrant authorizing a person named in the warrant to enter and inspect those premises.

(8) If a justice is satisfied by information, on oath or affirmation, that there are in a place books, documents, correspondence or other records that there are reasonable and probable grounds to believe will afford evidence relevant to a complaint, the justice may issue a warrant authorizing a person named in the warrant to

(a) search the place for those books, documents, correspondence or records, and

(b) remove those books, documents, correspondence or records for the purpose of making copies of them.

(9) If books, documents, correspondence or other records are produced under subsection (1)(a) or removed under subsection (8)(b), the commissioner of investigation and mediation or a human rights officer must:

(a) copy the books, documents, correspondence or records as quickly as possible, and

(b) promptly return the books, documents, correspondence or records to the person who produced them or to the place from which they were removed.

The *Ontario Human Rights Code*, R.S.O. 1990, c. H.19, s. 33 (1) to (8) provides:

Investigation of complaints — (1) Subject to section 34, the Commission shall investigate a complaint and endeavour to effect a settlement.

Investigation — (2) An investigation by the Commission may be made by a member or employee of the Commission who is authorized by the Commission for the purpose.

Powers on investigation — (3) A person authorized to investigate a complaint may,

(a) enter any place, other than a place that is being used as a dwelling, at any reasonable time, for the purpose of investigating the complaint;

(b) request the production for inspection and examination of documents or things that are or may be relevant to the investigation;

(c) upon giving a receipt therefor, remove from a place documents produced in response to a request under clause (b) for the purpose of making copies thereof or extracts therefrom and shall promptly return them to the person who produced or furnished them; and

(d) question a person on matters that are or may be relevant to the complaint subject to the person's right to have counsel or a personal representative present during such questioning, and may exclude from the questioning any person who may be adverse in interest to the complainant.

Entry into dwellings — (4) A person investigating a complaint shall not enter a place that is being used as a dwelling without the consent of the occupier except under the authority of a warrant issued under subsection (8).

Denial of entry — (5) Subject to subsection (4), if a person who is or may be a party to a complaint denies entry to any place, or instructs the person investigating to leave the place, or impedes or prevents an investigation therein, the Commission may refer the matter to the Tribunal or may authorize an employee or member to apply to a justice of the peace for a warrant to enter under subsection (8).

Refusal to produce — (6) If a person refuses to comply with a request for production of documents or things, the Commission may refer the matter to the Tribunal, or may authorize an employee or member to apply to a justice of the peace for a search warrant under subsection (7).

Warrant for search — (7) Where a justice of the peace is satisfied on evidence upon oath or affirmation that there are in a place documents that there is reasonable ground to believe will afford evidence relevant to the complaint, he or she may issue a warrant in the prescribed form authorizing a person named in the warrant to search a place for any such documents, and to remove them for the purposes of making copies thereof or extracts therefrom, and the documents shall be returned promptly to the place from which they were removed.

Warrant for entry — (8) Where a justice of the peace is satisfied by evidence upon oath or affirmation that there is reasonable ground to believe it is necessary that a place being used as a dwelling or to which entry has been denied be entered to investigate a complaint, he or she may issue a warrant in the prescribed form authorizing such entry by a person named in the warrant.

Execution of warrant — (9) A warrant issued under subsection (7) or (8) shall be executed at reasonable times as specified in the warrant.

CHAPTER 12

REVIEWING THE EVIDENCE

A. OVERVIEW

The primary task of the investigator is to be a neutral fact-finder. This entails digging up all the relevant facts. In most investigations, the facts come from disparate sources. The investigator must consider and assess all of the evidence and come to a conclusion regarding the validity of the complaint. Trained investigators often make judgment calls regarding the weight that should be given certain evidence, the credibility of the witnesses and the motivations of the complainant and the respondent. This is a huge responsibility and should be approached thoughtfully.

B. STANDARD OF PROOF

Standard of proof is a legal concept. It essentially refers to how persuaded a fact-finder must be before finding that a certain allegation is true. In civil cases, such as breach of contract, the standard of proof is known as the "balance of probabilities" or the "preponderance of evidence". Some law professors ask students to envision an old-fashioned scale and mentally stack the evidence for an allegation on one side of the scale and against the allegation on the other side of the scale. If the "for" side is heavier, the allegation has been established on a balance of probabilities.

By contrast, in criminal cases, the allegation must be established on the basis of "proof beyond a reasonable doubt". Allegations of criminal conduct may lead to the loss of liberty. The court system is vigilant against possible miscarriages of justice.

The courts have signalled that the more serious the alleged misconduct, the more convincing the proof should be.[1] The courts have indicated that the

---

[1] In cases of serious alleged misconduct, particularly where a person's continued employment and reputation is at stake, the employer will bear the onus of proof. The employer must have strong and cogent evidence that the allegations are true. The standard of proof is not "proof beyond a reasonable doubt", but it is beyond the

balance of probabilities approach is insufficient, particularly where the allegation of misconduct is significant. The investigator should be able to answer this question: *is there cogent and convincing evidence that the allegations against the respondent are true?* This is effectively an intermediate standard between the traditional civil and criminal tests.

C. ORGANIZING THE EVIDENCE

In complex cases, it can be useful to review the complaint (and any additional matters requiring determination) and summarize each allegation or incident in chronological order. For each separate allegation or incident, the investigator can create a point-form summary of the following:

- complainant's version;
- respondent's version;
- witness testimony (if any);
- documentary evidence (if any);
- matters requiring follow up (if any).

This process forces the investigator to focus on the specific evidence that has been accumulated. The exercise of trying to separate the evidence from the specific witness narrative or documentary source may draw the investigator's attention to further investigation that may be required. It may also highlight troubling inconsistencies or even reveal patterns that may shed light on the complaint in question. In many cases, this exercise establishes that the evidence clearly supports one version of the incident over another. In other cases, the investigator must resolve difficult questions of credibility.

"balance of probabilities" or "preponderance of evidence". The Supreme Court of Canada has held that in the context of dismissal for theft:

...in dealing with the burden of proof [the court] could properly consider the cogency of the evidence offered to support proof on a balance of probabilities and this is what he did when he referred to proof commensurate with the gravity of the allegations of the accusation of theft by the temporary driver. There is necessarily a matter of judgment involved in weighing evidence that goes to the burden of proof, and a trial judge is justified in scrutinizing evidence with greater care if there are serious allegations to be established by the proof that is offered. [*Continental Insurance Co. v. Dalton Cartage Co. Ltd.*, [1982] 1 S.C.R. 164 *per* Chief Justice Laskin].

D. ASSESSING CREDIBILITY

One of the most difficult tasks in an investigation is assessing the credibility of witnesses. In most investigations, the information provided by the parties to the complaint and witnesses conflict. Many cases fall within the "he says/she says" category. The investigator will have to decide whom to believe. Where appropriate, the investigator is entitled to assess the credibility of a witness and accept one witness's version of events over another. Ex-perienced police investigators have indicated that in most cases, one party is obviously less credible than another.

Resolving credibility is an art, not a science. Investigators do not possess an infallible lie-detector test that can advise who is telling the truth, who is lying and who is honestly mistaken regarding the facts. In the judicial context, the late Mr. Justice O'Halloran of the British Columbia Court of Appeal wrote this cautionary note:

> If a trial Judge's finding of credibility is to depend solely on which person he thinks made the better appearance of sincerity in the witness box, we are left with a purely arbitrary finding and justice would then depend upon the best actor in the witness box. On reflection, it becomes almost axiomatic that the appearance of telling the truth is but one of the elements that enter into the credibility of the evidence of a witness. Opportunities for knowledge, powers of observation, judgement and memory, ability to describe clearly what he has seen and heard, as well as others factors, combine to produce what is called credibility .... A witness by his manner may create a very unfavourable impression of his truthfulness upon the trial judge and yet the surrounding circumstances in the case may point decisively to the conclusion that he is telling the truth. I am not referring to the comparatively infrequent cases in which a witness is caught in a clumsy lie.
>
> The credibility of interested witnesses, particularly in cases of conflict of evidence cannot be gauged solely by the test of whether the personal demeanour of particular witness carried conviction of the truth. The test must reasonably subject his story to an examination of its consistency with the probabilities that surround the current existing conditions. In short, the real test of the truth and story of a witness in such a case must be its harmony with the preponderance of the probabilities which a practical and informed person would readily recognize as reasonable in that place and in those conditions.[2]

1. Self-Interest or Interest in the Outcome of the Investigation

An investigator should carefully assess the witness's interest in the outcome of the proceedings, their relationship to any party to the proceeding or any

---

[2]   *Faryna v. Chorney*, [1952] 2 D.L.R. 354 at 356-58 (B.C.C.A.).

possible motivations that might cause the witness to be less than candid. A complainant may want financial compensation or bear a grudge because of a lost promotion. A respondent has an obvious motivation to lie as his or her career may be devastated by the allegations.

Obviously, the specific parties to the complaint have the most direct interest in the outcome of the investigation. Nonetheless, in a harassment context, a subordinate may feel obliged to relate a story consistent with his or her superior's interests. A superior may wish to protect a valuable employee facing a complaint from an entry-level individual. Family members may not wish to jeopardize an individual's career. A witness who may have been somewhat complicit in the situation may be less than candid regarding his or her observations. Cultural pressures may also exist. Where the complainant and respondent come from different ethnic communities, there may be strong pressures to support a member of the community against an "outsider". In some workforces, women are considered to be interlopers and witnesses are swayed by "gender solidarity". Even witnesses who are completely unaffected by the complaint may wish to avoid becoming involved in a "messy" situation.

As part of the investigation, it is important to understand these undercurrents. These are critical to assessing credibility.

2. Consistency

One of the common tests of credibility is whether a witness has been consistent throughout or whether the story or salient details have shifted. Absolute consistency is not necessary. A truthful witness may honestly forget a detail or dismiss an aspect of narrative as being irrelevant. Documentation or follow-up questioning may jog a witness's memory. A witness who makes a mistake as to what may seem to be a less relevant detail may still be accurate about more material events. Nonetheless, a narrative that changes with respect to material details when the witness is pressed is cause for concern.

The investigator should also look for overall consistency among witnesses and any documentary evidence. Where most of the witnesses and/or documents support one version of events, that version of events will be more credible. Nonetheless, the investigator should be alert to the possibility of collusion. Particularly where the complaint is being made by a newcomer or perceived outsider, the investigator often encounters a workplace that is solidly behind the re-spondent, regardless of the truth of the allegations.

3. Plausibility

The internal plausibility of the story is also an important factor. A good investigator should try to visualize the entire scene, almost as if it were a re-enactment. If an explanation seems implausible, it may be appropriate to reject the explanation. A weak and implausible explanation on a peripheral matter should raise questions regarding the party's credibility on more central matters.

> ***Example 12.1***
>
> *Helena is a teenager. She accepted some temporary work at a charity casino. The normal shifts were 12 hours (10 a.m. to 10 p.m.). The second night, the senior manager told Helena to go home at 7 p.m. since it was cold, windy and rainy, and business was slow. Her immediate supervisor told her to stay to the end of the shift because there was work to do and he would take her home afterwards. She alleges that the immediate supervisor assaulted her in the parking lot of the casino after they closed up shop. The supervisor denies the allegation. In response to the investigator's questions, Helena indicated that at the supervisor's urging, she had kissed the supervisor on the cheek (and vice versa) as part of a social greeting common in her and the supervisor's ethnic community. Helena did not find this objectionable at all, as she was comfortable with the ways of the "old country". Helena added that the supervisor had never previously touched her in a sexual manner, or she would not have accepted the ride.*

During the investigation, the supervisor denied ever kissing Helena on the cheek or Helena kissing him on the cheek, even as part of a social greeting. The supervisor's denial, however, was ultimately rejected. Several witnesses noticed that Helena and the supervisor had exchanged this customary greeting. They also confirmed that Helena seemed perfectly comfortable in these interchanges. During the investigation, it also became evident that the business was very slow the night of the alleged assault. The senior manager indicated that he would always cut back on staff when business was slow and that the casual workers were cut first. The company maintained accurate records regarding the amount of business transacted. Due to the weather, the business was down by 50 per cent or more.

The senior manager did not know why his orders were countermanded by the supervisor. When the supervisor was confronted about the social greeting, he feebly responded that he "must have forgotten". When the supervisor was asked why he insisted on Helena staying late that night, he claimed that he thought it was busier. When asked why one of the permanent staff was sent home and not Helena, the supervisor explained it was just a "mistake". The other workers described the evening as "dead" and explained that it was both unusual and unfair for the casual worker to get the hours instead of the permanent worker.

The supervisor was ultimately not believed. He had lied about a relatively innocent matter: the kiss on the cheek. His explanation regarding why Helena had stayed late was not supported by the documentary evidence and the previous practice of the workplace. His lack of plausibility on two peripheral matters weighed heavily against him in the final analysis.

4. Strength of Witnesses

An investigator should also assess the perceptual abilities of witnesses. Witnesses have different capacities for observation and remembering what they have observed. Investigators routinely make decisions regarding which witness is a more accurate witness. Professional training or personal interest in the subject matter can make a difference. A bartender will probably remember what a customer drank, but may not remember what a customer was wearing. A valet may remember the details of the car he parked, but less about the owner of the car. A dress designer may be able to provide details about an individual's attire, but not remember the time when the person entered the room. These are all relevant factors in assessing credibility.

5. Watch for Cultural Biases

Cultural differences are also important. Certain cultural cues that create the impression of truthfulness in North American society, such as making eye contact or a firm hand shake, are not widespread in other cultures. In certain cultures, a man will not shake the hands of a woman who is not his family member. In other cultures, eye contact is considered rude. A loud voice may be considered boorish and uneducated. While these are broad general-izations, where cross-cultural factors are involved, an investigator should make sure that he or she has an adequate briefing regarding the cultural issues involved.

An investigator will also find it difficult to assess the information provided by a witness who gives evidence in a language in which he or she is not fluent. Investigators need to be aware that a witness may make an honest error because of a linguistic misunderstanding. Investi-gators should strive to ask straightforward questions without any use of slang or vernacular and listen carefully for any potential mistakes. Investigators should also recognize that it is easy to favour the testimony of individuals who have mastered the language and speak without an accent or hesitation. Consequently, it is appropriate to make allowances for a non- native speaker of the language.[3]

6. Body Language

An investigator should listen and watch a witness carefully. Body language, hesitation, and tone of voice are very important clues to the witness's comfort level and veracity. An investigator is entitled to evaluate the appearance and demeanour of the witness. While a certain amount of nervousness is under-standable, evasiveness and hostility are tell-tale clues.

7. Impairment

It is important also to assess if the witness's ability to observe was impaired in any way. Alcohol and drugs impair perception and memory. An individual who needs a hearing aid or glasses is at a disadvantage in providing evidence if he or she was not wearing the necessary items at the time of the incident. Exhaustion or fatigue play a factor as well.

8. Similar Fact Evidence

Most of this book has focused on eliciting evidence regarding whether a particular complaint can be substantiated on the evidence. What if the investigation turned up other instances of misconduct? Should the investigator consider previous misconduct in determining whether the particular complaint has been substantiated?

This type of evidence can be very dangerous. By focusing on instances of previous bad behaviour, the investigator may be sidetracked into focusing on the respondent's character and not on whether the events occurred as delineated in the complaint. On the other hand, a respondent's previous conduct may reveal a disturbing pattern.

Courts of law and tribunals have cautioned against the misuse of "similar fact" evidence. They are required to balance the "probative value" of the

---

[3] Example of a simple question that might cause confusion: "When did you call it a night?" instead of "When did you go to sleep?"

evidence against the "prejudice" to the respondent. In the criminal court system, similar fact evidence is treated very carefully.[4]

A sexual harassment investigation is not a criminal matter. Evidence does not have to be admissible in a criminal court in order to be considered by an investigator. Nonetheless, in reviewing similar fact evidence, the investigator should balance the relevance (*i.e.* probative value) of the evidence against the prejudice it may cause (e.g., making the respondent look bad for the sake of looking bad).

Example 12.2
A sixteen-year old female retail clerk, Angelica, complained that her supervisor, Giovanni, a male in his 50s, had offered her a ride late at night. It was pouring rain, and they lived within two miles of each other. She accepted. Angelica alleged that Giovanni had asked her intimate details regarding her sex life and her relationship with her boyfriend and had propositioned her during the ride. She claimed that he had kissed her hard on the lips and had touched her breast and groin. She was distraught. No one else had been in the car, however. Giovanni denied the charges. He emphasized that Angelica was a probationary employee who was having problems learning her job and that her employment would probably not be continued after the end of the month. The personnel file confirmed that there had been several discussions regarding Angelica's breaches of company protocol. In investigating a peripheral matter relating to the complaint, several current employees volunteered that it was well-known the supervisor was a "pervert" and that several ex-employees should be questioned. The ex-employees in question were all young female clerks. The ex-employees, questioned separately, confirmed that they had been asked about their sex life, whether they had boyfriends and had been propositioned by the supervisor. They had also been offered rides home by the supervisor, which they both had declined.

The investigators determined that the complainant and the ex-employees did not know each other. They did not come from the same ethnic community, geographic location, had not worked for the same time period or the same locations. The description by the ex-employees and the complainant of the supervisor's conduct were very similar. One of the two ex-

---

[4] For an excellent review of similar fact evidence in the harassment context, please refer to Walter S. Tarnopolsky, *Discrimination and the Law* (Toronto: Carswell, 2001) at para. 8.8(g).

employees had complained to her district manager at the time, but had been advised that nothing could be done since the supervisor denied the allegation. The second ex-employee had learned to avoid the supervisor and ultimately found another job. The investigator chose to consider the "similar fact" evidence after considering:

(1)   Is there a pattern of behaviour?
(2)   Is there a possibility of collusion?
(3)   Is there a way to deal with the potential prejudice?

The investigator noticed the following factors:

(1)   All of the ex-employees were 16 and 17.
(2)   All came from the same ethnic community as the supervisor.
(3)   The supervisor offered them rides.
(4)   The ex-employees did not know the present complainant and vice versa.

The investigator confronted Giovanni with the additional information. Giovanni denied those complaints as well. The work records of the ex-employees were superb. In determining that Angelica was more credible than Giovanni, the pattern of previous behaviour played a key role.

Example 12.3
In investigating a complaint of sexual harassment, the investigator learns from a witness that the respondent "Barry was always a bit of a cheat, looking to take the easy way out." The witness indicates that while he had never seen any sexual harassment, Barry always got his juniors to do his paperwork and take the self-learning tests for him. This type of behaviour was strictly prohibited by the company. The witness did not like Barry's attitude and believed it showed Barry did not "follow the rules". Barry has denied the charges of sexual harassment.

Although Barry's cheating on the paperwork may be a matter of interest to the company for different reasons, it does not assist the investigator in determining whether Barry has previously engaged in sexual harassment of an employee. In the circumstances, the investigator may wish to simply report, without comment, the allegation regarding the paperwork. However, the investigator ought not to use that information to establish that Barry has committed sexual harassment. The connection between cheating on paperwork and sexually harassing a subordinate is tenuous indeed.

In a well-known arbitral case, what seemed like similar fact was ultimately held not to be relevant at all. In *Samra v. Treasury Board,* an employee, Shinaaz Bhimani, made serious allegations of sexual harassment against Mr. Samra. She complained that he had touched her repeatedly, had used crude language to express his sexual interest in her and had made numerous personal and obscene remarks regarding her sex life. She indicated that she had rebuffed him.

On a previous occasion, Samra had engaged in an extra-marital affair with one of his subordinates. He indicated that he thought that the affair was consensual and in fact was shocked when the subordinate complained. Nonetheless, as a supervisor, he acknowledged that it was inappropriate to engage in a sexual relationship with a co-worker and accepted a three-day suspension as part of his discipline.

The investigators held that "on a balance of probabilities", the conduct probably occurred.[5] On review, the adjudicator disagreed. He looked carefully at the subordinate's complaint. He listened to the evidence of co-workers that the subordinate "threw herself" at Samra and that Samra had reciprocated. The co-workers had not seen or heard anything unusual between Ms. Bhimani and Mr. Samra and to the contrary, indicated that Ms. Bhimani appeared to be exceedingly fond of Mr. Samra. The adjudicator distinguished Mr. Samra's conduct in response to the Robinson complaint — *i.e.* taking responsibility and accepting discipline — from his complete denial in the Bhimani matter. Ultimately, the adjudicator ruled that the company had not made out the Bhimani complaint at all. The adjudicator ruled that the previous incident might be used to establish that Mr. Samra would be prepared to engage in an extra-marital affair, if propositioned. An extra-marital affair was significantly different from the type of conduct Ms. Bhimani alleged.

9. Adverse Inferences

In some cases, an investigator may not be able to access certain information without the consent of one of the parties or a witness. Whenever a witness denies the investigator access to information that may be useful to the investigation, the witness must be asked for the reason for the refusal. In some cases, the refusal may be legitimate. If the investigator is not satisfied with the explanation, it is appropriate to draw an adverse inference.

---

[5]   See Section B of this chapter for discussion regarding the Standard of Proof.

Complainants are often sensitive about disclosing comprehensive medical information, particularly if the investigator only needs to know a specific piece of information. Furthermore, complainants may not wish to waive solicitor-client privilege on any notes or records they are maintaining at the behest of their lawyer.[6] The investigator should consider these types of concerns seriously and determine if there is a way to meet the complainant's concern and still preserve the integrity of the investigation.

In other cases, the refusal is not justifiable and is suspect.

Example 12.4

Elena Martinoff complains that her manager, Nadeem Quereshi, called her one day and suggested they have dinner. They had a pleasant dinner and exchanged pleasantries. When they walked to the parking lot, Elena complained that the manager tried to pin her down to her car and fondle her. The company had a strict policy regarding managers socializing with their subordinates. Regardless of whether the assault had occurred or not, the invitation to dinner was considered by the company to be inappropriate. The manager denied inviting Elena to dinner. He stated that Elena had called him late that night because she had found work stressful and needed to discuss certain problems that had occurred on her shift. Because Nadeem had not eaten, he innocently suggested they grab a bite to eat. Elena denied initiating the call and pointed out that she only knew Nadeem's cellphone number. When asked for the cellphone records, Nadeem initially agreed. Despite numerous requests, he never produced them.

At the time of this investigation, it was not simple to track down telephone calls. In determining credibility, the manager's failure to produce the cellphone records was considered significant.[7]

---

[6] In an arbitration case, the adjudicator ruled that a complainant could not be forced to produce her diary that she had maintained at the request of the Ontario Human Rights Commission as part of the prosecution of her human rights case. *Brewers Retail Inc. v. United Brewers Warehousing Workers Provincial Board, UFCW - Local 326W*, [1998] Carswell Ont. 2068 (Aggarwal Arb.).

[7] Remarkable tools now exist to track down telephone calls. In addition to the telephone company, numerous companies will provide detailed information for a reasonable fee. These companies can track both land and cellphone usage. Most telephone companies insist on a formal complaint, a court order or a police investigation before providing usage records.

10. Motivations for False Complaints

The investigator must also consider any possible motives for fabrication. Deliberately false complaints of sexual harassment do occur and cannot be discounted.

(a) Pecuniary Motivations

One of the most highly-publicized cases in Silicon Valley, involved Larry Ellison, President of Oracle Corp. A former administrative assistant and former girlfriend, Adelyn Lee, claimed that Mr. Ellison had sexually harassed her. She further alleged that her termination from Oracle Corp. was at the instigation of Mr. Ellison. During the course of litigation, an e-mail surfaced, purporting to be from her supervisor to Mr. Ellison. The e-mail read, "I have terminated Adelyn per your request." The e-mail was subsequently proven to be a forgery. Cellphone records proved that the supervisor was in her car and could not have sent the e-mail at the time. The complainant was subsequently convicted of perjury. It appears that the complainant was motivated by the possibility of obtaining a financial settlement upon her termination.[8]

Similar factors appear to have motivated several of the contestants in the Miss Black America Pageant who falsely claimed that Mike Tyson had touched them on the rears and had committed sexual harassment. While Mike Tyson was convicted of rape, the additional complainants appear to have been motivated by the possibility of significant settlements or court awards.[9]

(b) Other Possible Motivations

There is little direct evidence studying false complaints of sexual harassment in the workplace. Some analysts have tried to draw inferences from false complaints of sexual assault and/or rape, where there is research with respect

---

[8] It is possible that this type of motivation is more prevalent in the United States than in Canada. The United States recognizes "at-will" employment. Accordingly, employers can terminate employees at any time without providing notice or a severance package. Employees are protected from termination if the termination is a result of sexual harassment.

[9] American situations do not necessarily have exact Canadian parallels. One author suggested that the complainants were expecting awards of approximately $20,000,000 *each*. This type of money is unheard of in the Canadian legal system, where awards of $5,000 and $10,000 are more prevalent. For more discussion regarding the false complaints in the Mike Tyson case, see W. Farrell, *The Myth of Male Power* (New York: Simon and Schuster, 1993).

to false complaints. In a controversial study commissioned by the U.S. Air Force, the authors suggested that 60 per cent of rape allegations in a military setting were *false*. In an earlier study of individuals who had admitted making a false allegation, there were a plethora of motivations, including:

- Spite or revenge (20 per cent)
- Compensation for feelings of guilt or shame (20 per cent)
- Fear of pregnancy (13 per cent)
- To conceal an affair (12 per cent)
- To test a spouse's love (9 per cent)
- Mental or emotional disorder (9 per cent)
- To avoid personal responsibility (4 per cent)
- Failure to pay or extortion (4 per cent)
- Thought she might have caught VD (3 per cent)
- Other (6 per cent).[10]

While it is difficult to draw a direct analogy between allegations of criminal conduct and workplace misconduct such as sexual harassment, the investigator should always consider whether there are possible motivations for fabricating a complaint.

(c) Consensual Relationships that Turn Sour

One of the most difficult types of cases involves seemingly consensual relationships that turn sour. In one difficult case, the fundamental issue was whether a 2-year extra-marital affair was consensual or not. The company's anti-nepotism policy did not forbid personal relationships, but required such employees not to be in a direct reporting relationship. The complainant was a young single woman, who reported to the respondent, a married man. The respondent admitted the sexual relationship, but stated it was consensual. The respondent acknowledged that he had broken the company's anti-nepotism policy, but strenuously denied any sexual harassment.

The respondent indicated that he had broken off the affair. He indicated that he had become a born-again Christian and found it difficult to reconcile

---

[10] Charles P. McDowell, Ph.D., M.P.A., M.L.S., "The False Rape Allegation in the Military Community," unpublished paper, Washington, DC: US Air Force Office of Special Investigations, March 1983 as quoted by Mike Rother in "Sexual Harassment: The Girl Who Cried Wolf?" at <http://www.geocities.com/Athens/6611/sh.htm>. Note that the study was based on a small group of 75 women who acknowledged they had made false allegations and also volunteered their motivations. See also, E.J. Kanin, "False Rape Allegations," 23 *Archives of Sexual Behaviour*, at 81-92, where the author concludes that 41 per cent of allegations regarding forcible rape were false.

his religion with his deceptive conduct. He had confessed to his wife as well. He indicated that the complainant did not take it well and openly told him, "I'll get you for this. You can't treat me like a used tissue. You'll regret this." The respondent had ignored the comment at the time, assuming it was just shock. The respondent had suggested that she take a few days off to calm herself and that her job would be waiting for her. She filed a sexual harassment complaint instead.

The complainant's co-workers had suspected the affair all along. They testified regarding the complainant's eagerness and willingness to seek out the company of the respondent. She would routinely stay late (without working) in order to talk to him after hours, had found excuses to deliver mail or other information to the respondent, would insist on sitting beside him during company social events and couldn't "keep her eyes or hands off" the respondent. The complainant had hand-knit Christmas gifts for the respondent and had purchased expensive Valentine's Day gifts for him. It was unclear who had initiated the affair, but it appeared that the respondent had made the first overt move after the complainant had made a few flirtatious remarks.

One co-worker indicated that after the break-up, the complainant was distraught and suicidal. She felt abused by the respondent, because he had promised that he would leave his wife and marry her. While there was a significant power imbalance in the situation (age and reporting relationship) and the respondent's conduct was immoral and reprehensible, the conduct was ultimately held not to be sexual harassment.[11]

In other cases, the initial consent may have ceased to exist. These types of cases pose great difficulties. Should the respondent have known that the complainant was no longer in agreement with what previously had been a consensual relationship? A close examination of both parties' conduct must be examined before a determination can be made on such a delicate issue.

---

[11] The respondent was terminated due to his flagrant violation of the anti-nepotism policy. Many of the co-workers indicated that the respondent unfairly favoured the complainant. She got better shifts and preferential treatment with respect to vacation requests. This demonstrated the wisdom of the anti-nepotism policy. The complainant was provided transition counselling and reimbursement of tuition fees to assist her to find another position. An extensive discussion regarding whether a relationship between superior and subordinate is inherently offensive can be found in Phyllis Coleman, "Sex in Power Dependency Relationships: Taking Unfair Advantage of the 'Fair' Sex", 53 Albany L. Rev. 95. The inequality of power between professor and student was a key factor in both *Mahmoodi v. Dutton (No. 4)* (1999), 36 C.H.R.R. D/8 (B.C.H.R.T.) and in *Dupuis v. British Columbia (Ministry of Forests)* (1993), 20 C.H.R.R. D/87 (B.C.C.H.R.).

E. MISTAKE

It seems absurd to suggest that complaints of harassment can be made by mistake. Many people believe that either a complaint is true or false. In reality, there are many shades of gray. In several instances investigated by this author, there has been a clear culture clash. Conduct that had been previously accepted in a company may no longer be acceptable due to changing demographics. It is hard to argue that an employee knew (or ought to have known) that conduct was unwelcome, if it had been condoned for the previous decade.[12] In other cases, different ethnic communities have ways of interacting that may be unacceptable in other ethnic communities. The test for harassment, *i.e.* "a course of conduct that is known or ought to have been known to have been offensive" is often not met. Training and open communication, however, can resolve many of these problems.

F. CONCLUSION

As a neutral fact-finder, the investigator must review all of the evidence. In reviewing the evidence, it is useful to consider the following simple, but revealing, questions:

(1)   What evidence supports the complainant?
(2)   What evidence supports the respondent?
(3)   Does the complainant have a motive for lying?
(4)   Is it possible the complainant is mistaken?
(5)   Does the respondent have a motive for lying?
(6)   Could the respondent be mistaken?
(7)   Do the witnesses have any reason to favour one side or another?
(8)   Do the documents corroborate one account or another?
(9)   Do I believe the complainant wholly or in part?
(10) Do I believe the respondent wholly or in part?

---

[12] The classic example: pornographic posters and swimsuit calendars in a male-dominated workplace. One of the author's friends was in the process of buying a car almost a decade ago. Several of the sales people had swimsuit/pornographic calendars in their work stations. In response to an off-hand comment regarding how offensive the calendars were, the dealership sent a written apology and thanked my friend for addressing the issue. The calendars and posters disappeared. The salesmen truly had no idea that their conduct was offensive as it had "never been addressed". There is a duty on the employer to advise employees that the unwritten rules of the workplace have changed.

After completing the review, the investigator should be able to come to a conclusion. There are effectively only five possible conclusions:

(1) The allegations are substantially true and constitute harassment (or other workplace misconduct);
(2) The allegations are substantially true, but do not constitute harassment (or other workplace misconduct);
(3) The allegations were made in good faith, but are not true;
(4) The allegations are false and were deliberately fabricated.
(5) The investigator is unable to come to a conclusion.

CHAPTER 13

PREPARING THE REPORT

A. OVERVIEW

After completing the investigative stage, the investigator must review all of the evidence in order to determine whether the allegations have been substantiated. After completing this review,[1] the investigator must determine whether a written report should be prepared.

In certain cases, the client has requested a detailed, written report. In other cases, the client seeks the investigator's input as to whether a report is warranted. The answer is not straightforward.

Some investigators are reluctant to submit their findings in a report. They express concern regarding the time, delay and expense of a formal written submission to the client. Certain commentators have also indicated that a written report can backfire on the client in a number of ways:

(a) the document may be used as ammunition against the employer by regulatory authorities, ex-employees or opposing counsel in litigation;[2]

(b) even when the document is protected by solicitor-client privilege, considerable pressure may be brought to bear against the company to disclose the report or, alternatively, an adverse inference may be drawn against the employer for its refusal to disclose the report;[3]

(c) the document may be used in subsequent proceedings not involving the complainant or respondent to establish that the company was aware of certain problems or that certain problems were widespread.

---

[1] See Chapter 12.

[2] These concerns are expressed in Scot W. MacKay, "A Primer for Lockheed Martin Corporation In-House Counsel: Handling Government and Internal Investigations," March 14-15, 2002 <www.acca.com/protected/legres/internal/investigationsprimer.pdf>.

[3] *Ibid.*

Many clients also wish to avoid the expense of a written report. Many investigators prefer to deliver a written report. They recognize that the discipline of writing a report requires them to:

(a) examine all of the events carefully;
(b) consider alternate explanations for incidents properly;
(c) present the results of the investigation in a thorough, fair and thoughtful manner;
(d) provide transparency to the process, so that parties can spot errors that may have been made and correct such errors, before drastic damage is done to individuals' reputations or careers.

Commissioning a report also records what the employer did in order to respond to the allegations of harassment. This may assist in reducing exposure in subsequent litigation or human rights hearings.[4]

Even when a detailed written report is not warranted, a point form outline or summary may be useful, particularly when accompanied by a thorough oral report. This intermediate approach appears to have gained popularity in the United States, in order to avoid the possibility of having a written report used against the employer.[5]

B.   CONTENTS OF THE REPORT

1. Scope of the Retainer

The written report should include a statement regarding the nature of the retainer undertaken by the investigator. This is particularly important when the investigator is a lawyer. In such cases, the description should make it clear whether the investigator was acting in a legal capacity (*i.e.* conducting the investigation as part of a legal retainer) or simply investigating the complaints in order to provide a neutral opinion as to whether the allegations have been substantiated.

---

[4] See discussion in Chapter 3 regarding employer's liability to a complainant in the context of sexual harassment.
[5] Thomas P. Hector, *et al.*, *Successful Partnering between Inside and Outside Counsel*, section 35:29.

2. Description of the Complaint

Depending on how the complaint arose, the report should either append a copy of the written complaint or provide sufficient details regarding the complaint.

The report should provide an overview of: (1) who complained; (2) when the complaint was made; (3) who was named as the alleged harasser; (4) the nature of the allegations; and (5) the response to the allegations.

This information is pertinent for the reader to determine what was investigated. In certain cases, the investigation will reveal further potential incidents of misconduct. In such cases, the expansion of the investigation should be explained by explaining what further incidents were investigated and why.

3. Description of the Investigator's Methodology

The next section should detail how the investigation was conducted. The reader should be able to ascertain who was interviewed, what documents were reviewed and whether there were any obstacles to the completion of the investigation. Furthermore, even if the investigator exercised his or her discretion to not pursue the particular avenue of investigation, the reasons for that judgment call should be delineated.[6]

(a) Special Considerations Arising from Witness Evidence

This section often causes concern. Some witnesses are understandably reluctant to participate in the process. They are legitimately concerned regarding the impact that this participation may have on their careers, *regardless of legal protections against reprisals*. They may have specifically requested that the investigator not reveal their identities, if at all possible.

The investigator is entitled to exercise discretion in drafting the report. In certain cases, the witness's information is not relevant and need not be referred to in the report. In cases where the evidence is merely corroborative of collateral issues, it may be possible to indicate that there is a witness who corroborates a certain detail. The investigator should indicate that the identity of the witness is being protected due to a concern with privacy.

---

[6] For example, in the Carruthers complaint (see Part II), the investigator chose not to interview a client who may have had some collateral information regarding how much the alleged harasser had to drink, but would not be able to shed light on the actual allegation of sexual solicitation.

In certain cases, a witness may be able to corroborate either the complainant's or respondent's version with respect to a critical issue. The investigator need not reveal the witness's identity by name, but could indicate that there is a corroborating witness who is afraid to come forward. In many cases, however, the identity of the corroborating witness can be easily guessed from the circumstances. Where the investigator determines that it is not feasible to protect the witness's identity, the investigator should warn the witness and repeat assurances regarding protection against reprisals.

Example 13.1

James Duthy, Elaine Ferguson and Arthur Molyneux recently returned from a conference. James is a senior manager and Arthur is a junior manager at the same company. Elaine reports to James. Due to bad weather, the drive back took much longer than anticipated. Arthur slept in the back seat of the car. James and Elaine could hear Arthur gently snoring. James and Elaine started talking. Elaine alleges that James began to talk about problems in his marriage and the fact that his wife isn't interested in him. He talked about how attracted he was to Elaine ever since he first met her. Elaine also alleges that James started touching her breasts and groin area. James denies the conversation. James stresses that Elaine is a probationary employee who has had some real problems adapting to the highly-computerized workplace of the company. There are performance reviews that express concern regarding Elaine's skills. Neither James nor Elaine realized that Arthur had woken up and heard most of the conversation, but did not see any of the touching. Arthur's evidence supports Elaine. Arthur begs the investigator not to mention anything, because he needs James' support in the workplace. Arthur has had to take a lot of time off because his wife is sick and James has covered for him.

Arthur's evidence is critical to the investigation. He is the only in-dependent witness. The investigator will clearly be influenced by Arthur's evidence in finding that Elaine's complaint is true. The report (whether written or oral) will have to indicate that an independent witness supports Elaine's account. Given the circumstances, it is clear that Arthur's identity will be revealed. In such circumstances, it is appropriate to advise Arthur that his evidence will be used and to discuss possible strategies regarding avoiding reprisals in the workplace.

(b) Documentary Evidence

The investigator should delineate what documentary evidence was reviewed and the source of the documentation. In certain cases, documents may not be available. For example, in the Carruthers case file, the respondent has refused to release his personal telephone records. An investigator has no power to compel these records. It is appropriate to outline what documents could not be accessed. In other cases, relevant documents may have been destroyed or misplaced. This should be noted as well.

(c) Third-party Assistance

In most cases, one (or a team of two) investigators handle most of the investigation and the report-writing. In certain cases, however, the investigator may have relied on third-party assistance and relies on the judgment and expertise of that third-party. For example, where computer analysis is involved, the investigator may not have the expertise to assess the credibility of that evidence. It is important to disclose the reliance on the outside expert and, where appropriate, to obtain a brief report.

> **Example 13.2**
> *Carter Hill has been retained to investigate a complaint of sexual harassment in the workplace. Part of the complaint involves obscene, but anonymous, e-mails directed specifically at certain women in the workplace. The women suspect that the e-mails are internal, because there are certain references to what the women have done at work. In conducting the investigation, Carter Hill retains a computer expert to investigate the source of the e-mails, who advises that the e-mails originate from an internet café. Carter Hill's further investigation, including interviews of personnel at the Internet café, lead him to believe that the e-mails came from Wally Augustus, a low-level IT employee.*

In this example, Carter Hill has relied on the forensic expertise of an outside consultant to provide critical information — the physical origin of the offensive e-mails. It is important to disclose this assistance. Where a report is commissioned, the computer expert should provide a letter, which can be used as an appendix to Carter Hill's report.

4.   Analysis of the Evidence

This is the key aspect of the report. The investigator's core task is to provide a neutral evaluation of the core of the evidence. The investigator should highlight the critical evidence in support and against the allegations. Where there is a discrepancy in the evidence or conflict in the witness account, the investigator should disclose his or her judgment regarding what evidence should be preferred and why. Many inexperienced investigators wish to avoid drawing conclusions where the evidence is of the "he says/she says" nature. This is inappropriate. Skilled investigators routinely make judgment calls regarding credibility.[7] As indicated earlier, there are effectively only five types of conclusion:

(1) The allegations are substantially true and constitute harassment (or other workplace misconduct);
(2) The allegations are substantially true, but do not constitute harassment (or other workplace misconduct);
(3) The allegations were made in good faith, but are not true;
(4) The allegations are false and were deliberately fabricated;
(5) The investigator is unable to come to a conclusion.

With respect to the last conclusion, it is appropriate to advise the client that given the evidence, a conclusion can not be safely drawn. No adverse inference should be drawn against the complainant.

5. Legal Analysis

If the investigator is a lawyer and if the retainer is of a legal nature, it is appropriate to provide legal advice to the client based upon the factual findings in the previous section. This legal analysis can delineate a client's potential exposure to regulatory authorities or civil litigation.

6. Recommendations

Where requested, the investigator may choose to provide recommendations regarding what the results of the investigation should be. These recommendations can cover a gamut of disciplinary measures, training measures, executive coaching, or broader undertakings to shift corporate culture.[8]

Before drafting recommendations, however, the investigator should ensure that the client wants written recommendations. Written recommendations regarding discipline or long-term changes to the workplace may backfire on the company. If a company declines to follow the recommendations,

---

[7] Review section D on Assessing Credibility in Chapter 12.
[8] For examples of possible responses, consider Chapter 14.

it can be extraordinarily difficult to justify that decision in subsequent litigation.[9]

It is often useful to call the client and double-check whether the client wants specific recommendations or not. Many clients prefer an analysis of the evidence, *i.e.* neutral fact-finding. Based on the investigator's fact-finding, the client will determine the appropriate remedies.

In certain cases, the company may simply want investigators to outline the possible choices that the company may wish to consider. This leaves the final decision to the company.

C. CIRCULATING THE REPORT

Investigators are routinely asked to provide a "draft" of the report by complainants and respondents. The parties are understandably concerned regarding the possibility that an investigator has misunderstood the evidence and may want to influence the report-writing, before an error is made. In this author's view, the report is being written for the benefit of the employer and not for either of the parties. The employer and not the parties should be apprised of the author's initial conclusions and recommendations. It is the employer's decision whether to release an investigator's report.

Some employers routinely refuse to release the investigator's report, citing litigation and/or solicitor-client privilege. Others release the investigator's report only after reviewing same and then inviting commentary from both parties, prior to making a final decision regarding the resolution of the complaint. Much depends on the nature of the report. Where the report deals exclusively with the parties' evidence, it makes sense to release the report. Where the report also reveals the existence of vulnerable witnesses or sensitive data, the employer may wish to withhold the report. The courts have given some latitude to employers. As long as the respondent knows of what he has been accused and has been given an adequate opportunity to respond, the requirement of fairness is met.[10]

---

[9]   For example, in the fictional *Carruthers* case report included in Part II, the investigator has recommended that Jack Andrews, the senior vice-president (Sales & Marketing) be terminated with cause. The company, may, notwithstanding the seriousness of the complaint, wish to retain Mr. Andrews for operational reasons. It may believe that a generous severance package to Ms. Carruthers accompanied by a reprimand and executive coaching for Mr. Andrews would be a better overall solution for it. While the investigator may not agree with the company, the investigator's recommendation in a written report may become a critical factor in any litigation which Janine Carruthers may choose to bring. A court would no doubt be highly influenced against the company for ignoring the recommendations made by the investigator.

[10]   *Masters v. Ontario* (1994), 115 D.L.R. (4th) 319 (Ont. Div. Ct.).

D. CONCLUSION

Writing a concise and objective report is difficult. Nonetheless, the parties deserve a thoughtful synopsis of the investigation. Subsequently, the investigation report may be used to defend the employer in litigation. A well-written report can be an invaluable tool for the employer.

APPENDIX 13.1

SAMPLE REPORT

Private & Confidential

To be opened by Addressee Only
Overnight courier

September 21, 200x

Mr. David Ricketts
Executive Vice-President, Operations
ABC Company
1288 Main Street
Toronto, Ontario M1M 1M1

Dear Mr. Ricketts:

Re: Complaint of Ms. Janine Carruthers

I am reporting to you pursuant to your written request[11] dated September 9th, 200x to have the undersigned investigate a complaint made by Ms. Janine Carruthers, Senior Sales Executive, against her immediate supervisor, Jack Andrews, Vice-President (Sales).

I acknowledge receipt of the formal complaint, formal response and the harassment policy.[12]

---

[11]   See Appendix 8.3 — sample retainer of external law firm.
[12]   See Part II.

SCOPE OF THE RETAINER

In the context of that request, you asked me to:

(1) review the complaint, response and harassment policy;
(2) provide you with legal advice regarding ABC's potential legal exposure to both Ms. Carruthers and Mr. Andrews;
(3) provide you with my opinion, after a full investigation, with respect to the validity of the complaint made by Ms. Carruthers;
(4) recommend possible resolutions.

The complaint and the response have not been appended to this opinion letter, as I understand that you have retained copies of those documents. The investigation was conducted by the undersigned.

OVERVIEW

The complaint was made on September 6th, 200x by Ms. Janine Carruthers, one of three senior sales specialists at ABC Company. Ms. Carruthers is 36 years old and has worked with the ABC Company for nine years. She complains about the conduct of Jack Andrews, the Executive Vice-President (Sales & Marketing). He has an excellent record at ABC Company. He is 43 years old and has worked for ABC for about 14 years. Both have exemplary work records and are valuable employees.

SUMMARY OF THE COMPLAINT

Ms. Carruthers' complaint makes five allegations:

(1) Pool incident — She alleges that on June 1, 200x, Mr. Andrews attempted to pull her bikini bottom while both of them were in the pool. This occurred during the summer picnic.
(2) Nice view incident — Ms. Carruthers states that on or about June 3rd, 200x, Mr. Andrews patted her on the rear and commented, "nice view".
(3) Car incident — Ms. Carruthers alleges that on June 8, 200x after a client dinner with Paul Sanderson, Jack Andrews made a number of sexually-suggestive remarks during a ride home.
(4) Hotel incident — Ms. Carruthers alleges that early on June 16th, 200x, Mr. Andrews pounded on Ms. Carruthers' hotel bedroom door.

(5)   Harassing telephone calls — Ms. Carruthers attributes a number of harassing telephone calls to her home number to Mr. Andrews.

Ms. Carruthers also expresses a concern whether she lost a promotion to vice-president (sales) because of her refusal of Mr. Andrews' propositions.

SUMMARY OF THE RESPONSE

(1)   Pool incident — Mr. Andrews does not recall the incident, but acknowledges that there may have been some inadvertent contact. The pool was crowded.

(2)   Nice view incident — Mr. Andrews denies touching Ms. Carruthers, but may have made a comment in reference to the view.

(3)   Car incident — Mr. Andrews denies propositioning Ms. Carruthers. He acknowledges making some comments regarding Ms. Carruthers being "nice to him" in reference to Ms. Carruthers' courtesy in driving him home.

(4)   Hotel incident — Mr. Andrews denies the episode completely and indicates he was in bed by the time that the incident occurred.

(5)   Harassing telephone calls — Mr. Andrews has made business calls to Ms. Carruthers at home, but denies any harassment or "hang ups".

Mr. Andrews indicates that he presented both Mr. Blackwell and Ms. Carruthers to you as candidates and, ultimately, you made the decision. He emphasizes that Mr. Blackwell's success in the international marketplace was the deciding factor and denies any suggestion made by Ms. Carruthers to the contrary.

CONDUCT OF THE INVESTIGATION

In the course of fulfilling the retainer with ABC Company, I conducted an investigation of the complaint made by Ms. Carruthers as well as the response made by Mr. Andrews. The following investigative steps were undertaken:

(1)   Ms. Carruthers was interviewed once;

(2) Mr. Andrews was interviewed once and was given an opportunity to be interviewed a second time. This second interview was cut short by Mr. Andrews' decision not to participate further;

(3) I conducted interviews of Timothy Blackwell and yourself;

(4) I determined that it was not necessary to interview Paul Saunderson (see below), as the incidents occurred after Ms. Carruthers and Mr. Andrews left the restaurant and in the car ride home. Mr. Saunderson would not have been able to shed light on that conversation.

(5) I reviewed computerized records of Mr. Andrews' use of his company computer using remote access technology;

(6) I conducted informal interviews of two employees at the LAX Hotel, Timothy Bridewell (Security) and Fazeela El-Esbir (Night Front Desk Clerk);

(7) I reviewed company cell phone records belonging to Jack Andrews;

(8) I reviewed expense reports submitted by Jack Andrews, Janine Carruthers and Timothy Blackwell with respect to various business expenses.

FINDINGS REGARDING THE VALIDITY OF THE COMPLAINTS

I have considered the evidence with respect to each incident separately and as a whole. In order to assist you, however, I have summarized the evidence we considered with respect to each incident.

1. The pool incident

With respect to the pool incident, I conclude that some contact did occur in the pool. It is, however, not possible to determine whether the contact was deliberate or accidental. Mr. Andrews indicates that he was in the pool and admits that he may have inadvertently bumped into Ms. Carruthers. Ms. Carruthers believes that she felt a tug on her bikini bottom. Mr. Andrews, Ms. Carruthers and Mr. Blackwell are in agreement that the pool was crowded. In the circumstances, it is our opinion that it is not possible to determine exactly what occurred in the pool.

2. Nice View Incident

There are no independent witnesses to this incident. Mr. Andrews categorically denies the touching. He admits that he may have made the comment "nice view", but would have been referring to the view outside the boardroom window. Ms. Carruthers is equally adamant that she was touched and that the comment "nice view" referred to her and not the external view. I took a view of the boardroom. The view outside of the boardroom consists of a parking lot and 2 dumpsters. The view is not particularly interesting or nice. Furthermore, in reviewing the evidence as a whole (see discussion below), Ms. Carruthers is a more reliable and credible witness. On the basis of Ms. Carruthers' evidence, I conclude that both the touching and the comment occurred. This type of touching (and the accompanying remark) do constitute sexual harassment. It is inappropriate for a supervising employee to touch the buttocks of a subordinate employee.

3. The Car Incident

Ms. Carruthers and Mr. Andrews have diametrically opposed versions of what occurred in the 25 minute car ride home from Toronto to Streetsville. Ms. Carruthers complains about sexually-suggestive remarks culminating in an open proposition to "f***". She also complains that Mr. Andrews suggested that if Ms. Carruthers was "nice", he would be "nice" in return. She indicates that she took that to mean a kind of crude "quid pro quo" in the context of his ability to influence her candidacy for the position of VP (sales). Mr. Andrews denies any kind of sexual banter or discussion. He states that the car ride home was quiet because Ms. Carruthers was not in a chatty mood. He acknowledges making some comment about Ms. Carruthers being "nice". He indicates that this comment was made in the context of expressing his gratitude for the lift.

There are no independent witnesses regarding what occurred during the drive home. Mr. Blackwell and Ms. Carruthers indicated that Mr. Andrews had been drinking somewhat heavily. Mr. Blackwell reported that there was some kind of "edge about him [Mr. Andrews]". Mr. Blackwell has known Mr. Andrews for over 20 years. Even at the time that Mr. Blackwell left (around 8:30 p.m.), Mr. Blackwell already had a concern about the level of Mr. Andrews' drinking and he had thought about warning Ms. Carruthers not to let Mr. Andrews drive. We have also obtained a photocopy of the records of the Red & Black Club with respect to the evening of June 8th. It confirms Mr. Blackwell's recollection that both single and double scotches were ordered. It is Mr. Blackwell's recollection that the client, Mr.

Saunderson, was drinking singles and that Mr. Andrews was drinking double scotches. The records suggest that Mr. Andrews drank significantly more heavily than he is prepared to admit. Ms. Carruthers drank sparingly.

I have also taken into account that Ms. Carruthers is deeply disappointed that she did not receive a promotion to vice-president (sales). Her colleague, Timothy Blackwell, has recently been awarded that position. She forthrightly expressed her doubt and anger about losing the promotion. Nonetheless, Ms. Carruthers acknowledged that Mr. Blackwell was genuinely qualified for the position and did not express any hostility against Mr. Blackwell. I have fully considered her motive for fabrication.

I recognize that Mr. Saunderson, ABC's client, may be able to substantiate who was drinking. I recognize that interviewing Mr. Saunderson is a sensitive matter, as ABC is in the process of concluding certain business dealings with this corporation. In light of Mr. Blackwell's evidence, I have determined that it is not necessary to interview Mr. Saunderson at this time.

On the basis of Ms. Carruthers' evidence (as corroborated on peripheral matters by Mr. Blackwell and the receipts), I conclude that there is cogent evidence supporting her allegation.

4. The Hotel Incident

Between June 15th and June 17th, 200X, the sales team (Jack Andrews, Janine Carruthers and Timothy Blackwell) attended at a marketing event. They all stayed at the LAX Hotel. Ms. Carruthers alleges that in the early morning hours (approximately 1:45 a.m. Pacific Standard Time), Jack Andrews pounded at her door and yelled at her to let him in. Mr. Andrews denies this allegation, and in fact, asserts that he was in bed (room 763) at the time.

Mr. Andrews indicates that he spent the evening with Janine Carruthers and Timothy Blackwell. According to him, they had a meal and he drank lightly. He then went to check his e-mail. Mr. Andrews' account is partially confirmed by the fact that he signed off on his e-mail at approximately 1:35 a.m. Pacific Standard Time or 4:35 a.m. Eastern Standard Time. This is a few minutes before the events occurred.

I have also obtained independent confirmation from hotel security that someone did make a disturbance on the 6th floor. Hotel security was not called by Janine Carruthers (room 622), but rather by an unnamed guest (room 624). Furthermore, elevator records show that the elevator was used between the 7th to the 6th floor and back again to the 7th floor in this exact time period. Hotel security appears to be very tight after 11:00 p.m. and no guests can access the guest room floors without a pass. Security reports that the elevator was called on the 7th floor and stopped on the 6th floor and returned back on the 7th floor in the very time period that the disturbance occurred. Stairs cannot be used between floors after 11:00 p.m. Stairs can only be used to exit the building for emergency purposes after 11:00 p.m.

Ms. Carruthers is firm in her recollection that she recognized Mr. Andrews' voice. She chose not to call hotel security. She says she simply changed rooms in order to avoid Mr. Andrews. The front desk clerk does recall that she was moved from the 6th floor to the 2nd floor in the early hours of June 16th, 200X. The front desk clerk specifically recalls the incident, because it is unusual for a person to complain about height phobia after having checked in. Furthermore, the 2nd floor is a smoking floor and Ms. Carruthers had specifically requested a non-smoking room. Both facts stick out in the front desk clerk's mind.

There is no question that someone pounded on Ms. Carruthers' door. Given Ms. Carruthers' recognition of the voice, the corroborating records of the elevator usage, Ms. Carruthers' subsequent actions in changing her room after the incident, and the nature of hotel security, it is our opinion that this incident occurred substantially as Ms. Carruthers describes it in her complaint. I have also obtained the receipt from the meal at the hotel. Mr. Andrews appears to have had substantially more to drink than he remembers. In my view, Ms. Carruthers' recollection is to be preferred. Despite her motive for fabrication (see above), I conclude that there is cogent evidence substantiating Ms. Carruthers allegations regarding the hotel incident.

5. Harassing Phone Calls

I have not been able to complete our investigation in this matter. Mr. Andrews has not provided us with his home telephone usage records. I am not in a position to compel same. I have been advised by the telephone company that it will not release home telephone usage records without a court order or a police investigation. Ms. Carruthers advises that she was considering a police investigation, but she has declined to do so because she has been told about the backlog of cases and feels that it would not be useful.

Company cell phone records, however, show a significant number of short (less than one minute) phone calls in July and August made from Mr. Andrews' business cell. They show approximately 50 calls of very short duration in July and August respectively. This is in marked contrast to his pattern of calls to the other two senior sales specialists in his department, where calls range from approximately three to 10 minutes or are of moderate duration.

Mr. Andrews was asked to explain his cell phone usage. He was also asked about the elevator usage records. The follow up interview was not completed, because Mr. Andrews chose to walk out of the interview and indicated that he would call his lawyer. We find that Mr. Andrews is not a credible witness on this point. His refusal to release home phone records, his weak explanation for the repeated (and anomalous) pattern of phone calls to Ms. Carruthers in July and August, all detract from his credibility.

I subsequently called Mr. Andrews to indicate that I would be prepared to meet with him to complete my interview with him with his lawyer present. He advised me that on the advice of counsel, he was not going to participate in the internal process.

I also note that the calls stopped immediately upon Ms. Carruthers making a complaint.

After a review of the evidence, I am convinced that Mr. Andrews is the author of the vast majority of the "hang up" telephone calls of which Ms. Carruthers complains.

6. The Promotion Issue

Ms. Carruthers is firmly convinced that she was passed over for promotion due to her inability to accede to Mr. Andrews' proposition. This is a significant concern. Your evidence confirms that Mr. Andrews has been consistently even-handed in his praise and support of his two senior sales specialists, Timothy Blackwell and Janine Carruthers. You are firm that it was your decision to promote Mr. Blackwell. The decisive factor appears to have been Mr. Blackwell's success in the international marketplace. Ms. Carruthers does not deny Mr. Blackwell's accomplishments in this and other areas, she simply expresses doubt in the validity of the decision-making process and wonders whether her chances of promotion were impaired because of her refusal of Mr. Andrews' propositions.

Although I recognize the legitimacy of Ms. Carruthers' concern, given your evidence, I am persuaded that the corporation made a decision to promote Mr. Blackwell instead of Ms. Carruthers on legitimate reasons, *i.e.* the importance of developing the international marketplace. Nonetheless, I must advise that it is open for a court of law or adjudicator to make a different finding.

LEGAL ANALYSIS[13]

You have asked me to opine about ABC's legal exposure to both Ms. Carruthers and Mr. Andrews. This analysis is predicated on the assumption that a court of law or tribunal would make similar findings of fact to the ones discussed in this report. While I have conducted our investigation in good faith, please recognize that another fact-finder might come to a different conclusion.

1. Issues Involving Janine Carruthers

In advising you regarding the potential liability to Ms. Carruthers, we have considered a number of legal issues including:

(a) Liability in tort (intentional infliction of mental distress), assault and battery;

(b) Liability under the Ontario *Human Rights Code*, which prohibits sexual harassment in the workplace;

(c) Liability under the common law of employment, particularly constructive dismissal.

As a general proposition, ABC Company is liable for the acts of Jack Andrews, even if it was unaware of the acts. Jack Andrews is a senior executive of ABC Company. Canadian law indicates that the actions of senior executives and managers of a corporation are considered to be the acts of the corporation itself.[14] Assuming that a court makes similar findings of fact as are contained in this report, ABC Company would be liable to Ms. Andrews.

(a) Tort Liability

In our opinion, Mr. Andrews' conduct in the boardroom constituted battery — *i.e.* unwanted touching. The battery itself was of a minor nature. The hotel incident may well constitute assault, *i.e.* "the intentional creation of the apprehension of imminent harmful or offensive conduct". The harassing phone calls, however, constitute a course of conduct that could be found to

---

[13] The legal analysis in this letter is considerably simplified and shortened. Employers should seek legal advice whenever there is a possibility of termination because of a finding of sexual harassment.

[14] There is an excellent discussion on point in Arjun Aggarwal *et al.*, *Sexual Harassment in the Workplace,* 3d ed. (Toronto: Butterworth, 2000) at 254-57.

be the intentional infliction of mental suffering. The repeated telephone calls also constitute criminal conduct.[15]

The medical notes from Dr. Schuller indicates that Ms. Carruthers has been affected. She has developed high blood pressure. She has been to the Upper Canada Sleep Disorder Clinic and has been prescribed anti-anxiety pills.

It is difficult to predict what type of damage award Ms. Carruthers might obtain under these various tort theories. Nonetheless, in Canada, damages (including general, aggravated, punitive) for mental distress, assault and battery are reasonably modest and range from a low of $5,000 to more generous awards of $50,000 or more. In addition, Ms. Carruthers would be entitled to any specific monetary losses she could demonstrate due to the inappropriate conduct. As discussed below (common law of employment/constructive dismissal), damages could escalate significantly if a court found that she lost the promotion to VP (sales) due to Mr. Andrews' tortious conduct.

(b) Common Law of Employment/Constructive Dismissal

The courts have held that there is an implied term in each employment contract that an employee will not be subject to illegal harassment. Ms. Carruthers would be entitled to resign her position and sue for damages on the basis that Mr. Andrews' conduct amounted to a repudiation of her employment contract, *i.e.* constructive (as opposed to actual) dismissal.

During the course of the interview, Ms. Carruthers indicated that she could no longer work with Jack Andrews and that her lawyer will be drafting a demand letter.

Damages for constructive dismissal are based largely on what Ms. Carruthers would have received had she been terminated without cause by ABC Company. The primary factors are job title, years of service with the company, age, and education. Ms. Carruthers has been with the company for nine years. She is one of the top ten earners in the corporation. She is 36 years of age. A basic package for Ms. Carruthers would probably be in the range of nine months of her total compensation (including base, bonus, commission, and benefits). Some courts have provided sales executives in similar circumstances as much as 12 months total compensation.

---

[15] Section 372 (3) of the *Criminal Code* provides: "everyone who, without lawful excuse and with intent to harass any person, makes or causes to be made repeated telephone calls to that person is guilty of an offence punishable on summary conviction".

Furthermore, the company is exposed to the "Wallace" factor, *i.e.* additional notice due to the circumstances and manner of her dismissal. This "Wallace" factor is unpredictable, but it is not unusual for an employee to receive another three months to six months of notice when the court finds the facts leading up to the termination/constructive dismissal to be reprehensible.

Courts can be unpredictable and ABC Company could be facing exposure of a minimum of nine months up to a maximum of 18 months on a constructive dismissal theory. This exposure would be reduced if Ms. Carruthers is able to find an equivalent job elsewhere after she left ABC. This is the concept of "mitigation of damages".

The court will also be influenced by the possibility that Ms. Carruthers lost a lucrative promotion due to the sexual harassment. You should note that a court could assess damages both for the constructive dismissal *and* on the tort grounds discussed above.

c. Human Rights Exposure

Under the Ontario *Human Rights Code*, a board of inquiry has the power to make an order for monetary restitution for any loss arising out of any infringement and monetary compensation, not exceeding $10,000, for mental anguish. Monetary restitution can encompass loss of income (including income that Ms. Carruthers might have earned as VP (sales)). Typically, however, damages awarded by the boards of inquiry are modest in comparison to the civil courts. Given the delays in the Ontario human rights system, I believe that ABC's most significant exposure rests on the tort and employment law grounds discussed above.

2. Issues Involving Mr. Andrews

You have also asked me to review the company's exposure to Mr. Andrews. Again, my comments are predicated upon my findings of fact. I am aware that Mr. Andrews has been with the company for 14 years. He is one of the top three earners of ABC Company. He is being groomed to take over the position of chief executive officer.

(a) Discipline and/or Termination

In cases involving sexual harassment, an employer has many options, ranging from a verbal reprimand at one end of the scale to termination at the other end of the scale. It is our opinion that it is unrealistic to expect Jack Andrews and Janine Carruthers to work in the same workplace. Janine

Carruthers is a senior sales specialist and is expected to interact routinely with the VP (sales & marketing). Given the size and structure of the company, alternatives such as transfers or demotions are unrealistic. The company has only one head office (Toronto) and all of the sales executives work out of Toronto. In our view, the company will not be able to retain the services of both Jack Andrews and Janine Carruthers. Given that it is Mr. Andrews' conduct that has precipitated these events, he should be asked to leave.

In our opinion, ABC Company is entitled to dismiss Mr. Andrews for cause, without compensation or notice. The type of sexual harassment was prolonged, severe and had a significant health impact on Ms. Carruthers.[16]

We have, in coming to our opinion, reviewed a number of cases, including those which recommend clemency where the conduct has been atypical, of short duration and where the respondent has expressed remorse.[17]

In this particular case, Mr. Andrews has repeatedly denied the complaint and has attributed malice to Ms. Carruthers. It has been suggested by Mr. Blackwell that the conduct is atypical and may be a result of Mr. Andrews' recent marital problems. It has also been suggested by Mr. Blackwell that Mr. Andrews may have a problem with drinking, also exacerbated by his recent matrimonial situation. Mr. Andrews has not admitted his conduct and has not provided any information which might support mitigating circumstances. Nonetheless, we cannot ignore that Mr. Andrews' conduct is both criminal and tortious. The ramifications on Ms. Carruthers' health have been significant.

We have also researched the exposure if a court of law held that there was no cause for dismissal. In our opinion, this is an unlikely result. The court would have to find either:

(a)   Ms. Carruthers' complaints are not substantiated; or

(b)   even if substantiated, the complaints are not significant enough to constitute just cause.

In such an unlikely event, the court would consider Mr. Andrews as a senior executive with 14 years of service. In Ontario, such executives would receive a package in the range of 12 months to 18 months of total

---

[16]   *Bannister v. General Motors of Canada* (1998), 40 O.R. (3d) 577 (C.A.) and *Gonsalves v. Catholic Church Extension Society of Canada* (1998), 164 D.L.R. (4th) 339 (Ont. C.A.).

[17]   For example, *Quirola v. Xerox Canada Inc.* (1996), 16 C.C.E.L. (2d) 235 (Ont. Ct. J. (Gen. Div.)) and *Tse v. Trow Consulting Engineers Ltd.*, [1995] O.J. No. 2426 (Ont. Ct. J. (Gen. Div.)).

compensation, including base, bonus, commission, stock options and benefits. The company may also face some exposure to an increased award due to the *Wallace* factor, discussed above. I would expect that the company's total exposure in this type of situation to be capped at 24 months.

OUR RECOMMENDATIONS

In the circumstances, it is my recommendation that the company enter into confidential discussions with Mr. Andrews with a view to permitting Mr. Andrews to exit the corporation gracefully with a small financial package. This package would not resemble the typical package afforded to senior executives being terminated without cause. Furthermore, Ms. Carruthers should be strongly encouraged to remain with the corporation, after Mr. Andrews' departure.

If, however, Ms. Carruthers does not wish to stay with the company even after Mr. Andrews' departure, it would be appropriate to consider providing her with a settlement package. This settlement package should include transition counselling to assist Ms. Carruthers to find another position, continuation of medical benefits including the employee assistance programs and a superb letter of reference from the corporation. It may be premature to discuss this option, as we have not yet received Ms. Carruthers' solicitor's demand letter.

If I can be of any further assistance, kindly let me know.

Yours very truly,

Donald DiLauro

CHAPTER 14

WHAT SHOULD YOU DO AFTER A FINDING OF HARASSMENT IS MADE: DEALING WITH THE RESPONDENT

A. OVERVIEW

In some ways, the investigative process is simply a prelude to the much more difficult issue: what should be done *after* the investigation. If the investigator has found no harassment or workplace misconduct, there is no cause to discipline the respondent.[1]

If a complaint has been substantiated, the company must determine what is the appropriate response. Some companies subscribe to a draconian "zero tolerance" approach to sexual harassment. In short, if a complaint is substantiated, the company will fire the harasser. Canadian law demands a more nuanced approach. It requires employers to determine whether termination is, indeed, warranted. A myriad of factors should be considered before the company makes a final determination regarding what is the appropriate response. The law requires the company to balance the conflicting interests of the complainant and the respondent.[2]

Regardless of the ultimate decision, the communication should be made in person. The on-going investigation will be a source of stress to the

---

[1]   Even if there is no reason to discipline the respondent, where an allegation may have been brought in good faith (but is subsequently proven to be incorrect, mistaken or false), it may be appropriate to consider the possibility of reconciling the complainant and the respondent. In some cases, the complaint of harassment uncovers systemic organizational issues that need to be addressed in a different forum.

[2]   See Chapters 3 and 4. Appendix 14.1 contains a series of questions that an employer should consider before making a final determination regarding the appropriate resolution.

employees involved. The courts prefer that sensitive communications be made in person and confirmed in writing. While this chapter gives examples of written correspondence, these documents should be handed over in person or sent by courier after an in-person discussion.

B. POTENTIAL RESPONSES TO A COMPLAINT OF HARASSMENT

An employer must consider the legal context in which it operates before considering a response to a complaint of harassment. In the unionized context, the employer's ability to discipline is circumscribed by the collective bargaining agreement.[3] In the non-unionized context, the employer is limited by the constraints of common law.[4] Consequently, it is important to consult with legal counsel prior to considering a serious disciplinary response.

1. Coaching and Training

In some cases, the company may be justified in using non-disciplinary measures. While the conduct may well constitute harassment, the lack of malicious intent may suggest that education and training will be more effective alternatives.

Example 14.1

Darren McFadyen has been a plant manager for 35 years. When he started, the workforce consisted of working-class Caucasians. Most of the employees used to be first- or second-generation immigrants from the British Isles. Lately, the workforce consists mostly of women and recent immigrants from Asia and the Caribbean. Darren is a tough, but fair boss. He believes in giving every worker a chance. Some of the women have indicated that they would prefer that Darren not call them "honey" or "darling". They also indicate that they feel he should not be touching them (e.g., pat on the back accompanied with an "attagirl"). He also uses obscenities when he gets frustrated, which bothers these employees. Darren does not deny the conduct. He points out that his conduct has

---

[3] One of the best resources on discipline in the unionized context is Chapter 7 of Donald J.M. Brown *et al., Canadian Labour Arbitration,* 3d ed. (Aurora: Canada Law Book, Inc. 1991). For a more specific discussion of discipline in the sexual harassment context, see Chapter 9 of Arjun Aggarwal *et al., Sexual Harassment in the Workplace,* 2d ed. (Toronto: Butterworths, 2000).

[4] See Chapter 3.

never been at issue. He indicates that he never wanted to cause offence and has already apologized privately to some of the workers.

Darren has been very good about responding to the complaint. He has been candid with the company. He has apologized to the workers. Darren could probably benefit from informal coaching. He needs to work on some of his verbal habits, *e.g.* "honey" and "darling". He could benefit from some pointers on how to deal with employees from different cultures, *e.g.* the different attitudes towards touching.

This training may be in the form of courses offered by consultants, schools of business or even one-on-one coaching. In short, a non-disciplinary response may work best with employees where:

(a) the complainants are comfortable, in general, with working with the respondent;

(b) the type of conduct was generally on the less serious side of sexual harassment;

(c) the respondent appears genuinely interested in resolving issues;

(d) the company is prepared to support coaching and training initiatives.

In some cases, the complaint may have revealed larger, systemic problems in the workforce that go far beyond the specific complainant or respondent. Alternatively, there may be no specific complaint. Nonetheless, there is a concern regarding the corporate culture of an organization.

Example 14.2

ABC is a powerful, well-known and large brokerage house. Its employees are legitimately proud of the company's pre-eminence in the industry. Many of the young stockbrokers socialize after hours. The socializing is an important part of the informal mentoring of young recruits. Rumours spread that one of the young recruits, Tom Robinson, was a gay activist at university. Since then, the young recruit has not been invited for drinks. He mentions this to human resources. Human resources tells him, "no one waits for an invitation. Just go and join the crowd." Tom tries to follow the advice. He feels a distinct "chill" when he tries to join the group. Although no one says anything to Tom, Tom's opinion is that there is a subtle homophobic culture in the brokerage house. The HR manager observes that there is not one gay employee in the workplace. Tom states that the HR manager is wrong, the gay employees just don't have the

confidence to come out of the closet. He states he understands why, but
challenges HR to do something about it. Tom does not want to complain.

The human resources department of ABC has a significant issue on its
hand. Tom's opinion that ABC's corporate culture is homophobic may
sound harsh, but is probably accurate. Is it realistic for a large brokerage
house to have no gay and lesbian employees? If there are other gay and
lesbian employees, why do they not have confidence to be open about their
sexual orientation at work?

The traditional complaint/investigation/resolution model is unlikely to
change corporate culture. It is, of course, difficult to justify reprimanding an
employee for not socializing after hours with a new employee.

Nonetheless, the HR manager is not without recourse. The HR manager
can review the company's recruitment and retention strategies in order to
improve mentorship opportunities for all young recruits. Furthermore, in the
longer term, a full-fledged diversity strategy is warranted. Where appropriate, the HR manager can emphasize diversity in its own communications
with employees. Discussions regarding same-sex benefits, for example, can
send a signal that ABC is open to gay and lesbian employees.[5]

2. Warnings and Reprimands

The first formal disciplinary step is often called a "verbal warning". This is a
misnomer. Even a verbal warning should be recorded. In most cases, the
difference between a verbal and written warning is the level of documentation and whether it is intended to impact on the employee's work record in
the future.[6] In the case of the verbal warning, most of the discussion is
verbal. The manager simply notes the substance of the discussion in the
personnel file. In the unionized context, a verbal warning may not be
intended as a formal disciplinary step.

For a "written" warning, the employee is presented with a formal letter or
memorandum outlining the discussion. The purpose of either warning
includes:

---

[5] See discussion in Chapter 7 for more ideas on how to deal with problems even in the
absence of a complaint.

[6] In the unionized context, a written warning is considered to be the least severe disciplinary sanction available to management. In order to constitute a disciplinary warning, it must form part of the worker's employment record and have the potential to
impact adversely on the worker's employment in the future. See Brown, *supra*, at note
3, at § 7:4210.

(a) to advise the employee that certain behaviour is unacceptable and why;

(b) to advise the employee what the employer's expectations are;

(c) to discuss the consequences if the employee fails to meet the requirements, including the possibility of termination;

(d) to document the employee's personnel file.

Depending on the nature of the complaint, it may be appropriate to monitor the situation closely for a period of time in order to ensure that the message has been clearly understood and that the problem has not re-occurred. Although most companies conduct annual reviews, in cases involving harassment, it may be appropriate to review the situation much more frequently.

Example 14.3

Phyllis Lamberton is always the subject of gossip at the workplace. At a recent company picnic, she proceeded to complain about the heat, stripped down to her skimpy underwear, danced suggestively in the quasi-nude and propositioned a number of the young male employees. Everyone laughed about it and no one took it seriously. Nonetheless, the CEO is furious. This is not the image he wants his employees to project. Phyllis is usually a stellar employee. On two previous occasions, however, she has been spoken to informally about her "sense of fun". This case was the worst. Phyllis does not understand why the CEO is furious. Her response to the complaint is mostly, "you are blowing it out of proportion. It was just a bit of fun."

Because Phyllis has been spoken to previously, it is appropriate to escalate this matter further. Despite Phyllis' perception that her conduct was just "fun", it is not acceptable in the workplace. Her response demonstrates a lack of understanding of the seriousness of her misconduct. A sample warning letter is reproduced at Appendix 14.2.

3. Suspensions

Employment lawyers often speak of "progressive discipline" when they refer to a series of steps prior to dismissal. In the unionized workplace, suspensions are recognized as a serious form of discipline, just short of dismissal. In the non-unionized context, the status of suspensions is still uncertain.

The traditional common law principle is that there is no right to suspend an employee for disciplinary matters — either the employee should be terminated for cause or alternatively, warned that a future re-occurrence will lead to termination for cause. More recently, courts have recognized that in certain cases, it is an implied term of the employment agreement that an employee may be suspended in certain circumstances.[7] A decision to suspend without pay should be made cautiously and only after consultation with legal counsel. Arbitrators have upheld suspensions from as short as three days to as long as one year in the context of sexual harassment.

4. Demotions

In the unionized workplace, demotion has been recognized as a possible disciplinary response to serious culpable behaviour. Particularly where the complaint involves a supervisor's serious misconduct against a subordinate, demotion has been accepted as an appropriate disciplinary measure. In the labour arbitration context, the underlying justification is that the supervisor has demonstrated his inability to fulfill the supervisory obligations of his position by sexually harassing a subordinate. In such cases, a demotion accompanied by a requirement to complete harassment training prior to applying for reinstatement or promotion may be an appropriate remedy.[8] In the non-unionized context, there is little case law on the use of demotions as a disciplinary response. Some courts have found that an employer must be able to establish just cause for dismissal before imposing a disciplinary demo-tion. In rare cases, courts have found that it was an implied term that an em-ployer could rescind a promotion or demote for unsatisfactory performance.

Demotions can be problematic. The complainant may be concerned that the harasser is still in the workplace. The harasser may find it intolerable to continue working at a company after a disciplinary demotion. In many cases, a demotion is easier to institute where it is accompanied by a change in geographic locale. The harasser and complainant are separated. The harasser does not have to face his former subordinates and peers on a daily basis. Both parties can make a fresh start. Demotions should be accompanied by careful monitoring and training, in order to ensure that the employee does not re-offend.[9]

---

[7]   *Reininger v. Unique Personnel Canada Inc.*, [2002] O.J. No. 2826 (S. Ct. *per* Howden J.); see also the general discussion in *Haldane v. Shelbar Enterprises Ltd.* (1999), 46 O.R. (3d) 206 (C.A.).

[8]   *Toronto Board of Education* (1997), 65 L.A.C. (4th) 174 (Howe).

[9]   See discussion regarding cause for demotion in Stacey Ball, *Canadian Employment Law* (Aurora: Canada Law Book, 1996) at para. 10:31.

5. Mediation

As indicated earlier, mediation is often used at a preliminary stage.[10] Surprisingly, mediation can also be very effective even after an investigation has been completed. In Ontario, Ontario Human Rights Commission investigators routinely attempt to "conciliate" the dispute during the course of the investigation. Mediation should only be used if both the complainant and the respondent have indicated a willingness to participate in the exercise.

6. Termination with Cause

Termination with cause is considered to be the most serious step an employer can take against an employee. There is no single test for just cause. All of the courts and commentators have emphasized the high legal standard which must be met by the employer to justify termination without notice (or compensation). The Ontario Court of Appeal observed:

> .... If an employee has been guilty of serious misconduct, habitual neglect of duty, incompetence, or conduct incompatible with his duties, or prejudicial to the employer's business, or if he has been guilty of wilful disobedience to the employer's orders in a matter of substance, the law recognizes the employer's right summarily to dismiss the delinquent employee.[11]

In the sexual harassment context, courts have recognized that the respondent's *denial* of the allegations may render warnings or other rehabilitative measures ineffective. The respondent's conduct in the context of the investigation may justify termination with cause. As the Ontario Court of Appeal stated in the *Gonsalves* case:

> Once the employer is satisfied that the complaints are well-founded, the denial has a significance in limiting suitable choices open to the employer. There is no opening for an apology to clear the air if employment is to be continued. Further, in this case, the pattern of behaviour was inconsistent with responsible management and suggests a profile that might benefit from treatment if employment was to be continued. *That alternative was eliminated by the denial.* Without some acknowledgement of fault and steps taken to reassure staff it is my view that Father Coughlan could not responsibly have left this small group of female employees in the charge of Mr. Gonsalves, subject only to a warning. It is a very sad and difficult task to tell an employee, with a long service record that was previously unblemished, that he must be dismissed at an age when his re-employment potential is questionable. However, persons in a supervisory capacity must not, over time, permit their position of power to supplant good judgment and responsibility. When

---

[10] See discussion in Chapter 6, section 5.

[11] *R. v. Arthurs, Ex parte Port Arthur Shipbuilding Co.* (1967), 62 D.L.R. (2d) 342 at 348 (Ont. C.A.), *per* Schroeder J.A.

credible evidence stands against denial, the employer's options may be limited and its obligations to the work force may have to supervene over the interests of an otherwise valued employee. (Emphasis added).[12]

In the unionized context, it is rare for an arbitrator to uphold an employee's discharge for cause. Nonetheless, employers have been successful in justifying summary discharge, particularly where the harasser was in a supervisory position.[13]

A decision to terminate for cause should always be made in consultation with a lawyer. The potential for litigation is high. In some cases, it may be appropriate to offer the harasser an option to resign with a small financial settlement. This financial settlement would not resemble the type of severance package an employee might receive in a "without cause" termination. Although employers often balk at the thought of "paying off the wrongdoer", it may represent an appropriate option. For example, in the *Gonsalves* case, the employer indicated it was terminating the employee for cause, but was still prepared to pay a package equivalent to 12 months in exchange for a release.[14] Mr. Gonsalves refused and sued for wrongful dismissal. As a result, the employer was forced to engage in a lengthy trial process and call the victim of harassment as a witness. The employer lost at trial and only won after an expensive appeal process. It is sometimes appropriate to consider the benefit of avoiding the trauma and publicity of the litigation process in deciding how to deal with the harasser.

In the sample case file, the investigator found that the complainant has substantiated her allegations of serious sexual harassment. Although the company may choose to terminate for cause, it may wish to consider the possibility of offering the harasser a small package in exchange for a release. Appendices 14.3 and 14.4 contain sample termination letters that the company may wish to modify.

---

[12] *Gonsalves v. Catholic Church Extension Society of Canada* (1998), 164 D.L.R. (4th) 339 at 346.

[13] See summary of arbitral jurisprudence in Chapter 9 of Arjun Aggarwal *et al.*, *supra*, at note 3, Chapter 9.

[14] (1996), 20 C.C.E.L. (2d) 106 (Ont. C.J. (Gen. Div.)). At the time of his termination, Mr. Gonsalves had completed 22 years of service and was 59 years of age. Both the trial and appeal court accepted that the prospects of his re-employment were poor. If there had been no issue of cause, Mr. Gonsalves could have expected a package equivalent to 20 months' compensation.

C. CONCLUSION

One of the most difficult exercises is to determine the just resolution of complaints involving sexual harassment. The investigator is able to assist with the neutral fact-finding exercise. Once a particular conclusion is reached, the employer must determine what to do with the parties to the complaint.

Any resolution can have devastating consequences for the harasser and the victim. The employer has a legal consequence to act. A refusal or reluctance to deal aggressively with the problem can be interpreted as condonation of the harasser's conduct. It may expose the company to significant damages if the harasser re-offends. The complainant may not be able to continue to work if the harasser is permitted to stay with the company.

Where an employer is considering termination of the harasser, legal counsel should be consulted before the termination is effected. The termination letter should be drafted carefully. Careful consideration should also be given to any corporate communications regarding the employee's departure from the corporation, in order to avoid fuelling any untoward speculation or exposing the company to a defamation claim.

APPENDIX 14.1

CRITICAL FACTORS TO BE CONSIDERED

(1) What is the legal context? Is there a collective bargaining agreement? If so, what is the union's position on discipline?

(2) Who is the respondent? Is the respondent an executive or manager with obligations to enforce the harassment policy?

(3) Does the respondent have responsibility for the enforcement of the harassment policy?

(4) Is he or she a manager?

(5) Does the complainant report to the respondent, either directly or indirectly?

(6) Do the respondent and complainant interact with each other on a regular basis as part of their job duties?

(7) What is the objective seriousness of the incident?
   (a) was it deliberate misconduct or causing offence inadvertently?
   (b) was it an isolated incident or a pattern of conduct?
   (c) did it involve criminal behaviour (*e.g.* assault, criminal harassment)?
   (d) did the harasser use his or her power at work to intimidate or coerce the respondent?
   (e) did the harasser impact on one or more individuals?
   (f) did it involve a minor (young) employee or complainant?

(8) What is the impact of the harassment on the victim?

    (a)   has the victim suffered job-related consequences (*e.g.* forced resignation, denial of promotion, wage increase or transfer)?

    (b)   has the victim suffered any physical or medical health consequences (*e.g.* blood pressure, anxiety, stress, teeth-grinding)?

(9)   What is the work record of the harasser?

    (a)   length of service;

    (b)   previous service record and any disciplinary issues;

    (c)   previous service record and any discipline for harassment-related matters.

(10) Are there any mitigating factors which should be considered? Mitigating factors could include unusual stresses (such as a death in the family), side-effects of medication, an undiagnosed mental or physical illness.

(11) Has the complainant indicated any concerns about continuing to work with the harasser?

(12) Was the respondent co-operative and candid in the investigative process?

(13) Has the respondent shown genuine remorse?

(14) Is the respondent prepared to apologize?

(15) Is the respondent prepared to participate in education and/or training?

(16) Is the organization large enough to be able to consider an alternative to termination, such as a transfer to another unit or demotion to another position?

(16) How have other employees in similar cases been treated?

APPENDIX 14.2

WARNING LETTER

ABC Company
Private & Confidential

To: Phyllis Lamberton, IT Specialist
     c.c.   Mark Crane, IT Manager

From: Niels Hansen, HR Manager

Date: August x, 200x

Re: <u>Your behaviour on July 31st, 200x , ABC Annual Picnic</u>

This memorandum confirms our discussion of today's date. On July 31st, 200x, you attended the ABC company picnic. During the picnic, you proceeded to strip to your underwear, danced in your underwear and sexually propositioned three of your employees. Approximately 20 to 25 employees (and/or their spouses) witnessed your behaviour. You justified your behaviour on the basis that it was just a bit of fun.

This is not the first time we have had to discuss this type of matter with you. On February 16, we advised you that it was inappropriate to send nude valentines to your co-workers. On May 8, we advised you that you were out of line when you sent a stripper to your boss as a 40th birthday gift. In both cases, you apologized and indicated it would not happen again. We believed you and gave you another chance.

As you know, ABC has a strict policy regarding workplace conduct. We expect our employees to act professionally with each other. In the future, you are to restrict your activities at the workplace or at work-related events to what is necessary to complete your duties as an IT specialist. Conduct which has a sexual overtone (flirting, propositioning employees, sending valentines, or sending a stripper) are strictly prohibited. If you have any doubt regarding whether certain conduct is appropriate, please do not hesitate to contact your boss or me.

Please note that any further re-occurrence of this type of behaviour will be subject to further discipline, up to and including dismissal for just cause.

*****

I have read this memorandum. I understand its contents.
_____   *Dated:* _____
Phyllis Lamberton

TERMINATION LETTER WITH CAUSE, BUT OFFERING SOME COMPENSATION

Private & Confidential
To be Opened by Addressee Only
Via Courier

September 25, 200x

Jack Andrews
1233 Kenilworth Lane
Streetsville ON L4V 3M6

Dear Mr. Andrews:

Re: Termination of your employment

This letter confirms our discussion of yesterday's date, in which we advised you that ABC had decided to terminate your employment with cause. This decision was not taken lightly.

We recently received a complaint of sexual harassment from Ms. Carruthers. During the last 2 ½ weeks, this complaint has been investigated and we have been apprised that there is cogent evidence supporting the allegation. Given the seriousness of the complaint, your senior position at ABC, the impact the conduct has had on Ms. Carruthers, and your repeated denials of any wrongdoing, ABC is of the opinion that it is not realistic to continue your employment relationship. Accordingly, ABC has decided to terminate your employment for cause.

On a totally gratuitous basis and without admission of liability, ABC is prepared to provide you with a lump sum equivalent to six months' base salary (less statutory deductions). *[Insert additional details re: offer, e.g. continued car allowance, benefits or other perquisites]* In order to receive this sum, you will be required to: (a) execute a full and final release of ABC, its employees and agents; and (b) undertake to abide by the post-termination provisions of ABC's Confidentiality and Non-solicitation Agreement that you executed when you were promoted to Executive Vice-President.[15]

You also asked us about references. We are not prepared to conceal from future employers that issues regarding a violation of the sexual harassment policy led to your departure from the company, but would be prepared to discuss your otherwise excellent contributions to the company.

Please let us know your response no later than October 8, 200x. You will receive your Record of Employment and your pay to today's date (including base, commission, accrued vacation pay and pro-rated car allowance) under separate cover.

Sincerely,

David Ricketts
Chief Executive Officer

---

[15] This is a simplified letter. Most termination letters contain lengthy detailed terms regarding exact amounts of salary and benefits and provide contact details regarding transition details. This simplified example is provided to assist the reader in considering how the issues surrounding sexual harassment should be dealt with.

APPENDIX 14.4

TERMINATION LETTER WITH CAUSE, BUT OFFERING NO COMPENSATION

Private & Confidential
To be Opened by Addressee Only
Via Courier

September 25, 200x

Jack Andrews
1233 Kenilworth Lane
Streetsville ON L4V 3M6

Dear Mr. Andrews:

Re: Termination of your employment

This letter confirms our discussion of yesterday's date, in which we advised you that ABC had decided to terminate your employment with cause. This decision was not taken lightly.

We recently received a complaint of sexual harassment from Ms. Carruthers. During the last 2 ½ weeks, this complaint has been investigated and we have been apprised that there is cogent evidence supporting the allegation. Given the seriousness of the complaint, your senior position at ABC, the impact the conduct has had on Ms. Carruthers, and your repeated denials of any wrong-doing, ABC is of the opinion that it is not realistic to continue your employment relationship. Accordingly, ABC has decided to terminate your employment for cause.

We have carefully considered your request for some kind of severance, particularly in light of your lengthy service record with ABC. With regret, we have decided that it would be inappropriate to provide a severance package to you, particularly given the nature of the harassment and your position as a trusted fiduciary and man-ager of ABC.

You will receive your Record of Employment and your pay to today's date (including base, commission, accrued vacation pay and pro-rated car allowance) under separate cover. Please note that your benefits will cease immediately.

Sincerely,

David Ricketts
Chief Executive Officer

CHAPTER 15

DEALING WITH THE COMPLAINANT

A. OVERVIEW

There are many legal and practical considerations when dealing with a complainant. In investigating a complaint, it is likely that an investigator will come to one of the following conclusions:

(1) The allegations are substantially true and constitute harassment (or other workplace misconduct);
(2) The allegations are substantially true, but do not constitute harassment (or other workplace misconduct);
(3) The allegations were made in good faith, but are not true;
(4) The allegations are false and were deliberately fabricated;
(5) The investigator is unable to come to a conclusion.

In each of the cases, the investigator and/or employer should meet with the complainant to discuss the results of the investigation.

The employer should be careful to ensure that nothing in the discussions (or subsequent correspondence) misleads the complainant to believe that he or she is precluded from addressing the concerns in another forum, such as:

(1) a civil case;
(2) a human rights complaint; or
(3) a criminal complaint.

The employer's responsibility is to address the issue of harassment from the perspective of an internal investigation. While the internal investigation may feature prominently if there is subsequent legal action, the employer should be reticent about discussing the complainant's options in these regards. The complainant should seek his or her legal counsel regarding any other steps that he or she may be entitled to take.

B. WHERE THE COMPLAINANT'S ALLEGATIONS HAVE BEEN SUBSTANTIATED

Where the complainant's allegations have been substantiated, an employer should consider what should be done on a going-forward basis. As indicated in the previous chapters, there are a host of considerations governing disciplinary measures against the respondent. Depending on the nature of the complaint, the employer must be prepared to handle the following questions:

(1)   What measures, if any, have been taken against the respondent?
(2)   What measures, if any, will be implemented to prevent a reoccurrence?
(3)   What measures, if any, will be implemented to protect the complainant against reprisal for having made the complaint?
(4)   Will the employer provide any monetary compensation to the complainant, if financial losses have been suffered by her?
(5)   Will the employer provide any non-monetary compensation or reimburse certain expenses, such as counselling, medical expenses, legal fees?

While it is imperative to discuss these issues candidly with the complainant, the employer should also confirm such matters in writing. Appendix 15.1 is a sample memo to a complainant in a situation involving serious sexual harassment, where the corporation has made the decision to terminate the employment of the harasser. In other cases, the company may choose not to terminate the harasser and the complainant may have legitimate concerns regarding future reprisals or retaliation.

C.   WHERE THE COMPLAINT IS NOT HARASSMENT

In some cases, an investigator may find that while the factual allegations are true, they do not constitute harassment in the circumstances. As indicated in Chapter 1, one of the key tests of establishing harassment was whether the harasser knew or ought to have known that the conduct is unwelcome. In Example 14.1,[1] it is quite possible that the old-school plant manager did not

---

[1]   See Chapter 14 in section B.1.

know that his conduct was considered offensive and given the past history of the plant, probably did not meet the "ought to have known" standards.

In other cases, the problem may not fall within the scope of the harassment (or any other policy), but still requires some type of response. In Example 14.2,[2] a gay employee voiced a concern regarding latent homophobia in the workplace. Because of the subtleties of the conduct, it may not be possible to establish a specific violation of the policy. Workplace bullying or "status-blind" bullying may not be contrary to a policy or the law, but may also need to be dealt with.

Many complainants do not care about the niceties of the legal scope of a policy. An employer should decide that even if conduct is neither illegal nor contrary to existing policy, whether a creative and non-disciplinary response can be devised.

Complainants will also want to be assured that there will be no reprisals for having made the complaint.

D. WHERE THE COMPLAINT WAS MADE IN GOOD FAITH, BUT IS NOT TRUE

A complaint may be made in good faith, but on investigation, is proven to be false. In Example 11.1, Lalita,[3] the employee, may have sincerely believed that her bad performance review was a reprisal because she had declined the supervisor's invitation to a date. The employee may have a genuine fear that she will suffer retaliation because of making a false complaint. The employee should be reassured in this regard. It may be appropriate to monitor the situation for several months to ensure that the supervisor's possible resentment regarding the investigative process is not manifested in conduct that could be viewed as retaliatory.

E. WHERE COMPLAINT IS A FABRICATION

In some cases, the investigator concludes that the complainant fabricated significant portions of the complaint. The entire complaint may be a lie or a consensual relationship may be maliciously recast as harassment. In such cases, disciplinary action against the complainant may be appropriate.

---

[2] See Chapter 14 in section B.1.
[3] See Chapter 11 in section D.

Example 15.1

Ingrid Blair worked as a stocker in a warehouse owned and operated by Matrix Logistics Services. In the fall of 1999, she accused her team leader, Errol George, of making sexually suggestive remarks and also accused him of making derogatory remarks about her to other members of her team. The HR manager in charge investigated, but Ingrid Blair refused (or was unable) to reveal the name of the other employees who had heard the remarks. Errol denied the complaints. Later that year, Ingrid Blair again complained about overhearing negative remarks from Errol George. She claimed she could not determine who was present, because she was on the mezzanine and Mr. George was directly below her. Mr. George denied the remarks and said that he only remarked about Ms. Blair to his co-team manager in a private office, not on the floor. In late December, Ms. Blair received a warning regarding excessive socializing and wandering from her workstation. In March, 2000, she repeated and reiterated her position that Errol George was making negative comments about her. She provided the names of two employees who could confirm her story. During the investigation, both denied hearing any such comments.[4]

Upon investigation, the company concluded that Ingrid Blair had deliberately fabricated complaints about Errol George and terminated her for cause. After the termination, Blair sued for wrongful dismissal, slander, malicious falsehood and deceit. When this matter proceeded to trial, the trial judge found that the complaints were false and were made in order to discredit her team leader and procure his dismissal.

Madam Justice Caswell recognized that not all acts of dishonesty justified summary dismissal. She reiterated a well-known two-part test:

(1)   Is the nature and seriousness of the dishonesty reconcilable or irreconcilable with sustaining the employment relationship? or

(2)   Does the dishonesty strike at the very heart of the employment relationship such that dismissal for just cause is warranted?

The court found that the unfounded allegations regarding Errol George undermined his authority as a team leader. Blair's dishonesty, the court concluded, was not reconcilable with a continuing relationship with her supervisor or the company. Accordingly, termination without notice or compensa-

---

[4]   The facts and the names are drawn from the case of *Blair v. Matrix Logistics Services Ltd.* (2001), Carswell Ont 2736 (S.C.J. *per* Caswell J.).

tion was appropriate. The *Blair* case illustrates the problems caused by a false complaint.

Before terminating or disciplining a complainant for a false complaint, legal counsel should be obtained. Nonetheless, a simple precedent termination letter is included at Appendix 15.7.

F. WHERE THE INVESTIGATOR IS UNABLE TO COME TO A CONCLUSION

In the Carruthers complaint,[5] one of the minor complaints was an incident in a pool. The complainant alleged that the respondent had pinched her buttocks. The respondent denies doing anything deliberately, but admits that there may have been inadvertent contact in the pool. The description suggests that the pool was crowded, people were engaged in horseplay and it is possible that the complainant was mistaken about the nature of the contact or who was responsible. On the other hand, the investigator may find Ms. Carruthers quite believable. In such circumstances, the investigator may not feel comfortable in making a conclusive finding. This ambivalence is not the fault of the complainant or the respondent. If the pool incident were the only issue in the scenario, it would have been appropriate to advise the complainant of the failure of the investigator to arrive at a definitive conclusion. The company will wish to reassure the complainant that the failure to draw a conclusion, however, will have no negative impact on the complainant. A sample memo is reproduced at Appendix 15.1.

G. DEALING WITH THE WORKPLACE'S REACTION TO THE COMPLAINANT

Some complainants have indicated that a harassment complaint inevitably leads to members of the workplace choosing "sides". Even when a complaint is found to be valid, other employees may sympathize with the harasser. It is not unusual for employees to express opinions, such as:

(1)   Blame the complainant — "well, she over-reacted. She shouldn't be so thin-skinned. If she had said something right away, none of this would have happened."

(2)   Empathy for the respondent — "Jack's a nice guy and has responsibility for a wife and kids. Who does she think she is?"

---

[5]   See Part II.

(3) Focusing on the respondent's contribution to the work — "Jack's the only reason the company made money last year. Doesn't she care about the company at all?"

(4) Focusing on friendships — "Jack was always there for me. He's the only reason why I've done so well here. I can't believe he would do anything bad enough to justify throwing him out of the company."

(5) Anti-feminist backlash — "This is why I hate feminists. Everything is gender politics. A guy just can't be a normal guy any more."

Despite efforts to maintain confidentiality, word leaks out. Employees who did not have the full story or who only heard the respondent's view, may align themselves against the complainant. Although overt management support of the complainant may help alleviate some of these stresses, the complainant may find the workplace a hostile place.

The employer often finds itself in a quandary. The pressure to maintain confidentiality and respect the complainant's privacy can backfire against the complainant. Some workplace experts maintain that it is important to try to "heal" the workplace after the stresses of the investigation.

Several human resource consultants suggest that team-building exercises can be an excellent way to strengthen the workforce after a stressful investigation, even if there is no specific reference to the investigation itself. It forces the employees to focus on something positive, instead of a divisive investigation.

Example 15.2

Margaret Woods complained about sexual harassment against her co-worker, Todd Jenkins. Margaret and Todd had been in a permanent, consensual relationship for some time. Their co-workers were aware of the relationship. Margaret is quiet, thoughtful and introverted. Todd is gregarious and was generally well-liked. The co-workers also knew that Margaret broke off the relationship with Todd. They didn't knew that Todd had been physically abusive to Margaret during the relationship. They also didn't know that Todd began to stalk Margaret both in the workplace and elsewhere. When Todd is dismissed, many co-workers feel that Margaret had it in for Todd. They are coldly polite to her, but shun her from the normal social interactions in the workplace.

Although the anti-reprisal or anti-retaliation policy may protect Margaret from management actions, it cannot make the employees "like" Margaret.

Formal and informal team-building exercises may help co-workers appreciate Margaret in a different light, without requiring her to discuss the painful details of her relationship with Todd.

Some experts would recommend that the employer consider involving Margaret and her co-workers in a workplace reconciliation. While this can be very effective, it requires Margaret to be prepared to discuss in public some matters she has kept fiercely confidential. This strategy can be very effective, but should only be used in circumstances where the complainant is comfortable with the parameters of the process.

H. CONCLUSION

Unless there is a finding of a deliberate malicious complaint of harassment, the complainant should feel comfortable continuing to work regardless of the result of the complaint. The employer should institute measures to ensure that the complaint does not lead to retaliation or reprisals.

APPENDIX 15.1

MEMO TO COMPLAINANT

To: Janine Carruthers

From: David Ricketts

Date: September 30th, 200x

Re: Complaint of Sexual Harassment

As we discussed, we retained an investigator to investigate your complaint of sexual harassment. As indicated in our discussion, the investigator has concluded that while he is unable to draw any conclusion regarding the incident in the pool, the balance of the complaints are true. We confirmed that Mr. Andrews is no longer with the corporation. You will continue in your current position.

Although we recognize that you may believe that you were denied a promotion because of the harassment by Jack Andrews, we want to assure you that your suspicion is this regard is incorrect. In making the decision to choose another candidate, we looked at ABC's future growth in international markets. We chose a candidate we believed had a proven track record in this area.

We want to thank you for bringing the complaint to our attention. We want to assure you that the complaint will have no bearing on your career with ABC. You have indicated to me that you have found this process very stressful and if you wish, we would be prepared to extend to you a paid authorized leave of absence for a period of four to eight weeks so that you can focus on your health. This leave will not affect your vacation, bonus or other entitlements at work.

Should you need a longer period of absence, we will assist you in obtaining coverage through our short-term and long-term disability insurance.

Furthermore, you have indicated that your doctor has recommended that you get one-on-one assistance from a trained psychologist. To the extent that this assistance is not covered by our insurance plan, we will reimburse your out-of-pocket costs upon receiving receipts. ABC's EAP provider also has excellent resources and we encourage you to consider them. A brochure about the EAP provider is included. We would appreciate getting a sense of when you might be able to return to work.

During our discussion, you indicated that you are thinking of quitting. I would encourage you to defer any decision. We recognize that the last four weeks have been exceptionally stressful for you and I would not want you to make a decision that you may subsequently regret. You indicated that you were worried how "people" might view Jack's departure and blame you for it. If necessary, I will ensure that the appropriate people know the true circumstances and that you are to be commended and not blamed. If you have any problems, call me.

APPENDIX 15.2

MEMO TO COMPLAINANT (WHERE HARASSER NOT TERMINATED)[6]

To: Devraj Choudhry

From: Tony Robinson, HR Manager

Date: August 9, 200x

Re: Complaint of harassment

I wanted to follow up on yesterday's discussion. My investigation confirms your complaint about harassment and in particular, Mr. Ralph Ng's repeated use of the derogatory terms "fag" and "poufter" in reference to you and homosexuals in general.

As you no longer work in the IT department, Mr. Ng no longer has any direct or indirect responsibility with respect to you. Please be assured that we take this matter seriously. We have taken the following steps:

(1)   Mr. Ng will be participating in a three-day management course, which includes managing a diverse workplace in September, 200x;
(2)   We will continue to monitor Mr. Ng's department for any offensive or anti-gay remarks or conduct;
(3)   Mr. Ng has indicated that he will be apologizing to you in private. We cannot force Mr. Ng to apologize, but believe that he is honestly trying to make amends;
(4)   Mr. Ng will not be eligible for bonus consideration for this fiscal year;

---

[6]   This memo is drafted in response to the complaint of Devraj Choudhry, described in Example 10.2 in section C.4 of Chapter 10.

(5)   We will recirculate our materials on harassment and anti-discrimination in the workplace;

(6)   We will include expanded materials on harassment and anti-discrimination in the workplace in our orientation materials.

You expressed concern that you might suffer reprisals because of making a complaint against Mr. Ng. Please call me directly if you feel that there is any kind of backlash or reprisal. The company takes its obligations with respect to human rights seriously and will intervene quickly and promptly in this regard. Thank you for making the complaint and for your cooperation and input in the process.

Appendix 15.3

Memo to Complainant (Where Facts Correct, but no Illegal Conduct)[7]

To: Tom Robinson

From: Brenda Pratt, HR Manager

Date: March 2, 200x

Re: Concerns regarding workplace

Tom, I wanted to thank you for bringing your concerns regarding certain "cultural" issues to my attention. I have reviewed our various workplace policies and they do not apply to the concerns you raised. I do want to confirm that I recognize the importance of what you have brought to my attention and will be working to implement strategies that may assist in shifting some of the cultural issues.

In the meantime, I have instituted an informal mentoring program for all new hires and 1st year hires. The mentoring program is intended to include formal business, client development opportunities as well as social events. Your mentor for the 200x to 200x period will be Pierre Desjardins. Mentors for other new hires and 1st year hires will be assigned separately. We will organize both formal and informal events for networking, both within the company and elsewhere.

I want to assure you that I have kept your complaint confidential. Should you have any concerns in the future, please direct them directly to myself.

---

[7]   See facts as described in Example 14.2 in section B.1.

APPENDIX 15.4

MEMO TO COMPLAINANT (COMPLAINT FALSE, BUT MADE IN GOOD FAITH)[8]

To:	Lalita Persaud
From:	John Smythe, HR Manager
Date:	February 12, 200x
Re:	Your performance review

We have had an opportunity to review your complaint in great detail. We understand that your fundamental concern is that the review was not fair, but retaliation for your refusal of your supervisor's proposition at last year's office Christmas party.

We have taken great care to investigate your complaint. In the course of your complaint, we have reviewed:

(a)   your previous performance reviews;
(b)   your interim performance review;
(c)   objective measures regarding your productivity;
(d)   previously documented concerns regarding issues of delegation/ productivity/computer skills;
(e)   other relevant departmental documents.

After careful review, we believe that the performance review was not retaliatory or unfair.

---

[8]   This memo is drafted in response to the complaint of Lalita Persaud, described in Example 11.1, in section D.

We want to assure you that we believe that you made the complaint in good faith. Our company policies protect you against reprisals, even when a good faith complaint is ultimately disproven. Nonetheless, the company has a right to provide you with appropriate feedback. As indicated in your performance review:

(a) you will attend the next scheduled computer skills class offered by the company, which will be held on February 19, 200x;

(b) you will train and then delegate to David, routine tasks regarding account reconciliation and follow up;

(c) you will continue to work with your supervisor with respect to improving your productivity in the areas identified as "needing" improvement.

If you wish to discuss this report or any other concerns, please call me directly.

APPENDIX 15.5

MEMO TO COMPLAINANTS (WHERE FACTUAL ALLEGATIONS TRUE, BUT NOT HARASSMENT BECAUSE OF THE LACK OF KNOWLEDGE OF THE ALLEGED HARASSER)[9]

To:	Noor Mohammed, Ranjit Singh, and Sayeeda Ahmad
From:	Andrew McGowan, HR Manager
Date:	February 28, 200x
Re:	Your concerns

I wanted to follow up on your complaint about Darren. We have briefly reviewed this matter. We are persuaded that Mr. McFadyen did not know that his language and patting you on the back were offensive to you (and others). We also recognize that in the past, our plant has been a somewhat rough workplace, where a certain amount of profane language and physical horseplay was common.

---

[9] See facts described in Example 14.1 in section B.1.

I understand that Darren has already apologized to you. Darren understands and respects your position. He has committed to working on these issues with us. In the meantime, let me know if you run into any other problems. I want to thank you for bringing this matter to our attention. We have learned a great deal about how to work with recruits from different backgrounds.

APPENDIX 15.6

MEMO TO COMPLAINANT (WHERE INVESTIGATION INCONCLUSIVE)[10]

To: Janine Carruthers

From: David Ricketts

Date: September 30th, 200x

Re: Complaint regarding Jack Andrews

Janine, I just wanted to recap our discussion regarding your complaint regarding Jack's conduct during the office summer picnic. As you know, our investigator interviewed Jack and various witnesses. Unfortunately, our investigator was unable to draw any firm conclusion. Our investigator found that both you and Jack were credible witnesses and he believed that it was possible that whatever interaction occurred in the pool may have been due to the overcrowding and inadvertent contact.

We have taken this opportunity to remind all executives, including Jack Andrews, of the importance of the company's anti-harassment policy.

I want to reassure you that your complaint was taken seriously. As I indicated to you, the company policy protects you against any reprisal for having made the complaint. I will be monitoring matters carefully and you should not hesitate to contact me if you feel that you have experienced retaliation.

---

[10] The complex complaint of Janine Carruthers is reproduced in Part II. In this version, there was only one complaint — a relatively minor complaint of horseplay in the pool at the summer office picnic.

Appendix 15.7

Memo to Complainant (Where False Complaint)[11]

Dear Ms. Blair:

Re: Termination of employment

This is to confirm our conversation that effective immediately, your employment with the company will end.

This termination is based upon just cause. In particular, on three separate occasions you have alleged that your team leader either: (a) sexually harassed you verbally; or (b) made derogatory remarks amounting to harassment about you to your colleagues in the open.

During the investigation, you were unable to provide us the name of even one witness who confirmed that Mr. George had made the remarks in question. The two witnesses you suggested strongly denied overhearing any such complaints. We have warned you about the dangers of false complaints previously.

You will be provided pay to today's date and accrued (but not used) vacation pay. Your benefits will cease effective today. You will receive a Record of Employment under separate cover.

Sincerely,

---

[11] See the summary of facts provided for Example 15.1 in section E.

CHAPTER 16

POST-INVESTIGATIVE MATTERS

A. OVERVIEW

An investigator's job is not finished with delivering the report or dealing with recommendations. There are a number of significant matters that ought to be considered before the file is marked "closed".

B. PROTECT THE FILE

The investigator must institute reliable precautions against the inadvertent disclosure of material gathered during the course of the investigation, such as the complaint, response and documentary evidence. Furthermore, the investigator's work product, such as witness statements and notes, should also be protected. Depending on the nature of the investigation, it may be appropriate to:

(1) Shred duplicates of documents;

(2) Download computer files onto a CD-Rom that is physically kept in a safe place and/or password protect any networked files;

(3) Change names of any computer file names to reduce chance of inadvertent disclosure – *i.e.*, "Janinecarruthersinvestigation.doc" could be renamed as "investigationseptember200x.doc";

(4) Seal files and keep in a locked cabinet where only the investigator and/or trusted designates have access;

(5) Where harassment has been found, there should be a confidential note in the personnel file referring the reader to the investigation file. Details of the investigation, however, must not be placed in the personnel file, where it may be inadvertently revealed. It is appropriate to note the action taken in the personnel file: *e.g.* employee terminated with cause after investigation into complaint of sexual and racial harassment.

Particularly where an employee is cleared or the results of the investigation inconclusive, an investigator may be asked to destroy the file. This is inappropriate, as the file may become highly relevant even after the investigation has been concluded.

Regardless of the investigator's conclusions, there may be subsequent legal action that calls into question the accuracy or validity of the investigation. For example, if the complainant is dissatisfied with the results of the internal investigation, he or she may seek to complain to a human rights commission or even press criminal charges. The investigator's file may become relevant. The investigator will have difficulty justifying his or her conclusions without the full file.

In some cases, it may be appropriate to re-open the investigation. For example, an investigator may find it impossible to reach a conclusion about one complaint of harassment. If several years later, an employee makes a similar complaint, the first, inconclusive, investigation may become relevant. Witnesses may have to be re-interviewed and the notes reviewed. It may be easier to reach a conclusion on the validity of a complaint if a pattern of misconduct is subsequently discovered.

Example 16.1

Four years ago, an HR manager was called upon to investigate the allegations of Claudia Yu, a recent immigrant from Hong Kong who worked in the packaging department of a large plant. Claudia claimed that Eric, the foreman in the packaging department, demanded sexual favours in exchange for keeping her job.

The respondent, Eric Bellegarde, was very well regarded. There were no independent witnesses. Both witnesses seemed credible and the HR manager was unable to reach a conclusion. Eric had many female subordinates and co-workers who spoke highly of him. The conduct seemed uncharacteristic.

Despite the HR manager's efforts to the contrary, Claudia found a job at another plant and resigned. Two years later, Gian Xu, another recent female immigrant from Hong Kong, made a complaint that echoed the allegations of Claudia Yu. In reviewing personnel files, the HR manager noticed that eight female recent immigrants — three from Hong Kong, three from Taiwan and two from Bulgaria — had resigned from the packaging department both before and after the Yu complaint. After redoing the investigation, the HR manager realized that Eric targeted recent female immigrants only.

Example 16.1 is an example of how an old "closed" case can become relevant. While Eric was "cleared" of the allegations of the Yu complaint, the HR manager was able to discern a pattern many years later. If the HR manager had destroyed her notes and records, it would have been difficult to review the details of the Yu complaint four years later. Witness memories fade and ex-employees are notoriously reluctant to re-open "ancient history".

C. MONITOR THE WORKPLACE

Regardless of the result of the investigation, a harassment investigation can create a significant amount of tension. Witnesses and complainants may fear reprisal. A vindicated respondent may feel that the investigation process was unfair. Where the investigator works in-house, he or she can take active steps to monitor activity in the part of the workforce that was most acutely affected by the complaint and subsequent investigation. As indicated in Chapter 15, section G, the company may wish to consider steps to help the workplace move forward after the stresses of an investigation.

The employer should also scrutinize any disciplinary or termination decisions involving complainants or witnesses carefully. Even where such decisions are completely unrelated to the complaint, they may be perceived as retaliation. In most cases, the onus of proof that the decision was not retaliatory is on the employer. Proving a negative is notoriously difficult.

Example 16.2
Elsa Chambers complained about sexual harassment against her manager in the company, Gary Waddell. While the investigation was ongoing, the employer decided to downsize the workforce and focused on three com-ponents:

(a)   seniority within the organization;
(b)   language skills (because of an international service com-ponent); and
(c)   training in certain software.

Elsa was offered a package, while employees with less service were retained. Elsa immediately complained to the Human Rights Commission, both about the initial harassment and the retaliation. It took six hearing days to establish that the decision-makers with respect to the downsizing knew absolutely nothing about Elsa's complaint and that the termination was not a reprisal. Elsa, however, successfully established her claim on the basis of sex harassment against both her manager and the company.

Example 16.2 illustrates the importance of good internal controls within the employer's human resources function. It is highly likely that Elsa would have had confidence in the internal process, if she had not been terminated within a week of making a complaint. Elsa had no way of knowing whether she was being included on the downsizing list as a way of ridding the company of an "inconvenient" employee. Because her trust in the internal process had been shattered, she sought help externally. The cost to the company was significant.

D. LEARN FROM THE PAST

A good investigation does more than establish facts and suggest resolutions with respect to the complaint. In investigating the complaint, the company may also be able to obtain invaluable feedback about many important workplace issues, including:

(1) whether it has good hiring practices;[1]
(2) whether it trains its employees well;
(3) whether it has established good communication practices;
(4) whether it supervises employees well;
(5) whether its disciplinary process works; and
(6) whether its anti-harassment policies actually function as they ought.

Although it is critical to address the specific complaint properly, a good investigation may allow an employer to subject itself to some critical self-analysis. An employer that uses the results of the investigation to improve the workplace has made a true commitment to meeting its obligations under human rights law to eradicate harassment.

---

[1] In two cases the author investigated, the company had failed to conduct reference checks of the respondent. In one of the two cases, the respondent had been previously fired for harassing an under-age employee.

PART II

CASE FILE: RE COMPLAINT OF JANINE CARRUTHERS, SENIOR SALES SPECIALIST

SAMPLE HARASSMENT COMPLAINT FORM

Harassment Complaint Form

Date: September 6th

Name of Person Making Complaint: Janine Carruthers

Person(s) Against Whom Complaint Made: Jack Andrews

Nature of Complaint: Sexual Harassment

Details of Incident: I believe that I have been sexually harassed by Jack Andrews. During the summer picnic (June 1), Jack and I were in the pool. Jack swam under water and reached and tugged my bikini bottom and pinched me. I turned around, but he went swimming further and surfaced about 10 feet away. I left the party right away. After the June 3rd Sales Department meeting, Jack asked me to stay behind. He patted my rear and commented "nice view." I left right away. On June 8th, Jack, Timothy Blackwell and I went out for drinks with Paul Saunderson. Paul is an important client. Jack drank too much and I didn't think it was safe for him to drive home. I drove him home. On the way there, Jack made a number of suggestive remarks. He said he wanted to "f***" me. I told him to smarten up. He didn't. When I dropped him off at home, Jack turned around and said, "you know, Janine, you should be nice to me. I would be nice to you." I drove away, thinking that he was just being silly. On June 15th, we arrived in LA. Early on the 16th, Jack pounded on my hotel bedroom door in the early hours of the morning. I could hear him through the door. He scared me so much, I almost called security. Since then, I have received numerous harassing telephone calls. I know Jack is calling me. I've changed my telephone number, but company policy requires that we give team members our home number. I feel that I've been sexually harassed.

page 1 of 2

Harassment Complaint Form

What impact has this conduct had on you? I used to be very happy at ABC Company. I am only 1 of 2 female Senior Sales Specialists in the company out of 58 in total. I used to like working with Jack Andrews. Now I feel that I have no future with the company. I know that he did not recommend me for promotion to Vice-President. I deserved that promotion, but feel that because I didn't play ball with Jack, I lost out on an opportunity of a lifetime. The phone calls have ruined my sleep and I've been referred to the Upper Canada Sleep Disorders Clinic. I'm jumpy. My doctor has prescribed an anti-anxiety drug.

How do you want this complaint treated? I want Jack Andrews to stop bothering me. I want to be compensated for losing out on the promotion.

"Janine Carruthers"

ABC Company takes every complaint of harassment very seriously. A person making a complaint is encouraged to provide as much information as he or she can to assist the company in handling the complaint.

Please note that a deliberately false or malicious complaint is considered to be a serious matter and subject to disciplinary action.

SAMPLE RESPONSE FORM

Response Form

Date: September 9th

Name of Person Making Complaint: Janine Carruthers

Person(s) Against Whom Complaint Made: Jack Andrews

Nature of Complaint: Sexual Harassment

Response: I have never sexually harassed Janine. I think she is a terrific employee. I think she is making this up because she is upset that Timothy Blackwell got the promotion. I never thought she was malicious. Here's my recollection of the various dates: June 1, I was at the summer picnic. I spent most of the time in the pool, either horsing around or playing waterpolo. I did not tug at Janine's swimsuit or pinch her. June 2, I do remember the Sales Department meeting. I did have a few items to discuss with Janine after the meeting on a specific deal we were working on. I did not touch her on the rear at all. June 8, I remember the Saunderson meeting. Janine did drive me home that night. It was really nice of her and remember saying that she was very nice to me and I would have to be nice to her. I never tried to kiss her. I felt guilty about getting a bit loaded. I probably was over .08 that night. I got home and just passed out a bit. June 15th, The whole thing about the business trip to Los Angeles is a complete fabrication. Tim and I stayed in the bar well past midnight and I went straight to bed. I have never made any harassing calls to Janine. I have called her at home for business reasons.

Witnesses: Timothy Blackwell and Mary Anne Thomas.

Jack Andrews

INVESTIGATOR'S NOTES OF THE INTERVIEW WITH JANINE CARRUTHERS

Introductory Formalities[1]

☐   Investigator introduction

☐   Investigator confirms that she is retained by company:
"

I have been retained by ABC Company to investigate a formal complaint of sexual harassment made by you against Jack Andrews. I want you to understand that as an investigator, I am a neutral party. My job is to interview witnesses, look at evidence and deliver a report to ABC Company. [*If investigator a lawyer*] You should understand that although I am a lawyer, I am not *your* lawyer."

☐   Confirm that Complainant has made a formal complaint

☐   Ask Complainant to review complaint

☐   Ask Complainant if he/she needs to change or amend complaint

☐   Confirm that Complainant has copy of harassment policy

☐   Explain general process — interview, information gathering, report to employer, employer makes decision

☐   Explain timetable

☐   Advise witness to listen to question carefully and to answer question honestly. If witness does not know or remember, best to advise that. If witness subsequently wishes to correct or add to statement, he/she may contact investigator

☐   Explain record-keeping methods. Explain recording interview, *etc.*

☐   Permission to tape interview

Background Questions

1. Tell me a little bit about yourself?

I'm Janine Carruthers. I'm 36 years old. I've worked with ABC Company for nine years, always in a sales role. Before ABC, I worked two years in a marketing research position with George Franklin & Co., but I realized that I could make more money and get further ahead in a sales position. I applied for about 10 positions, but ABC Company was the only one who would take a chance on me. Since then, I've worked really hard. I've been promoted three times and I'm one of two female Senior Sales Specialists. I'm single and don't have kids. I'm pretty much a workaholic.

---

[1]   These formalities are shown as a checklist as many investigators use checklists to ensure certain basics are covered every time.

It's a great job. I make good money. I love the product line.

I thought I was on track for promotion to Vice-President when Emil Pascale retired. I'm used to working in a "boys" club and I never thought I would be someone who would ever complain about sexual harassment.

2. Tell me about Jack Andrews?

Jack is an absolute whiz kid at sales. He's 42 years old. Everyone says that he's probably one of three being considered who will replace David Ricketts when David retires. I used to like working with Jack. I never had a problem with him before. He used to flirt with me a little bit, but nothing I couldn't take. I think things changed a bit when his wife left him. She just couldn't tolerate Jack's long hours any more. I noticed that, well it's hard to say. I thought I noticed something a bit different about his teasing and comments in May. I think his wife left him at the end of April. Nothing specific and nothing I would dream of complaining about and nothing I couldn't handle. It was just an impression. Maybe it was body language or the tone of voice, but there was a different edge to the comments. It just made me a bit more careful about what I said or did.

Questions Based Upon Complaint

3. Tell me a little bit more about what happened in the swimming pool?[2]

June 1st, ABC Company had its annual picnic. It's usually a great time. ABC Company rents out the whole Yacht Club — tennis courts, swimming pool, dining room. It's a great spread. The weather soared over 34 degrees and a whole bunch of us were in the pool, cooling off. All of a sudden, I felt someone pull my bikini bottom and pinch my rear. I turned around to see who it was and it was someone under water. I realized it was Jack when he surfaced about 10 – 12 feet away from me. He gave me a little smile.

I was really upset. I thought it would be a good idea to get out of there. A few people, including Jack, had had too much to drink and well, I didn't want there to be an incident. I was pretty angry and I didn't trust myself not to blow up at Jack.

---

[2] This is an example of a question that invites a narrative. It is completely open-ended and allows the witness to tell the story in his or her own words.

I dried myself off and went to Timothy Blackwell to get a cab chit and went straight home. I think it was around 1:30 p.m. I went home — it took about 1/2 hour or so and I went to bed. I woke up about two hours later and felt a lot better. I think I might have had a little too much wine and sun. That's about it. It was pretty stupid and juvenile. A little bit of horsing around, I suppose. I didn't like it, but it wasn't a big deal.

4. How much wine?[3]

I knew you were going to ask me that. Look I wasn't drunk and I know what happened. I had two white wines. One when I got to the Yacht Club at noon and one after I finished lunch — about 1:00 or so. I jumped into the pool right afterwards.

5. Did anyone see anything?

I doubt it. I mean a whole bunch of us were in the pool, but Jack was underwater and I doubt anyone would have noticed. The only way I noticed was because I followed him. Tim will tell you I left early, but that's about it.

6. I notice you wear glasses. Did you wear glasses in the pool?[4]

No, I didn't.

7. Do you know your prescription?

Around – 4.25. Look I know what you are implying. Even without glasses, I can recognize him. He was wearing dark blue or black and yellow striped swim trunks. He was pretty hard to miss. He was trying to look "cool" in that surfboard style.

8. Did you recognize him by his swim trunks or could you actually see his features?

When he was underwater, I could just make him out — trunks, dark hair, fancy watch, that sort of thing. When he surfaced, I recognized him. He was a little out of focus, but I work for the guy. I can recognize him at 10 feet even without glasses. I'm not that blind.

---

[3] This is an example of a review question. The issue of alcohol may go to the accuracy of the witness.

[4] This is another review question, again to explore the accuracy of the witness's observations.

9. Why didn't you complain right away?[5]

That's not a fair question. What did you expect me to do? Jack's my boss and I wasn't going to make waves.

A pinch on the bottom is pretty juvenile. Things happen at a company party. I just chalked it up to experience. Avoid Jack when he's had one too many. It wasn't a big deal.

10. Did you confront Jack about it afterwards?

No. It wasn't worth mentioning. If the company picnic was all that had happened, I wouldn't be here.

11. What happened next?

I went to work the next day. I didn't see Jack, except in passing. Our next meeting was the staff department meeting a couple days after the picnic. It's a regular 8:00 a.m. meeting with department staff.

12. What happened at the department sales meeting?

The meeting itself was pretty routine. We were under some pressure to compare our current year projections with last year's and produce a presentation for the board. Jack promised he'd work on the first draft. There were about seven or eight of us at the sales meeting. As the meeting was breaking up, Jack asked me to stay behind.

You know, I actually thought he was going to apologize for his juvenile behaviour at the office party. He asked me if I could locate the soft copy of the financial results as soon as possible. Mary-Anne had had to leave early and he wanted me to get them from her. I said I would. I turned around to leave and he patted me on the bottom and made a comment, "nice view".

13. What did you do?

I don't think I did anything. I was a bit in shock. Jack was perfectly sober this time. I might have given him an ugly look or something, but I just high-tailed it out of there. I did run into Mary-Anne and asked for the financial results. That's about it.

---

[5] This review question challenges the witness. It is a difficult type of question, but must be asked in order for the investigator to later assess credibility.

14. Did anyone see or hear anything?

I don't think so. Everyone had left when Jack and I were in the boardroom.

15. Did you mention anything to anyone?

No.

16. Why not?

Same reason as before. I thought I could handle things. I wasn't going to jeopardize my career at ABC Company over something so trivial. I was pretty angry though.

17. What happened next?

There was this meeting with Paul Saunderson. Saunderson's a pretty big client for us. Jack, Timothy and I had tried to meet him for weeks. I wanted to be at the meeting with Saunderson. I had a few misgivings, but since both Paul and Timothy were going to be there, I decided to go through with it. Besides, I didn't have a convincing excuse to bow out of it.

18. What happened at the meeting?

The meeting went really well. Timothy left early though. He had to catch the last train back home. Paul and Jack hit it off real well. They both liked single-malt Scotches. Paul nursed a few, but Jack started drinking heavy. Nothing he couldn't handle, but I didn't think he should drive. Around 9:30 p.m., we decided to call it a night. I offered Jack a ride. He lives about a mile from my place. I didn't want him behind the wheel of a car.

19. What happened while you went home?

Nothing at first. It's about a 25 minutes drive home. Jack started insinuating things. He started, "the night doesn't have to end". I tried to deflect him, saying I needed to get an early start on my day. He talked about how he "wanted to see more of me" ... how "we could be a great partnership". He then got pretty vulgar. He talked about wanting to "f*** me" and how he hadn't had a great "f***" in months.

20. What did you do?

We were almost in front of Jack's place. I dropped him off. I said, "Smarten up, Jack." He said to me, "you know Janine. I could say really nice things about you if you were only a little nicer to me" or something like that. I thought it was the booze. I went home and told myself that I was a fool to let myself be alone with him when he had a few too many.

21. What did you understand his comment about "really nice things, etc." to mean?

Look, it was no secret. Emil Pascale, the VP (Sales) had had a massive coronary and there are rumours that he would not be returning to ABC Company. I knew that there was a strong possibility that ABC would appoint an interim or even permanent replacement. The choice was between Tim or me.

I'd always been candid about my ambitions at ABC. I knew exactly what he meant: Sleep with him and he'd support my candidacy.

22. Why didn't you call a cab for Jack?

You obviously don't know Jack. He's 42 going on 18. He would never admit that he had had one too many or take a cab. I didn't want him to get into an accident. It seemed like the right thing to do. I had worked for him for years and I would have felt really guilty if he got into an accident and hurt himself or worse, some innocent bystander.

23. Did anyone witness anything?

Timothy left pretty early. I suppose Paul Saunderson could comment on the drinking, but nothing untoward happened at the bar. Other than that, no. I don't want you to talk to Paul Saunderson. He's an important client and I can't afford to get him involved and lose the account.

24. Who picked up the bill?

Jack did. Or more accurately, ABC Company. We were at the Red & the Black. ABC Company had an account there. Jack signed for it.

25. Did you tell anyone about this incident or any of the other incidents?

Sort of. I had a medical checkup at the end of June/beginning of July. My blood pressure was a little up. I told my doctor, Dr. Schiller, that I had a bit more stress at work and some problems with my boss. She asked me if I wanted to talk about it or wanted a referral. I told her it was nothing I couldn't handle. She told me to call her if I had a problem.

26. Why didn't you tell her what happened?

It wasn't a big deal. I thought that I could handle it.

27. Anyone else?

Indirectly. I told my neighbour I was having some problems at work. She's a law clerk and works for an employment lawyer. I told her I might have a problem with harassment and did she know anyone. She told me that I could drop by her office any time and she'd arrange a free consultation. But no one else. My parents are elderly and they couldn't handle the stress.

28. I'd like to turn to the Los Angeles incident. What happened there?

We had a pleasant flight to LAX. Jack, Timothy and I grabbed a cab together. We had a quick bite and a drink and I headed upstairs. Timothy and Jack were still at the hotel restaurant when I left. About 1:30 a.m. or 1:45 a.m., Jack started banging on my door, demanding to be let in. He said he needed to talk to me. He was loud. I threatened to call hotel security. He left.

29. How do you know it was Jack?

Are you kidding? I've worked with him for eons. I can recognize his voice easily.

30. Did you call hotel security or police?

No, I did not. Jack left. I didn't want to get him in trouble. We had a huge sales presentation the next day and we needed to be sharp.

31. What happened next?

Well, I guess I got really spooked. I don't know what got into me. I decided I needed to change rooms. I didn't want Jack knowing what room number I had. I had not even really unpacked. I threw my toiletries and a few items into my overnight bag. Called the front lobby. Asked to have my room changed. The hotel clerk was a bit startled and asked me if there was something wrong with the room. I told her that I wanted to be closer to the ground. It was the only excuse I could think of. She was a really nice person. She got me a nice upgraded room at the same price on the 2nd floor.

32. What did you do the next morning?

I showed up for breakfast. I didn't mention anything specific to anyone.

33. *Anything else happen while in Los Angeles?*

No, not really. Jack and I only met at breakfasts and during the evening cocktail hour to debrief. Timothy was always there. I was making real efforts to make sure I wasn't alone with Jack.

34. *What happened when you returned?*

Nothing at first.

35. *Why didn't you complain?*

I came very close. I really did. The hotel incident really threw me for a loop. I got a security company to install an intruder alarm — one of those alarms where they have video and voice monitoring as well as a silent alarm. I got some bars for my lower windows and upgraded the locks to the house. My doctor had to prescribe anti-anxiety drugs. Part of me felt I was over-reacting. Part of me didn't want to "rock the boat". Part of me was really angry.

36. *Are you prepared to provide me access to your doctor?*

I have to think about that. I don't think my general medical history is relevant at all, but I might be prepared to let you talk to Dr. Schiller or get her notes regarding what I told her. Dr. Schiller has been my doctor for almost 15 years and I don't feel comfortable about her telling you everything.

37. *Are you prepared to let me talk to your neighbour/law clerk?*

I don't think so. I've retained the firm to represent me and ABC will be getting a formal demand letter. I've been advised that I should not waive solicitor-client privilege.[6]

38. *Did you tell anyone about Los Angeles?*

Not really. Some people asked about the trip. I told them about the great business opportunities and left it at that.

---

[6] This is not unusual. While the investigator may wish to draw an adverse inference, asserting solicitor-client privilege makes sense at this preliminary stage.

39. *Do you have the receipts for the hotel in Los Angeles?*

I've submitted them to ABC's accounting department already. I didn't keep copies. You can get them from ABC.

40. *What happened next?*

Well, it was kind of spooky. When I got back, I started getting phone calls and hang ups. I thought they were wrong numbers. Then there was the heavy breathing. I got three or four calls some nights. They were caller blocked ID calls, however. I changed my telephone number. I let the sales team know right away about the change because we are all required to be accessible. The calls continued. It started affecting my sleep.

41. *Why do you think it is Jack?*

Well, I never used to get these kinds of phone calls. The only other calls I get are from people whom I know and whose names I can see on call display. The sales team — Timothy, Mary-Anne, Jack and their assistants are the only ones who have access to my new phone number at work. I'm convinced its Jack. I tried to get the phone company to tell me who it was and they told me that they needed a formal complaint and/or a court order. They also said it could take weeks before they got to it. I called the police, they told me to call the phone company. The lawyer told me it would be expensive to get a court order. I was sick and tired of the run around. I don't see much future anymore at ABC. I need to move on. I decided I might as well complain.

42. *Why didn't you complain to Human Resources right away?*

Don't take this the wrong way, but the HR managers are a bunch of "yes men and women" who don't have a lot of clout. Jack is one of the four most influential people in the company. I don't have a lot of confidence in the department. Most of them rose through the ranks and have little or no training. I guess it was the phone calls. The phone calls were the worst, because they disturbed my sleep. I didn't feel comfortable taking the phone off the hook. I have elderly parents and they sometimes need me at odd hours. We're also expected to be accessible at night — sometimes, a sales person is overseas and can only reach you late at night. I thought about it. It took me a while to figure out it must have been Jack. Anyone could have gotten my old number. I'd had it for nine years. The new number — the caller didn't miss a beat. As I said, everyone else who called me were people I knew and to whom I gave my number. I wasn't even on the telemarketing lists yet. But I still got the phone calls. I figured it had to be someone at work — Timothy, Jack, Mary-Anne. Jack's the only one who has been pestering me.

43. Are they still continuing?

No, I got the last one the night I lodged a complaint with HR. They've never happened again. That's a relief.

44. Why didn't you complain to the police?

I did speak to both the telephone company and the police. It's quite an elaborate process and there is a huge backlog. I was considering laying charges, but the police weren't supportive at all.

45. Why did you finally decide to complain?

After all I put up with and all I've done for the company, I got passed up for promotion. I like Timothy. He's a great guy, that's not the point. The promotion was mine. Do you have any idea how few women are in technical sales? Do you have any idea how hard it is to be in sales, when 95 per cent of the technical buying decisions are made by men? I really resented being passed over. I guess if all this hadn't happened, I would have accepted it. Timothy's numbers are great, too and he's a good manager — a rare combo. But, I can't help remembering Jack suggesting that night that I should be nice to him. I will now never know whether I got subtly blackballed because I didn't go along with Jack.

46. Is there anything else you want to add? Anything else I should know?

I guess you should know that I am consulting the lawyer about a potential civil suit or maybe a human rights case. I wanted you to find out about it from me, not indirectly.

47. Are there any witnesses or documents I should consider?

I guess you need to ask David Ricketts why I didn't get the promotion. Other than David, Timothy and Jack are the only ones who might have additional information. You should get Jack's phone bills and stuff — he won't give them to you, but maybe the company has access.

48. Do you have any suggestions regarding how to resolve your complaint?

What kind of question is that? I'm so angry. I've worked hard in this company. I've sacrificed my personal life for this company. Jack decides to come unravelled because Alison left him and I have to put up with this sh**. Either he goes or I go. I'm never going to trust him again. You might as well tell the company if I go, it won't be cheap. The demand letter is going out in the next week or so.

> *I have read over this transcription of the investigation. I agree that it is accurate. I understand that I have an opportunity to provide the investigator with any additional information or corrections. I also understand that this interview is part of a confidential process and I undertake to keep the contents of this interview confidential.*

<u>*September 15th, 200x*</u>   <u>*Janine Carruthers*</u>

INVESTIGATOR'S NOTES OF THE INTERVIEW WITH JACK ANDREWS

Introductory Formalities

- ☐ Investigator introduction
- ☐ Investigator confirms that she is retained by company:

"I have been retained by ABC Company to investigate a formal complaint of sexual harassment made against you by Janine Carruthers. I want you to understand that as an investigator, I am a neutral party. My job is to interview witnesses, look at evidence and deliver a report to ABC Company. [If applicable] You should understand that although I am a lawyer, I am not your lawyer."

- ☐ Confirm that Respondent has received copy of complaint
- ☐ Explain general process — interview, information gathering, report to employer, employer makes decision
- ☐ Confirm Respondent has copy of harassment policy
- ☐ Explain timetable
- ☐ Provide copy of harassment policy if respondent does not have one
- ☐ Advise witness to listen to question carefully and to answer question honestly. If witness does not know or remember, best to advise that. If witness subsequently wishes to correct or add to statement, he/she may contact investigator
- ☐ Permission to tape record interview

Background Questions

1. Tell me a little about yourself?

I'm Executive Vice-President (Sales & Marketing). I've been with the company for almost 14 years. I'm 43 years old. I started life as an architect and realized that I missed working with people. I went back to school, got my MBA, graduated summa cum laude. I worked with a small company. It became a medium-sized company and got bought out by one of the giants. I didn't like being a small fish in a big pond and started looking. ABC head-hunted me. It was a good fit and I've stayed.

2. What about your personal background?

I'm married, well separated actually. Alison and I just drifted apart. I guess I worked too hard and she found someone else. We have two phenomenal kids, Justin (seven) and Alexa (11). They are both into competitive sports — and they keep us both pretty busy. I play a half-decent game of golf. Other than that, it's work work work.

3. Have you read Janine Carruthers' complaint?[7]

Yes, of course. It's a lie. I can tell you what is really going on. Janine Carruthers is getting back at me for being passed over for promotion. She's always been incredibly ambitious and work is her entire life — no kids, no husband.

4. Are you aware of ABC's sexual harassment policy?

Yes, it was distributed about five years ago and put on the intranet thereafter. The first thing when I found out about Janine's complaint was check the policy out.

5. What I'd like to do is go through her complaint and your response. Why don't we start at the summer picnic?

Pretty much the whole sales department was there. The heat was brutal. Most of us ended up in the pool, trying to keep cool.

---

[7] This investigation is being conducted in the context of a formal investigation policy which provides that the respondent does get a copy of the complaint. In other situations, the investigator will simply advise that there is a complaint about something that occurred in a particular context and request the respondent to provide his or her recollection of the events in that context.

6. Do you remember Janine being there?

Yes, I do. She was there when I arrived. I arrived late because I had to finish a golf game with a client.

7. Was she ever in the pool with you?

I assume so, there were about 20 or 25 of us going in and out of the pool that afternoon. We'd run to the bar or the food line up, get a drink or snack and head back. It was pretty crowded.

8. How many drinks did you have?

I don't really remember. Look, it was the summer picnic and we traditionally cut loose. Probably five or six, maybe more throughout the afternoon. I was there until 5:30 or so.

9. Do you remember touching Janine in the pool?

Not at all. I did swim underwater a couple of times, just to get from one end to the other and I suppose I might have brushed her accidentally, but I honestly don't remember anything unusual involving her. The pool was crowded. The weather was scorching and everyone was trying to cool off a bit.

10. What were you wearing at the summer picnic?

I went in shorts and golf shirt. I changed into swim trunks for the pool, of course and stayed in them. I threw the shirt on top later to keep the sun off. I got quite a sunburn and somewhat dehydrated.

11. Describe your swim trunks

I'm not sure. I think I was wearing yellow and navy blue striped trunks. My other trunks are pretty faded.

12. Do you remember Janine leaving?

Not really, I noticed she wasn't there around 4:00 o'clock or so. A couple of the guys were suggesting a game of water polo. Janine's a good athlete and I wanted her on my team — but she wasn't there.

13. Anything else about the summer picnic?

No, I ran into Janine a couple of days later. She didn't say anything and seemed perfectly normal. Why wouldn't she say anything to me if she thought I had done something so juvenile?

14. Did anything of note happen between the summer picnic and your next departmental meeting between Janine and you?

No, not at all. We don't normally interact on a daily basis. Janine's pretty independent in her operations.

15. I'd like to turn to the departmental meeting please. What do you recall?

I remember asking Janine to stay behind and then asked her to get the financial reports for last year for me. Janine and Mary-Anne Thomas had actually finalized them for the department for the previous year. Mary-Anne had had to leave early from the meeting. That's all that happened.

16. Did you make any comment about nice view?

I don't think so. If I did, I must have been referring to the view out the window.

17. Did you touch Ms. Carruthers on the rear?

Are you kidding? She's no shrinking violet. I wouldn't ever risk it.

18. Did anything else of note happen at the meeting?

No, it was a good meeting. We were trying to figure out how to meet our previous year's numbers, which had been extraordinary.

19. I understand that you, Timothy Blackwell and Janine Carruthers met Paul Saunderson for drinks. Tell me about Paul Saunderson.

Paul is an important client and has the potential to be one of our top five clients world-wide. He controls strategic technical buying for the entire XYZ group of companies. He's smart and he's no nonsense. He wanted to meet with us to determine if we could streamline the process and sharpen our pencils if he made a longer term commitment. Tim and Janine have run into Paul a couple of times before. This was the first time I met Paul. We hit it off. We shared a love for premium Scotches — and did an informal tasting. It was great. Tim left early to catch the train, but it was clear that Paul was still enjoying himself, so Janine and I continued.

20. Who was drinking and how much drinking?

I was doing more tasting than drinking. I think Paul and I might have ordered three different kinds of Scotches — for a comparison. It was a nice evening. Janine was into red wine — she says that Scotch reminds her of bad mouthwash. Tim's been dry since I've known him. He says it is for religious reasons, but I know that he needed to get dried out after university. I knew him back then and he was definitely heading for a fall. His career was going nowhere for a while. You could say that I rescued his career. I gave him a second chance. He needs to stay off the booze and he does.

21. I understand that Janine drove you home?

Janine lives about a mile from me and she offered to drive me home.

22. Don't you have a car?

Yes, it is a company car. But Janine was really pushy about not letting me drive and it was just as easy for me to cadge a lift.

23. Do you recall what was said in the car?

Not much. Janine had the radio on and she didn't seem to be in a chatty mood.

24. Did you say anything to her or suggest that you guys continue the evening?

No, not at all. I've read what Janine has suggested and it's not me. Look, I really like Janine. She's a terrific sales executive. I made some comment about Janine being really nice — but it was my way of thanking her for taking me home and being supportive. I can't believe that she is making this up about me. She's sabotaging my career. I never took her for being a sore loser.

25. Did you have any interactions between the staff meeting and the trip to Los Angeles?

No, not really. We were all swamped trying to get ready for L.A. I passed Janine a couple of times down the hall and we may have exchanged greetings. She and I sat next to each other in first class in the plane. She seemed pretty focused on some work in the lap top, but perfectly cordial.

26. What happened when you arrived in Los Angeles?

We shared a cab to the hotel. We freshened up and then met at the hotel lobby. We went for drinks and a meal. The time difference, even though it is only three hours, really throws me. I wanted to adjust to pacific standard time right away. Janine turned in early.

27. How much did you have to drink?

Not much. I'm pretty careful about jet lag and booze. It's a bad combo. A scotch and soda, maybe two.

28. When did you turn in?

About 1:30 P.S.T. I went to my room and checked e-mail and voicemail messages for an hour or so and then went to bed. It was a bit "early" by E.S.T., but it made sense to try to adjust to local time.

29. Did anything else happen of note?

Not really. I read what Janine said. I did not knock on her door. I'm not saying it didn't happen, but she has made a mistake — it wasn't me.

30. Anything else about the LA meeting?

No, it was a very good meeting. We met some of our high-level buyers and ran into a few people we've been trying to meet for months. It was a very productive set of meetings. We headed back on the same flight. Janine sat next to me. She was fine, a bit tired — she didn't say anything to me at all.

31. Anything else of note?

No, not really.

32. Janine claims she received harassing phone calls. Do you know anything about them?

Just what I read in the complaint. I feel badly for her. She must really have been scared. I had nothing to do with them and I'm disappointed that she suspects me. We've worked together for almost a decade. She should know I wouldn't do something like that to anyone.

33. Did you ever call Janine at home?

Yes, of course. When I'm on a business trip, I'd call Janine, Mary-Anne and Timothy. I'd probably call Janine the most, because she sometimes dropped papers or files at my home on her way from the office.

34. How often would you call Janine at home?

I don't know. Not that often, maybe three or four times max when I'm on a business trip.

35. How often would you call Timothy or Mary-Anne?

Maybe the same, maybe a little less, two to three times a business trip.

36. Would you call at the office?

More often, I'd leave voice mail messages via the system or respond by e-mail. If I called them at home, it's because I needed time to chat longer with them.

37. Are there any witnesses you think I should contact?

I guess Timothy was at the Saunderson event and in LA. Don't call Paul Saunderson. He means a lot of business to ABC and I'd hate for this to jeopardize our relationship. If we have to settle with Janine, that's fine, but we're talking huge dollars if we lose Paul as a client.

38. Can I get your personal telephone records please?

Look, I'm cooperating. I don't like what is going on, but I don't think it is right that I be treated as a suspect. My telephone calls are personal and none of your business.

39. Do you understand that I might draw an inference from your lack of cooperation?

I resent that. I am cooperating. I'm been fair and frank with you. I have a personal life and my personal telephone calls are none of your business. Janine should simply go to the police and leave me alone.

40. Is there anything else you want to add?

Yes. Look you have got to understand that this complaint is politically motivated. Maybe Janine has had a run of bad luck. Maybe somebody did pound on her door that night and maybe someone has been telephoning her, but it is not my fault. Janine is just angry that Timothy got promoted instead of her. It has nothing to do with harassment or discrimination. She's just trying to make a point with ABC and I don't like it. Most of this stuff occurred in June. She didn't make a complaint in September until she learned Tim got the promotion. It doesn't take a genius to know that Janine is trying to extort a settlement from ABC.

41. Are there any witnesses or documents I should consider?

You should talk to Timothy I guess. David will back me on the promotion issue and Timothy was at L.A.

> *I have read over this transcription of the investigation. I agree that it is accurate. I understand that I have an opportunity to provide the investigator with any additional information or corrections. I also understand that this interview is part of a confidential process and I undertake to keep the contents of this interview confidential.*

September 18th, 200x   *Jack Andrews*

INVESTIGATOR'S NOTES OF THE INTERVIEW WITH DAVID RICKETTS

Introductory Formalities

☐   Investigator introduction

☐   Investigator confirms that she is retained by company:

"I have been retained by ABC Company to investigate a formal complaint of sexual harassment. I am not at liberty to discuss the specifics of the allegation, but have been advised you might be a relevant witness. I want you to understand that as an investigator, I am a neutral party. My job is to interview witnesses, look at evidence and deliver a report to ABC Company."

☐   Advise witness to listen to question carefully and to answer question honestly. If witness does not know or remember, best to advise that. If witness subsequently, wishes to correct or add to statement, he/she may contact investigator

☐   Describe note taking process

☐   Permission to tape record interview

Background Questions

1. Can you tell me about yourself?

I'm the VP, Operations. I know all about the complaint made by Janine Carruthers. I've read it. I'm the one who told HR to hire someone external. I know the drill. You have 25 minutes before my next meeting. Let's cut to the chase.

2. What is your relationship like with Jack Andrews?

I've known him almost 10 years. He's been on the executive board for the last five years with me. He's smart, ambitious, talented and hard-working. I wouldn't be surprised if he succeeded me. It's openly acknowledged that he and Timothy Blackwell were responsible for ABC expanding its sales in Mexico and Latin America. When he was married, the four of us used to get together every so often. I don't see him socially as often, but we occasionally do a round of golf.

3. What is your relationship like with Janine Carruthers?

Very cordial. I run into her about two times a week or so. We occasionally grab lunch. She's a lot like Jack — smart, ambitious and hard-working. I don't socialize with her after hours, although a couple of times I've joined the sales group for drinks. I like her. She's smart. She's done superb work with the North American market.

4. Since you've read the complaint, tell me what you know about any of the allegations.

I read about the pool incident. I wasn't there. About the department meeting, the pat on the rear, I wasn't there. You'll have to ask the department people there if they noticed anything. I can't help you about LA, I was stuck here.

5. What about the suggestion that Janine Carruthers was passed over for promotion because of the harassment?

Janine lost out on a promotion — fair and square. Timothy is a great guy. Timothy has great international experience and he expanded a market that we didn't even realize we had. He earned the promotion.

6. What role did Jack Andrews play in the decision to promote?

Jack's recommendation carries weight. The two leading candidates reported to him.

7. Whom did Jack Andrews recommend?

He didn't really. He gave a very fair synopsis of what Janine and Timothy had accomplished and assured me that either would do an amazing job in the position. He said we were lucky to have such stellar internal candidates.

8. Do you recall why ABC picked Timothy?

Look, decisions about Vice-Presidents are a question of fit. It's not like assessing a secretary's typing speed. Timothy and Janine were matched on the numbers, I'll give you that. Timothy, however, had handled some amazing multi-national deals with some really complex issues. It's the direction the company wanted to go and Timothy had the edge. It also made a lot of sense. Jack and Tim had worked like dogs to expand the international market. If Jack moved from Exec VP to fill the CEO's shoes (which was widely discussed) Tim would be able to fill Jack's shoes. It would make for a smooth transition. Janine was a great candidate and I would have no hesitation recommending her, but Tim had the edge. The decision was a board decision.

9. Had the issue of promotion ever come up before?

Yes, twice. We knew that one of the VPs was taking early retirement for health reasons and we began considering replacements about six months ago. Emil's heart attack just accelerated the process. Jack mentioned Janine and Timothy both times and said that they both were amazing.

10. Did he lean either way?

Hard to say. He indicated that he would support either candidate and the decision was really up to the executive group as a whole. Look, he was being groomed to take over. Everyone knew that. Either candidate would be able to take over Jack's position. It was clear that we were in a transition period. This new VP would ultimately become Exec VP. At the end of the day, Tim's international experience really impressed us. Jack was very careful about being neutral. You could tell he was really torn. He and Tim go a long way back and he's been a great mentor to Janine. He gave her a chance in sales when there were no women in the industry and she's proved herself more than capable. I was thinking about a long-term transition plan.

11. Can you remember what he said back then?

No, not verbatim.

12. Are there notes or minutes?

No, there was a discussion and a consensus. No real notes of the discussion.

13. When was the decision made to promote Timothy Blackwell?

At the mid-August board meeting. The position was empty for about two months. The former VP, Emil Pascale, had had a heart attack and had let me know confidentially that he wasn't going to be able to come back. It was clearly time.

14. How was the decision made?

It was clear that the decision was between Janine and Timothy. Jack discussed both candidates. He was very fair about both. All the Execs gave input. There was a preference for Tim because of his international experience and that ultimately trumped Janine's candidacy.

15. Is there any information you think might be helpful or any witnesses I should interview?

Not really, no.

16. Who should I talk to if I want copies of expense reports or any other documents?

Just e-mail me the request and I will courier what you need to you.

I also understand that this interview is part of a confidential process and I undertake to keep the contents of this interview confidential

I have been advised that the law protects against reprisals for having participated in this investigation.

September 19th, 200x   *"David Ricketts"*

INVESTIGATOR'S NOTES OF THE INTERVIEW WITH TIMOTHY BLACKWELL

Introductory Formalities

☐   Investigator introduction

☐   Investigator confirms that she is retained by company:

"I have been retained by ABC Company to investigate a formal complaint of sexual harassment. I am not at liberty to discuss the specifics of the allegation, but have been advised you might be a relevant witness. I want you to understand that as an investigator, I am a neutral party. My job is to interview witnesses, look at evidence and deliver a report to ABC Company. You should understand that although I am a lawyer, I am not *your* lawyer. [*If investigator is a lawyer*] Do you understand?"

☐   Advise witness to listen to question carefully and to answer question honestly. If witness does not know or remember, best to advise that. If witness subsequently wishes to correct or add to statement, he/she may contact investigator

☐   Permission to tape record interview

Background Questions

1. Can you tell me about yourself?

I'm Timothy Blackwell. I recently was promoted to Vice-President (Sales) of ABC Company. I've been in sales all my life, pretty well since university. I've worked for ABC Company almost eight years.

2. What about your personal life?

I'm married with two children. They're almost grown now — 16 and 18. My wife, Daphne, is a well-known artist. She does portraits of children and some landscape work. Very much in demand. I have a quiet personal life. I'm a deacon in our church. When Daphne and I can, we love to travel. We've been to Japan, Bali, Indonesia, India, Nepal. I don't golf and I'm not much of a drinker — both of which are a bit of a handicap.

3. I'm going to ask you a series of questions arising from a formal complaint of harassment. It has been suggested that you might be a relevant witness. I am not at liberty to discuss specifics, but would like your cooperation.

Sure.

4. I understand that you were at the office picnic on June 1st, 2002. Can you recall anything unusual that happened that day?

Not really. It was brutally hot. It was a typical summer party. Food, loud music, drinks, pool. Nobody played tennis. It was too hot. Most of us ended up in the pool.

5. Do you remember anything involving Janine Carruthers?

Janine's no doubt upset about the promotion. (Pause) The summer picnic was hot. Janine left early. She looked a bit upset. I quizzed her about it. She said she wasn't feeling well. No surprise there. Janine has never liked the heat at all. I gave her a chit and she went home.

6. Do you remember anything involving Jack Andrews?

No. Jack was having a blast. He was captain of a water volleyball team and trounced the other side. He was one of the last to leave. He's a real party animal. He hasn't changed one whit.

7. What do you mean by that?

I knew Jack back in college. We were both party animals. My body couldn't take it and I avoid alcohol. Jack can still drink and be completely fit for work the next morning. He has the metabolism of a 20-year old.

8. Were you involved in a department sales meeting on June 3rd?

Yes.

9. Did you notice anything unusual?

No, not at all.

10. Did you see Jack touching Janine in any way at that meeting?

No, I don't think so. I think I left right after we finished discussions, though. I was late for another meeting.

11. *What about afterwards?*

No, I ran into both Jack and Janine after the meeting. Nothing unusual. Oh yes, Mary-Anne left a bit early. She had a conflict.

12. *Were you at a meeting with Paul Saunderson on June 8th, 2002?*

Yes, Janine and I set it up. We wanted Paul to get to know Jack. It was a great meeting. The two hit it off.

13. *Do you recall who was drinking what?*

I was drinking my usual, sparkling water. Janine likes red wine. Jack and Paul started to taste premium Scotches.

14. *How much?*

Look, I don't want to go into this. I have my own opinions about drinking.

15. *I need you to answer my questions. Is there a reason you are un-comfortable?*

I want to go off-the-record. Turn the tape recorder off.

16. *I respect the fact you are uncomfortable about something, but I can't promise you this information won't come up. All I can say is that I will do my honest best to keep my source of information con-fidential. But you have to understand that this investigation may go further and your name may have to be revealed.*

All right. This is my opinion. Jack was drinking a bit heavily. Paul was tasting. Jack was drinking. Jack was having doubles to Paul's singles. He wasn't slurring or anything. Jack can drink heavily and still perform. I think that his breakup with Alison has really been tough on him. I was almost going to say something to Janine, but didn't. Janine's a smart cookie and I knew she wouldn't let Jack drive. They live only a mile apart or so. I left at 8:30 or so to catch the last train out of town. I told the waiter to keep an eye on Jack. There was something odd about Jack. I couldn't put my finger on it.

17. *What were you going to say to Janine?*

Just to make sure that Jack doesn't drive and if she had to, to take his keys away. You know — the basic "friends don't let friends drive drunk" warning.

18. Anything else?

No.

19. You said there was something odd, what did you mean?

I don't know. It just seemed that there was an edge to Jack. I can't explain it. Look, Jack is normally a really happy, mellow drunk. That evening, he seemed to have an edge on him.

20. Did you ever talk to Jack about this?

No. Jack was fine the next morning. The meeting with Paul had gone well. Janine told me that she had driven Jack home. There was nothing to talk about.

21. How did Janine seem the next morning?

Fine.

22. Were you involved with the trip to Los Angeles?

Absolutely. It is the premier sales event in North America.

23. Do you recall dinner in LA?

Yes, Janine, Jack and I got together in the hotel restaurant. The food was pretty plain, but okay. Janine looked wiped and headed up early. Jack and I continued with dinner for a while longer.

24. How much longer?

Quite a bit longer. Jack believes in adjusting to local time right away and was working on staying awake. We had a few drinks.

25. How many?

Can't remember.

26. Who was drinking what?

Janine had wine. I had sparkling water. Jack had scotch I think.

27. How did Jack seem that evening?

We talked business and then Jack started talking about how tough it was to be away from the kids and how much he missed Alison. I let him talk. I think he needed to get things off his chest.

28. Was Jack under the influence?

He probably couldn't drive, but he wasn't staggering drunk. As I said, he's got a great constitution.

29. What time did the evening end?

Maybe 11 P.S.T. Around then, I turned in. Jack stayed behind to pay the bill.

30. Were you on the same floor as Jack or Janine?

Jack was on a higher floor than I was. I always get a low floor — a phobia about heights. Janine got a non-smoking room on the 6th floor.

31. Do you recall anything about Janine during that trip?

Yeah. Janine seemed a bit "off" the next morning. I asked her if there was something wrong and she just told me, "everything's fine". She clearly wasn't telling the truth, but I didn't feel like it was my position to pry. I told her that she had to keep focused on this trip and she told me to f*** off. I remember thinking Janine must be under stress. I have rarely heard her swear.

32. Anything else?

No, I saw Janine at the breakfast and after the meetings to debrief. She pretty well kept to herself.

33. Was that typical?

Yes and no. Janine's usually a bit more gregarious, but she tends to turn in earlier in the evenings, because she's a morning fitness addict. You know — the 10k run — the whole bit.

34. Does Jack phone you at home?

Yes, every so often.

35. How often?

Maybe once or twice when he's on a business trip. I guess six or seven times a month.

36. Why would he call you?

Usually, if something came up involving one of my files or if he needed something right away.

37. Do you have any idea how often he would call Janine or Mary-Anne?

Probably the same. Maybe a tiny bit more if he needed Janine to drop something off at his place on the way home. We have similar kinds of work loads and accounts.

38. I understand you were recently promoted. I am wondering if I could ask you when you were advised that might happen?

It was no secret. Look, our former VP (Sales) had had a heart attack and there were rumours he didn't want to come back. It was between Janine and me. I thought I had the edge because I had done some great stuff in Mexico, but Janine would have been a great choice and she would have been the first female VP in the company.

39. Why do you think you got the nod and not Janine?

I was told by David [Ricketts] that my multi-national sales experience was really invaluable. I earned that promotion.

40. Do you think you were Jack's favourite for Vice-President?

No, I think he was genuinely torn between Janine and myself. I got the sense that the decision was made by David.

41. Is there anything else you want to add?

Yes — this complaint could tear apart the sales team. I don't think Jack could do anything like sexual harassment, but if he did — it's because he's going through a traumatic time now. I just hope that you can figure out a way to fix things. I like Janine and Jack. I don't want this to go further, I really don't. I know how messy these things can get.

I also understand that this interview is part of a confidential process and I undertake to keep the contents of this interview confidential.

I have been advised that the law protects against reprisals for having participated in this investigation.

September 19th, 200x   *"Timothy Blackwell"*

DOCUMENT 1

Red & Black Club
129 Ontario Blvd.
Toronto ON M1L 2L2
416.555.1288

June 8th, 2003
4 guests
Server: Andy Sammut

1 Arctic Char	15.50
1 T-bone (12 oz)	25.75
1 Surf & Turf	29.95
1 Pasta Special	14.95
1 bottle sparkling water	7.95
2 glasses White Wine (house)	11.00
3 premium scotch (single)	24.00
4 premium scotch (double)	64.00

billed to the account of ABC Company
taxes and gratuities not included

"Jack Andrews"

DOCUMENT 2

	AIRPORT HOTEL LAX SECURITY INCIDENT REPORT
June 16th, 200x	1:54 a.m. Guest in room 624 complained about noise in hallway, described as "banging and shouting". Arrived on floor 1:58 a.m., but hallway empty. Called guest to advise. Guest confirms that banging stopped less than a minute after call. Apologized to guest. Checked elevator access records. Someone accessed elevators to go from 7th to 6th floor at 1:52 and returned at 1:57 a.m. Patrolled 6th and 7th floor every 15 minutes. No further disturbances. Todd Bridewell, Employee 332

DOCUMENT 3

Cozy's Restaurant
Airport Hotel
LAX

June 15th 2002 at 11:52 p.m.

Roast Beef Special	$18.95
Soup & Sandwich Platter	$11.00
Blackened Chicken with Salad	$15.00
2 Sparkling Water	$5.00
2 Red Wine	$10.00
6 Premium Drinks	$36.00
3 Coffee	$3.00

Gratuity and taxes not included
Charge _____ Room 740
Signed: "Jack Andrews"

We wish you a pleasant stay with us.

DOCUMENT 4

Security Log	
Dial-in Records (Jack Andrews)	**Usage**
June 16th, 2002	3:01:10 a.m. to 4:35:02 a.m.

Note that all time records are eastern standard time. Subtract 3 hours to get to pacific standard time. Consequently, Andrews on-line between 12:01 and 1:35 a.m. on June 16th

DOCUMENT 5

LAX Hotel

Guest
Jack Andrews
ABC Company

June 15th, 2003	$201.00
Room 763 (business room/conf special)	
June 16th, 2003	
Room 763 (business room/conf special)	$201.00
Mini-bar (1 juice, 2 scotches, 1 crackers & cheese)	$32.00
Internet/fax/dataline usage (flat charge)	$15.00

NOTES OF DISCUSSION WITH FAZEELA EL-ESBIR, FRONT DESK CLERK

September 23, 200x

- • F.E. was night clerk on the 14th, 15th, 16th, and 17th
- • recalls Janine Carruthers real well, because hotel pretty quiet during the graveyard shift until the morning
- • wanted room changed
- • on the 6th floor — room 622 — non-smoking

- computer records show that she called down at 1:55 a.m. on June 16th
- given upgraded room on 2nd floor (but smoking floor)
- note on computer says, "guest nervous on 6th floor and wants lower floor"
- thought unusual — usually guest asks for lower floor right at check-in and usually non-smokers are fussy about being on a smoking floor
- not aware of any disturbance, but should talk to security
- thought there was something going on, but guest wouldn't say

NOTE OF DISCUSSION WITH TODD BRIDEWELL (SECURITY)

September 23, 200x

- received call regarding disturbance from guest on June 16th, 200x
- will fax security report
- remembers that night — unusual to have problem regarding noise that late
- hotel caters to business crowd — early to rise, early to bed — etc. etc.
- very tight security after 11:00 p.m.
- guests have to show passcard to security in order to get into elevator banks or stair case from lobby
- believes that disturbance would probably be another guest, because hard to get access after 11:00 p.m.
- cannot use staircase between floors after 11:00 p.m. — only to exit to ground floor or parking garage (mostly for emergency exit purposes)
- checked elevator access records after the complaint
- shows elevator used on 7th floor to access to 6th floor and immediately thereafter returned to 7th floor
- not aware of any room changes that night
- bellhop or front desk would know about any check-ins or room changes, not security. Security in different section
- elevators are subject to video surveillance, but videos *not* kept after 1 week
- did not think to review tapes — admits he should have

NOTES OF DISCUSSION WITH MARK BEAUREGARD, IT DIRECTOR, ABC COMPANY

September 23, 200x

- log-in system very secure

- uses local time of server (*i.e.* E.S.T.)
- requires password from employee
- employees forbidden from sharing passwords
- time records kept for usage, billing and security purposes
- review of records show that during LA trip, Jack Andrews signed in and out two times and was active during the session
- security logs out after five minutes if there is no activity

REVIEW OF COMPANY CELLPHONE RECORDS (JACK ANDREWS) FROM JANUARY, 200X TO AUGUST, 200X

- Jack Andrews heavy user of cellphone — routinely has over 1000 minutes a month
- routinely uses cellphone to check company voicemail during business trips and leave messages (corporate numbers all are prefaced with 416.555.2000 as they go through central automated switchboard)
- through the months of January to June, 2003 — makes two to five calls to home numbers of team members (Janine, Timothy and Mary-Anne). Calls of moderate duration (three minutes to 10 minutes). Mostly correlate with business trips outside city
- does not use cellphone while in office. Corporate policy discourages use of cellphone if land line available

Month of July, 200x and August, 200x

- routinely uses cellphone to check company voicemail during business trips and leave messages (corporate numbers all are prefaced with 416.555.2000 as they go through central automated switchboard)
- makes three to eight calls home numbers of team members (Timothy and Mary-Anne). Calls of moderate duration (three minutes to 10 minutes)
- in July, 30 calls to Janine's home number (three are of moderate duration — eight to 10 minutes) 26 appear to be short duration (under a minute — company charged by the minute — includes hangups)
- in August, 57 calls to Janine's home number (5 are of moderate duration — seven to 10 minutes) 52 calls appear to be short duration (under a minute — company charged by the minute — includes hangups)

NOTES OF VIEW OF COMPANY BOARDROOM — SEPTEMBER 23, 2002

- sales boardroom overlooks company parking lot
- parking for approximately 30 cars
- two dumpsters
- large air conditioning unit
- no trees
- abuts parking lot for grocery store
- can see loading docks of grocery store and trailers

INVESTIGATOR'S NOTES OF THE SECOND INTERVIEW WITH JACK ANDREWS

Introductory Formalities

☐ Investigator introduction

I am still investigating a formal complaint of sexual harassment made against you. As part of that investigation, I have some follow-up questions.

1. Thank you for agreeing to see me again. I wanted to follow up with you on a number of issues that have arisen since we last spoke. Do you recall me asking you about your cellphone usage and calling Janine at home?

Yes, I do.

2. I had ABC Company pull the company cellphone records from your cellphone. I've circled the calls to Janine Carruthers. It looks like you made a lot of calls to Janine's number in July and August. The calls are pretty short, less than a minute. Do you have an explanation?

(Angrily) Who gave you the right to look at my personal calls? Who do you think you are? It's obviously a mistake. Like I told you before, I only called Janine on business.

3. The records belong to the company. As I asked you, is there any explanation for the number of short calls in July and August?

(Calming down) No, I don't remember calling her this many times. I suppose I could have been trying to locate her and not having luck. That must have been it.

4. I also want to clarify an issue with you. I understand that you had a few drinks at the restaurant after you arrived in LA.

Yes, I remember that. I told you I had a scotch and soda or two.

5. Yes, that's what I want to clarify with you. I've got the receipt from Cozy's Restaurant. It looks like six premium drinks, two wines and two sparkling waters were ordered. Timothy Blackwell says he was drinking the water. Janine says she had some wine. Everyone agrees that you had the scotches. Can you explain the six premium drinks?

You sound like my wife. I had a bit more to drink than I thought. It's not like I can't handle it or anything.

6. I also had a chance to look into the LA hotel incident. Did you know that security keeps a video-tape of the elevator and that there are logs of elevator usage for that night?

No, I didn't know that.

7. The elevator log shows that someone used the elevator from the 7th floor to the 6th floor and back to the 7th floor exactly at the same time that Janine says she had a problem.

(Angrily) There you go again. Making innuendos. I told you, I turned in for the night right after dinner. I can't help it if some weirdo went after Janine. It wasn't me. I'll bet you haven't seen the elevator videotapes, have you? You would have told me that right away. You're just trying to trick me.

8. *I'm not trying to make innuendos. I have to tell you that I have to consider that there was someone using the elevator from your floor to Janine's floor the same time she complained about noise. She says she recognized your voice.*

I'm telling you, I didn't do it. I'm not that stupid. I had a big sales meeting the next day. Look I'm finished talking to you. I can see the direction this is going. I'm calling my lawyer.

9. *I also want to discuss your recollection regarding what you did after dinner. I had a chance to look at the computer log-in records and it looks like you worked on your computer after dinner with Janine and Timothy and logged off around 1:35 a.m. P.S.T.?*

So what? I did some work. Look, you are obviously trying to blame everything on me. I should have gotten a lawyer ages ago. I heard Janine's got a lawyer. I thought if I cooperated with you, you'd see how Janine was trying to manipulate the system. Look, it's not personal — but I'm not answering any more questions until I talk to my lawyer.

(Investigator notes that Jack Andrews leaves interview room)

September 24, 200x

NOTES OF TELEPHONE CALL WITH JACK ANDREWS
September 25, 200x

- has no confidence in process
- clearly tainted
- not fair process
- Janine's motives not being considered
- on the advice of his lawyer, Jack will not participate in any more interviews at all
- explained adverse inference
- "he doesn't care about what inferences I draw — the truth will out".
- believes this is "witchhunt".

PART III

APPENDIX A

EXCERPTS OF RELEVANT FEDERAL AND PROVINCIAL HUMAN RIGHTS LEGISLATION

Federal *Canadian Human Rights Act* R.S.C. 1985, c. H-6 s. 14	*Harassment* 14. (1) It is a discriminatory practice, (a) in the provision of goods, services, facilities or accommodation customarily available to the general public, (b) in the provision of commercial premises or residential accommodation, or (c) in matters related to employment, to harass an individual on a prohibited ground of discrimination. *Sexual harassment* 14.(2) Without limiting the generality of subsection (1), sexual harassment shall, for the purposes of that subsection, be deemed to be harassment on a prohibited ground of discrimination.
Ontario *Human Rights Code* R.S.O. 1990, c. H.19 Part I s. 2; s. 5	*Harassment in accommodation* 2.(2) Every person who occupies accommodation has a right to freedom from harassment by the landlord or agent of the landlord or by an occupant of the same building because of race, ancestry, place of origin, colour, ethnic origin, citizenship, creed, age, marital status, same-sex partnership status, family status, disability or the receipt of public assistance.

	Harassment in employment 5.(2) Every person who is an employee has a right to freedom from harassment in the workplace by the employer or agent of the employer or by another employee because of race, ancestry, place of origin, colour, ethnic origin, citizenship, creed, age, record of offences, marital status, same-sex partnership status, family status or disability. *Harassment because of sex in accommodation* 7.(1) Every person who occupies accommodation has a right to freedom from harassment because of sex by the landlord or agent of the landlord or by an occupant of the same building. *Harassment because of sex in workplaces* 7.(2) Every person who is an employee has a right to freedom from harassment in the workplace because of sex by his or her employer or agent of the employer or by another employee.
Quebec *Charter of Human Rights and Freedoms* R.S.Q., c. C-12 Part I s. 10	*Harassment.* 10.1. No one may harass a person on the basis of any ground mentioned in section 10.

Manitoba *The Human Rights Code* C.C.S.M. c.H175 s. 19	*Harassment* 19.(1) No person who is responsible for an activity or undertaking to which this Code applies shall (a) harass any person who is participating in the activity or undertaking; or (b) knowingly permit, or fail to take reasonable steps to terminate, harassment of one person who is participating in the activity or undertaking by another person who is participating in the activity or undertaking. *"Harassment" defined* 19.(2) In this section, "harassment" means (a) a course of abusive and unwelcome conduct or comment undertaken or made on the basis of any characteristic referred to in subsection 9(2); or (b) a series of objectionable and unwelcome sexual solicitations or advances; or (c) a sexual solicitation or advance made by a person who is in a position to confer any benefit on, or deny any benefit to, the recipient of the solicitation or advance, if the person making the solicitation or advance knows or ought reasonably to know it is unwelcome; or (d) a reprisal or threat of reprisal for rejecting a sexual solicitation or advance.
Newfoundland and Labrador *Human Rights Code* R.S.N.L. 1990, c. H-14 s. 8; s. 12 (as am.)	*Harassment of Occupant Prohibited* 8. A person, directly or indirectly, alone or with another, by himself or herself only or by the interposition of another, shall not harass a person or class of persons who is an occupant of a commercial unit or a self-contained dwelling unit because of the race, religion, religious creed,

	political opinion, colour or ethnic, national or social origin, sex, sexual orientation, marital status, physical disability or mental disability of that person or class of persons. *Harassment in Establishment Prohibited* 12. A person in an establishment shall not harass another person in the establishment because of the race, religion, religious creed, sex, sexual orientation, marital status, physical disability, mental disability, political opinion, colour or ethnic, national or social origin of that person.
Northwest Territories *Human Rights Act* S.N.W.T. 2002, c. 18 s. 14	*Harassment* 14.(1) Harassment No person shall, on the basis of a prohibited ground of discrimination, harass any individual or class of individuals (a) in the provision of goods, services, facilities or accommodation; (b) in the provision of commercial premises or residential accommodation; or (c) in matters related to employment. *Definition of "harass"* 14.(2) In subsection (1), "harass", in respect of an individual or class of individuals, means engage in a course of vexatious comment or conduct that is known or ought reasonably to be known to be unwelcome by the individual or class.

Nova Scotia *Human Rights Act* R.S.N.S. 1989, c. 214 s. 5	*Prohibition of discrimination* 5.(1) No person shall in respect of (a) the provision of or access to services or facilities; (b) accommodation; (c) the purchase or sale of property; (d) employment; (e) volunteer public service; (f) a publication, broadcast or advertisement; (g) membership in a professional association, business or trade association, employers' organization or employees' organization, discriminate against an individual or class of individuals on account of (h) age; (i) race; (j) colour; (k) religion; (l) creed; (m) sex; (n) sexual orientation; (o) physical disability or mental disability; (p) an irrational fear of contracting an illness or disease; (q) ethnic, national or aboriginal origin; (r) family status; (s) marital status; (t) source of income; (u) political belief, affiliation or activity; (v) that individual's association with another individual or class of individuals having characteristics referred to in clauses (h) to (u). *Sexual harassment* 5.(2) No person shall sexually harass an individual.
Yukon *Human Rights Act* S.Y. 1987, c. 3 s. 13	*Harassment* 13.(1) No person shall (a) harass any individual or group by reference to a prohibited ground of

	discrimination, (b) retaliate or threaten to retaliate against an individual who objects to the harassment. 13.(2) In subsection (1), "harass" means to engage in a course of vexatious conduct or to make a demand or a sexual solicitation or advance that one knows or ought reasonably to know is unwelcome.
Alberta *Human Rights, Citizenship and Multiculturalism Act,* R.S.A. 2000, c. H-14 s. 7	*Discrimination re employment practices* 7.(1) No employer shall (a) refuse to employ or refuse to continue to employ any person, or (b) discriminate against any person with regard to employment or any term or condition of employment, because of the race, religious beliefs, colour, gender, physical disability, mental disability, age, ancestry, place of origin, marital status, source of income or family status of that person or of any other person. (2) Subsection (1) as it relates to age and marital status does not affect the operation of any bona fide retirement or pension plan or the terms or conditions of any bona fide group or employee insurance plan. (3) Subsection (1) does not apply with respect to a refusal, limitation, specification or preference based on a bona fide occupational requirement.

British Columbia *Human Rights Code* R.S.B.C. 1996, c. 210 Part 1 s. 13	*Discrimination in employment* 13.(1) A person must not (a) refuse to employ or refuse to continue to employ a person, or (b) discriminate against a person regarding employment or any term or condition of employment because of the race, colour, ancestry, place of origin, political belief, religion, marital status, family status, physical or mental disability, sex, sexual orientation or age of that person or because that person has been convicted of a criminal or summary conviction offence that is unrelated to the employment or to the intended employment of that person. 13.(2) An employment agency must not refuse to refer a person for employment for any reason mentioned in subsection (1). 13.(3) Subsection (1) does not apply (a) as it relates to age, to a bona fide scheme based on seniority, or (b) as it relates to marital status, physical or mental disability, sex or age, to the operation of a bona fide retirement, superannuation or pension plan or to a bona fide group or employee insurance plan. 13.(4) Subsections (1) and (2) do not apply with respect to a refusal, limitation, specification or preference based on a bona fide occupational requirement.
Prince Edward Island *Human Rights Act*, R.S.P.E.I. 1988, c. H-12 (as am.) s. 6	*Discrimination in employment prohibited* 6.(1) No person shall refuse to employ or to continue to employ any individual (a) on a discriminatory basis, including discrimination in any term or condition of employment; or (b) because the individual has been convicted of a criminal or summary conviction offence that is unrelated

	to the employment or intended employment of the individual.
New Brunswick *Human Rights Act* R.S.N.B. 1973, c. H-11 (as am.) s. 7	7.1.(2) No employer, representative of the employer or person employed by the employer shall sexually harass a person employed by the employer or a person seeking employment with the employer.
Saskatchewan *Saskatchewan Human Rights Code* S.S. 1979, c. S-24.1 (as am.) s. 2; s. 16	*Interpretation* 2(1)(m) "person", in addition to the extended meaning contained in *The Interpretation Act*, includes an employment agency, employers' organization, occupational association or trade union; (m.01) "prohibited ground" means: (i) religion; (ii) creed; (iii) marital status; (iv) family status; (v) sex; (vi) sexual orientation; (vii) disability; (viii) age; (ix) colour; (x) ancestry; (xi) nationality; (xii) place of origin; (xiii) race or perceived race; and (xiv) receipt of public assistance. *Discrimination Prohibited in Employment* 16.(1) No employer shall refuse to employ or continue to employ or otherwise discriminate against any person or class of persons with respect to employment, or any term of employment, on the basis of a prohibited ground. 16.(2) No employee shall discriminate against another employee on the basis of a prohibited ground.

APPENDIX B

CONTACT INFORMATION FOR HUMAN RIGHTS COMMISSIONS

Canadian Human Rights Commission
National Office
344 Slater Street, 8th Floor
Ottawa, Ontario K1A 1E1
Tel: (613) 995-1151
Toll Free: 1-888-214-1090
TTY: 1-888-643-3304
Fax: (613) 996-9661
<http://www.chrc-ccdp.ca>

Ontario Human Rights Commission
180 Dundas Street W., 8th Floor
Toronto ON M7A 2R9
Tel: (416) 314-4500
Fax: (416) 326-9520
<http://www.ohrc.on.ca>

Yukon Human Rights Commission
201-211 Hawkins St.
Whitehorse, YT Y1A 1X3
Tel: (867) 667-6226 or 1-800-661-0535
Fax: (867) 667-2662
<http://www.yhrc.yk.ca>

The B.C. Human Rights Tribunal
1170 - 605 Robson Street
Vancouver, B.C. V6B 5J3
Tel: (604) 775-2000
Fax: (604) 775-2020
TTY: (604) 775-2021

Toll Free (in B.C.): 1-888-440-8844
<http://www.bchrt.bc.ca>

Alberta Human Rights and Citizenship Commission
Northern Regional Office
800 Standard Life Centre
10405 Jasper Avenue
Edmonton, Alberta T5J 4R7
Confidential Inquiry Line (780) 427-7661
Fax: (780) 427-6013
<http://www.albertahumanrights.ab.ca>

The Manitoba Human Rights Commission
Winnipeg
7th Flr-175 Hargrave
R3C 3R8
Tel: (204) 945-3007
Toll Free: 1-888-884-8681
TTY: (204) 945-3442
Fax: (204) 945-1292
<http://www.gov.mb.ca/hrc/english>

Saskatchewan Human Rights Commission
Saskatoon Office
8th Floor, Sturdy Stone Building
122-3rd Avenue North
S7K 2H6
Tel: (306) 933-5952
Fax: (306) 933-7863
Telewriter: (306) 373-2119
Toll Free: 1-800-667-9249

Regina Office
3rd Floor
1942 Hamilton Street
S4P 3V7
Tel: (306) 787-2530
Fax: (306) 787-0454
Telewriter: (306) 787-8550
Toll Free: 1-800-667-8577
<http://www.gov.sk.ca/shrc>

Quebec Human Rights Commission
360, Street Saint-Jacques 2nd floor
Montréal (Québec) H2Y 1P5
Tel: (514) 873-5146
Toll Free: 1-800-361-6477
Fax: (514) 873-6032
<http://www.cdpdj.qc.ca/en/home.asp>

New Brunswick Human Rights Commission
Head Office
New Brunswick Human Rights Commission
P.O. Box 6000, Fredericton, NB E3B 5H1
Tel: (506) 453-2301
Fax: (506) 453-2653
TDD: (506) 453-2911
<http://www.gnb.ca/hrc-cdp/e/index.htm>

Nova Scotia Human Rights Commission
Halifax office
6th Floor, Joseph Howe Building
1690 Hollis Street
P.O. Box 2221
Halifax, NS
B3J 3C4
Tel: (902) 424-4111
Fax: (902) 424-0596
<http://www.gov.ns.ca/humanrights>

Prince Edward Island Human Rights Commission
98 Water Street
P.O. Box 2000
Charlottetown, P.E.I.
C1A 7N8
Tel: (902) 368-4180
Fax: (902) 368-4236
Toll Free: 1-800-237-5031
<http://www.gov.pe.ca/humanrights/index.php3?number=72418>

Newfoundland and Labrador Human Rights Commission
P.O. Box 8700
St. John's, NL
A1B 4J6
Tel: (709) 729-2709
Fax: (709) 729-0790
Toll Free: 1-800-563-5808
<http://www.gov.nf.ca/hrc>

APPENDIX C

SAMPLE MEDIATION AGREEMENT

Note that most mediators have a preferred form. This sample is provided in order to illustrate how mediators set up the "ground rules" right up front in the form of an agreement that all parties must sign.

AGREEMENT TO PARTICIPATE IN MEDIATION

BETWEEN

THE MEDIATOR _____
(insert name)

- and -

_____ (complainant's name)

- and -

_____ (respondent's name)

The parties voluntarily commit themselves to the mediation process with a view to resolving their disputes according to the following terms and conditions:

1. The parties agree to have mediation services provided by
    _____.

2. The parties agree that the primary responsibility for resolving their disputes rests with them and that the mediator will act as a neutral facilitator and does not have authority to force a settlement on the parties and will not make decisions on their behalf. The parties also agree that the mediator, who may or may not be a lawyer, will not provide them with legal advice and is not acting as their lawyer.

The parties agree and understand that they are at liberty to bring their own legal counsel to the mediation.

3.   The mediator agrees to help the parties discuss the matters in dispute between them and to assist the parties in effecting a diligent, fair, full, final, and mutually acceptable settlement of the matters in dispute.

4.   The parties agree to follow the ground rules set by the mediator, to act in good faith, diligently and with an open mind to make every effort to resolve the dispute. These ground rules include: (a) they shall take turns in speaking; (b) they shall not use rude, offensive or profane language; and (c) they shall keep an open mind regarding any possibilities suggested by the other side or the mediator. The mediation process is voluntary. Nonetheless, if a party wishes to exercise his or her choice to stop the mediation process, he or she undertakes to give the mediator a 15-minute advance warning of the decision.

5.   The parties and the mediator agree to keep all discussions in the mediation proceedings and all documents generated for the purpose of effecting a settlement of the matters in dispute confidential.

6.   The parties agree that the mediation process is without prejudice and that the statements made during the course of the mediation are inadmissible in any other disputes related to the matters being mediated.

7.   The parties agree that none of them will subpoena or otherwise require the mediator to testify or to produce notes or documents in any other proceedings related to the matters in dispute or dealt with under this agreement.

8.   If the parties arrive at an agreement, the mediator will assist the parties to compose a draft agreement for the review and signature of all parties. The mediator will be acting as scribe and not as counsel in this regard. This agreement will bind the parties and will end the dispute between them. The parties agree that the settlement will be confidential and will not create a precedent.

9. By signing this agreement, all of the parties and the mediator acknowledge that each has read this agreement and agrees to proceed with the mediation on the terms contained in it.

10. The fee for the mediation shall be $_____for one-day session starting at 10:00 a.m. and ending at 5:00 p.m. Additional time shall be charged out at $____ per hour.

Signature of complainant _____

Signature of complainant's lawyer _____

Signature of respondent _____

Signature of respondent's lawyer _____

Signature of mediator _____

INDEX